Discrimination

Discrimination

Its Economic Impact on Blacks, Women, and Jews

Robert Cherry
Brooklyn College of the
City University of New York

Lexington Books
D.C. Heath and Company/Lexington, Massachusetts/Toronto

Library of Congress Cataloging-in-Publication Data

Cherry, Robert D., 1944–
   Discrimination : its economic impact on blacks, women, and Jews / Robert Cherry.
      p.   cm.
   Includes index.
   ISBN 0–669–20418–8 (alk. paper). ISBN 0–669–20419–6 (pbk. : alk. paper)
   1. Discrimination—United States.   2. Minorities—United States—Economic
conditions—1981–   I. Title.
E184.A1C446   1989
305.8′00973—dc19   88–31841
                                                                              CIP

Published simultaneously in Canada
Printed in the United States of America
Casebound International Standard Book Number: 0–669–20418–8
Paperbound International Standard Book Number: 0–669–20419–6
Library of Congress Catalog Card Number 88–31841

The paper used in this publication meets the minimum requirements of American National
Standard for Information Sciences—Permanence of Paper for Printed Library Materials, ANSI
Z39.48–1984. ∞™

   89 90 91 92 8 7 6 5 4 3 2

Contents

Tables

Preface and Acknowledgments

This book highlights the broader theoretical underpinnings of contrasting theories of discrimination. Beginning with the detailing of general viewpoints, the book then applies them to contemporary issues that affect blacks, women, and Jews. Historical background is included when necessary, but the emphasis is on presenting the range of current economic research on the varied aspects of discrimination presented.

By presenting material on blacks, women, and Jews in one volume, readers are able to compare and integrate evidence and theories. Without understating the distinctive quality of each area of discrimination, care is taken to draw out the common threads. The consistency of each viewpoint in its approach to all areas of discrimination is highlighted.

I have attempted to avoid partisanship, particularly in the general presentations (chapters 2, 3, and 4). Each of the competing perspectives is developed in the most persuasive manner possible. One value of a nonpartisan presentation is that the role of empirical evidence is not overstated. While empirical evidence is used, sometimes providing important insights, I do not believe it can be decisive in determining the relative merits of competing views. A number of times I present hypothetical data to highlight statistical issues rather than trying to emphasize the superiority of a particular data set. I hope that readers will have an enhanced understanding of important data issues encountered when measuring discrimination and testing theories.

I wrote this book so that it would be accessible to noneconomists. I avoided specialized terminology and provided no graphical analysis. While the book does have some areas of primary research—assessment of black–Jewish relations and the evolution of conservative and liberal views—its primary strength is its ability to synthesize and summarize current research. The book is intended to give readers a firm understanding of the research findings on a wide variety of topics related to discrimination. Since all viewpoints are covered, the source references are comprehensive, providing a starting point for students and faculty wishing to research further particular topics.

Not only is this an excellent reference book for individuals, it is quite usable in undergraduate classes. The nonpartisan approach forces students to think seriously about what *they* believe, not what the author thinks; it also increases their appreciation of the importance of theory rather than reliance on evidence. Students can gain a better understanding of interpreting evidence as a result of the way data are presented in this book. Finally, the comprehensiveness allows students a broad choice of term paper topics, which they can relate to the material presented within the book. Students can go back to references quoted and write papers on more detailed topics or relate historical or sociological material to the economic studies presented.

The book was organized to be equally valuable for courses that desire an emphasis on racial or gender discrimination. The foundation chapters (2, 3, and 4) integrate examples of racial and gender discrimination. This integration enhances the presentation and is valuable when topics that cut across race and gender lines, such as welfare policies, are discussed.

This book also would be useful for students in various labor courses, since labor texts often make competitive assumptions that minimize their treatment of discrimination. In addition, this book can supplement political science courses that emphasize political strategies and coalition building.

This book has benefited from the constructive comments made by many individuals. I am indebted to Robert Blecker, Ann Davis, Jane Farb, Dana Frank, Gertrude Goldberg, Tom Michl, Joseph Schneider, Stephen Steinberg, and Roger Waldinger for their suggestions and encouragement. I would also like to thank my editor at Lexington Books, Karen Hansen, for her advice and help, as well as for overseeing the final stages and production. Finally, the patience of my family with my (extended) moments of preoccupation made it possible for me to complete this book.

1
Introduction

Beginning with the Carter administration, there has been a curtailment of programs and policies intended to reduce the discrimination faced by members of disadvantaged groups. The Reagan administration claimed that these programs interfere with the free market system. Many economists joined forces with the administration, contending that the programs actually worsened the situation for black and female workers.

This would not be a cause for concern if economic data indicated that discrimination in labor markets had been eliminated. Indeed, if women and blacks had attained earnings and occupational distributions similar to comparably skilled white males, the elimination of special policies would be cause for celebration. This is exactly the posture taken by Reagan administration officials, and it has been reinforced by studies conducted by conservative economists. For example, James Smith and Finis Welch (1986) suggest that discrimination against blacks, particularly black males with a postsecondary education, has been virtually eliminated. They note that by 1980 almost 30 percent of black males had incomes above the median income of white males, and that since 1970 the economic benefits from a college education for black males exceeded the benefits for white males. Smith and Welch believe that rising educational attainment and not government antidiscrimination policies have been responsible for these results. They believe focusing on government policies to aid minority groups is counterproductive. Smith and Welch claim, "The three issues that dominate the recent political debate—the safety net, affirmative action, and busing—are a good illustration of the problem. All three issues have their merit, but if history provides useful lessons, they are not the key to long-run reductions in black poverty" (p. 27).

Evidence also appears to indicate that there are no labor market barriers impeding women from attaining incomes as high as their male counterparts. Data demonstrate a dramatic rise in the number of women in highly visible professions. By the 1980s, more than one-third of the entering classes in medical and law schools were women (Parrish 1986). These gains have undercut contentions that women face significant discrimination. Indeed, President Reagan's appointment to head the U.S. Civil Rights Commission, Charles Pendleton, has labeled recommendations that the government adopt comparable worth procedures to reduce female–male wage gaps "a proposal as loony as 'Loony Tunes' " (Sorensen 1988, 33).

Despite these upbeat findings, evidence continues to indicate that wage differentials by race and by gender persist. Indeed, many liberal and radical economists contend that after making certain adjustments, these differentials are almost as great as they were at the beginning of the civil rights era. When either family or individual income is used as the measure, median black incomes are still less than 75 percent of white incomes (see table 5–1), and median female earnings are less than 70 percent of median male earnings even if we restrict comparisons to full-time year-round workers (see table 8–1). The only change has been the closing of the gap between black and white women.

The next three chapters in this book present the reasoning behind conservative claims and the opposing views of their liberal and radical critics. Central to the conservative viewpoint is the belief that competitive market forces are beneficial to groups that suffer from discrimination. Conservatives contend that competitive forces make discrimination so costly that it discourages discriminatory behavior in the marketplace. Liberals agree that competitive forces can be beneficial, but they do not believe that these forces are strong enough to have a significant impact on discriminatory behavior. For this reason, liberals believe that government antidiscrimination programs must supplement the marketplace. In contrast, radicals contend that competitive forces may encourage discriminatory behavior. For government policies to be effective, they must supersede, not simply supplement, the marketplace.

The perspectives presented in these three chapters differ substantially from those presented by sociologists and psychologists. These noneconomists usually begin their analysis with cultural and psychological explanations for the presence of discriminatory attitudes. They contend that policies that reduce discriminatory attitudes are necessary if we desire less discrimination in labor markets.

Economists, in general, have a different perspective on the relationship between discriminatory attitudes and discriminatory behavior. Conservatives tend to believe that discriminatory behavior can be eliminated without changing discriminatory attitudes. They believe that costs incurred will be sufficient to discourage discriminatory behavior in the marketplace. Discriminatory attitudes will remain, but conservatives believe that it is not the business of government to legislate attitudes. Thus, conservative economists do not think it is important for people to know the source of these attitudes and do not believe it is warranted to develop policies to change them.

Radicals believe that discriminatory attitudes are strongly influenced by the economic effects, both real and imagined, of discriminatory behavior. Discriminatory attitudes often function to rationalize exploitive relationships. It was comforting for plantation owners to believe that slavery was a benevolent institution that cared for blacks who could not care for themselves. The belief that this was the white man's burden was a useful outlook for those engaged in imperialist conquests.

Radicals contend that as long as groups perceive that they benefit from the maintenance of unequal relationships, they will continue to cling to discriminatory attitudes. Thus, radicals claim that changing attitudes cannot be accomplished without changing the perceptions held by those who believe they benefit from discriminatory behavior. Some radicals believe that white male workers benefit from discriminatory practices. Other radicals believe that within racially or gender-divided labor markets, white male workers are harmed by discrimination. For this reason, these radicals claim that it is possible to build a united movement of black and white working-class men and women.

Only liberal economists hold views consistent with those of sociologists and psychologists. Liberal economists believe that few groups either benefit from or are significantly harmed by their discriminatory behavior. Liberals believe that people's attitudes are not influenced by economic factors and will be changed only by policies advocated by sociologists and psychologists.

These three theoretical perspectives also differ in their assessments of government intervention. Many conservative economists believe that government intervention has had a harmful effect on disadvantaged groups. They contend that government programs often reduce incentives for firms to hire the most efficient workers. Without this incentive, it is more likely that the employer will rely on prejudicial attitudes. Conservatives also contend that government programs create a disincentive for disadvantaged groups to attempt to better themselves. In particular, conservatives claim that government social programs have generated a welfare dependency among the poor that discourages their labor market effort.

For entirely different reasons, radicals also do not believe the government can be relied on to end discrimination. Radicals contend that discrimination is profitable to important interest groups, which are powerful enough to circumvent most antidiscrimination policies. Indeed, radicals suggest that in the past governments have justified and protected discriminatory policies. Thus, radicals contend that only a mass movement that consistently pressures the government to enforce antidiscrimination regulation has any possibility of reforming the system.

Only liberal economists are optimistic that government programs are capable of reducing discrimination. They reason that much of the discrimination that takes place is unintentional and has no economic value to firms that discriminate. For this reason, they believe that there will be little organized resistance to government antidiscrimination policies. Since liberal economists believe efficiency will be improved, they believe antidiscrimination policies will be accepted by the corporate community once their benefits are realized. Thus, liberals are confident that together with the educational programs advocated by sociologists and psychologists, government antidiscrimination policies will eliminate discriminatory attitudes and behavior.

Following the detailing of each of these perspectives, chapter 5 presents assessments of the black–white income gap and affirmative action programs. This chapter also describes competing histories of the origins of the 1960s civil rights legislation and its impact on discriminatory practices. Whereas liberals believe the civil rights legislation was indispensable, conservatives believe it was unnecessary, resulting in reverse discrimination. Radicals believe it diverted activists away from building militant multiracial movements that would benefit both black and white workers.

There are a number of reasons why this book was organized to present empirical evidence only after a full presentation of each of the perspectives. First, while black male income is only three-quarters that of white male income, each theoretical framework may have a different interpretation of the data. Thus, we must understand the theoretical structures of each viewpoint in order to assess the different interpretations. Second, the most relevant information consists of those facts that can help us decide the relative merits of each perspective. Only after presenting each viewpoint can we determine the data we desire. Third, even if empirical evidence is consistent with one theoretical perspective, it is incorrect to leap to the conclusion that this demonstrates the accuracy of that viewpoint. The same data may be consistent with alternative perspectives.

Finally, we should expect that there will be little empirical evidence that can provide a decisive basis for choosing one theoretical perspective over another. If this evidence was available, we would not have the persistence of alternative perspectives. Social science data have severe limitations and often require relatively arbitrary assumptions to be made. For example, suppose we look at a simple hypothesis that discrimination rather than skill differences explains the female–male wage gap. How do we measure skills and discrimination? Do we compare only full-time workers or all workers? Even if we could obtain unbiased sample data, the results might be extremely sensitive to the choices made. Measuring skills by educational attainment might give entirely different results from those obtained by measuring skills according to on-the-job training. For this reason, it might be more appropriate to emphasize the foundations of each perspective than to try to obtain data that will enable us to determine the "correct" theory.

Chapters 6 through 11 apply the theoretical perspectives developed to a number of specific aspects of discrimination. Even the most upbeat assessments of the progress made by blacks in the post–World War II period do not ignore the employment problems of black youths, which is the subject of chapter 6. Since the 1960s, the unemployment rate of black youths has been double that of white youths and has generally been over 30 percent. Conservatives and many liberals suggest that racism has little to do with black youth unemployment problems and that minimum wage legislation has been harmful. Conservatives tend to believe that cultural deficiencies are the principal cause and reject all government initiatives. In contrast, liberals believe that some government programs are helpful. They support targeted educational programs and improved matching of job locations with job seekers.

Most radical economists claim that the assumptions necessary to justify minimum wage legislation as an aid to the poor are reasonable. They also note that empirical studies do not provide strong support for conservative contentions. Radicals suggest that other factors cause black youths to be trapped in unstable employment situations. They suggest that black youths have become an important component of the industrial reserve army of the unemployed and that only a militant confrontational movement might significantly reduce black youth employment problems.

Chapter 7 evaluates the impact of government social welfare programs on the behavior of low-income groups. It summarizes conservative contentions that government welfare programs have undermined individual incentives and been responsible for the growth of poverty and female-headed households. Most liberals believe that conservatives overstate the size of the welfare-dependent population and the impact of welfare programs on family structure. While liberals reject welfare cutbacks, they favor welfare reforms that encourage work. In addition, liberal proposals provide funding for day-care, education, and training programs. This chapter also presents radical criticisms of liberal welfare reform proposals. It details radical contentions that the plight of the poor will be improved only if welfare reform is combined with policies that raise the wage level of low-wage workers.

Chapter 8 further develops the theoretical structures presented in earlier chapters to include discrimination against women. Discrimination against women differs somewhat from racial discrimination. First, whereas society is very segregated by race, it is highly integrated by gender; individuals tend to marry, and children tend to be enrolled in coeducational institutions. Thus, female stereotypes may operate in ways that differ substantially from the ways in which racial stereotypes operate. Second, jobs are much more segregated by gender than by race. Hence, interoccupational wage differentials have a greater impact on male–female wage differences than on black–white wage differences. Third, whereas most theories of the racial earnings gap assert that educational disparities are a significant explanation, there is little educational disparity between men and women; the male–female earnings gap must be explained by other factors.

Chapter 8 details conservative theories that link female stereotypes to choice of occupation and skill development. Conservatives find that women choose occupations and education that are consistent with their preferences—preferences that differ dramatically from male preferences. In contrast, both liberals and radicals believe that the gravitation of women to lower-paying occupations is not due to female preferences. Both viewpoints identify discrimination against women as the dominant reason why women work in lower-paying occupations, but they differ in their views of how discrimination works. Whereas liberals tend to emphasize the need for stricter enforcement of affirmative action guidelines, radicals believe that the government should uphold comparable worth as an appropriate method of determining wage rates.

The analyses in chapters 7 and 8 contain only occasional references to discrimination against women outside the labor market. Many feminists have argued that the source and perpetuation of discrimination against women in the marketplace is the unequal patriarchal relationships found in the family. They argue that only by ending these patriarchal relationships will it be possible to end discrimination in the marketplace. Chapter 9 presents these feminist views.

Chapter 9 begins with an outline of the reasons why feminists believe it is impossible to assess accurately labor market discrimination against women without a systematic analysis of family relationships. It continues with a presentation of mainstream and traditional Marxist assessments of the nuclear family. Whereas mainstream theorists believe that the nuclear family benefits both men and women, Marxists believe that it serves only the interests of capitalists.

This chapter presents left-feminist criticisms of both mainstream and traditional Marxist views. In contrast with mainstream theorists, these feminists believe that the nuclear family is patriarchal—that is, males have power and privileges over females. In contrast with traditional Marxists, they believe that the patriarchal family persists because it serves the interests of working-class men as well as capitalists. Traditional Marxists suggest that left feminists incorrectly analyze the impact of patriarchy on capitalists, the ability of working-class men to enforce patriarchy, and the conflict between bourgeois and working-class women.

In response to contentions that the persistence of racial income differentials results from discrimination, conservatives point to the economic success of other minority groups that have experienced similar levels of discrimination. While black West Indians and Japanese Americans are mentioned, the preeminent comparison made is with the eastern European Jewish immigrants. Chapter 10 assesses the experiences of these immigrants and the relevance of their success to the black experience. While Jewish immigrants have been more successful than other immigrant groups, Jewish poverty and deviant behavior were more widespread and lasted longer than many histories indicate. Moreover, the anti-Semitism experienced by Jewish immigrants has been different from the racism experienced by black Americans.

Other factors external to Jewish values and culture may have been responsible for Jewish success. These factors differentiate the Jewish experience from the black experience. One factor has been the ability to use small businesses as a stepping-stone to further upward mobility. Whereas Jewish immigrants were able to enter the middle classes through entrepreneurship, blacks have been unable to sustain even a small number of business enterprises. Chapter 10 identifies various explanations for the lack of a large black business class.

Just as women have a distinctive occupational distribution, Jews are often disproportionately situated in middleman occupations. This fact has given rise to numerous theoretical explanations. These middleman theories are quite similar to some radical split labor market theories. In both, more privileged workers benefit from the discrimination against minority workers. Thus, it is alleged that Jewish success reflects the Jews' monopolization of middleman positions at the expense of other groups. Moreover, some theories claim that these middleman positions directly exploit poorer sections of the working class. Chapter 11 assesses these middleman theories and their relevance to the experience of American Jews. In particular, it evaluates theories stating that the black–Jewish relationship is fundamentally antagonistic as a result of the occupations in which Jews are concentrated.

Having outlined the contents of this book, I would like to point out some of its limitations. First, a number of groups that suffer from economic discrimination are not discussed. There is scant reference to the experience of Hispanic Americans even though their earnings, occupational distribution, and educational attainment are quite inferior to virtually all other ethnic groups. While there are some similarities between the situations of black and Hispanic Americans, it would be a mistake to claim that theories applied to the black experience can automatically be applied to the Hispanic experience. Moreover, it would be a distortion to claim that the Hispanic experience can be summarized without reference to the differences within that community. Although there are similarities, the experience of Puerto Rican immigrants to the Northeast differs substantially from the experience of Mexican immigrants to the Southwest, and both groups have a radically different experience from Cuban refugees. Given the complexities of the Hispanic experience, a brief chapter would have created more distortions than insights.

Second, this book is limited to the United States. Discrimination is not unique to the United States, and it would be useful to assess relationships in other countries. Just as blacks experience discrimination in the United States, they experience it in France and South Africa. Just as Jews seem to have become middlemen in the United States, the Chinese appear to have attained the same economic position throughout Southeast Asia. Just as white and black workers form a split labor market in the United States, native and foreign-born workers form split labor markets in Western Europe, while ethnic divisions are prominent in Malaysia, Sri Lanka, and India. Unfortunately, all these comparisons are beyond this book's scope, but the analytical structures developed herein provide a foundation for those who are interested in exploring other parts of the world.

References

Parrish, John. 1986. "Are Women Taking Over the Professions?" *Challenge* 28:54–58.

Smith, James P., and Finis Welch. 1986. *Closing the Gap: Forty Years of Economic Progress for Blacks.* Santa Monica CA: Rand Corporation.

Sorensen, Elaine. 1988. "The Comparable Worth Debate: An Evaluation of the Issues." In *The Imperiled Economy: Through the Safety Net,* ed. Robert Cherry, et al. New York: Union for Radical Political Economy, 133–140.

2
The Conservative View

Conservatives universally believe that discrimination is at most a minor blemish on a generally open, equitable economy. Indeed, conservatives such as Milton Friedman claim that capitalist development has been responsible for the dramatic decrease in the extent to which particular groups have operated under special handicaps in their economic activities. Thus, Friedman (1962) finds it paradoxical that it has been "minority groups that have frequently furnished the most vocal and numerous advocates of fundamental alterations in a capitalist society" (p. 111).

The first section of this chapter details the reasons why conservatives believe capitalism discourages discrimination. It begins by demonstrating that factors other than discrimination may be responsible for the wide gap between group incomes. Next, this section describes the basis for conservative claims that competitive pressures discourage discrimination. This section concludes with an analysis of the process by which market forces were responsible for the elimination of discriminatory (racially based) hiring practices by major league baseball teams.

Since conservatives believe that market mechanisms are sufficient to discourage discriminatory hiring practices, they believe that government antidiscrimination policies are unwarranted. The second section of the chapter discusses why some conservatives believe that particular government policies can make matters worse. First, this section details conservative contentions that the most discriminatory hiring practices are found in government and government-regulated industries. Next, this section describes the conservative criticisms of government educational and legislative antidiscrimination programs. Finally, this section indicates why conservatives believe government welfare and labor legislation are harmful to disadvantaged workers.

The third section of this chapter presents some historical examples of the conservative viewpoint. It summarizes the views of Thomas Malthus and Booker T. Washington concerning the reasons for economic inequality and the role of government policy. Parallels between their views and those of contemporary conservatives are presented.

Conservative Explanations of Income Differentials

Earnings data indicate that blacks earn less than whites and women earn less than men. Conservatives believe that factors other than discrimination are responsible for these large income gaps. They also note that a number of disadvantaged groups have family incomes above the national average and that the income of West Indian blacks is at the national average. Let us begin by demonstrating that wide income differentials can be explained by factors other than discrimination.

Income Differences

Just because two groups have different earnings does not mean there is labor market discrimination. Only if these groups have identical productive skills would we consider the earnings differential to be the result of discriminatory behavior. Thus, we must first adjust data so that we are comparing groups with the same productive skills.

Table 2–1 illustrates how unadjusted group averages can give a distorted view of income differentials. Let us assume skills can be approximated by years of education completed. Table 2–1 lists both overall average income (column 2) and average income by schooling completed (columns 3 and 4) for five groups (A–E). The analysis is simplified by assuming that within each group, individuals are either high school or college graduates.

Let us assume that A is the majority group. Column 2 indicates that the overall average income for groups B, C, and D is 80 percent of that of group A. When we look at the average income standardized for educational level (columns 3 and 4), however, it is clear that the overall income differentials disguise more than they clarify. Group B has the same differential in each of its subgroups; its high school and college graduates have incomes that are 80 percent of those of comparably educated group A members. In this case, we would judge that none of the income differences can be explained by skill differences.

When standardized for educational attainment, group C members have incomes that are 90 percent of those of group A. The overall 80 percent ratio occurs because the proportion of group C workers who are high school

Table 2–1
Average Incomes When Standardized for Educational Attainment

Group	Average Incomes (thousands of dollars)			Percent of Group	
	Overall	High School	College	High School	College
A	20	10	30	50.0	50.0
B	16	8	24	50.0	50.0
C	16	9	27	61.1	38.9
D	16	10	30	70.0	30.0
E	21	9	27	33.3	66.7

graduates is greater than the proportion of group A workers who are high school graduates (61 percent to 50 percent). In this case, half the income differential between group A and group C workers may be explained by educational (skill) differences. For group D, the entire income differential can be explained by educational differences, since once group A and group D workers are standardized for educational attainment, they have the same average incomes.

The most startling example is the comparison between group A and group E workers.[1] It would seem that group E workers cannot suffer from discrimination because their overall average is higher than that for group A workers. When standardized for educational attainment, however, group E workers actually earn less on average than comparably educated group A workers. The overall averages are the opposite only because of the extraordinary educational attainment of group E workers. This demonstrates that it is impossible to make solid judgments based on overall group averages alone.

Suppose that after adjusting for educational differences, group income differences remain. Other factors can influence incomes, such as age of head of household, family size, and residential location. Given the same level of educational attainment, we would expect older workers to earn more than younger workers. Since minority households tend to be younger, they tend to have lower incomes than comparably trained majority group households. Similarly, average family size among blacks and Hispanics is much higher than among other groups, and this may have a negative impact on incomes since large families are less likely to allocate funds for education. Finally, incomes differ by location within the United States. Individuals on the West Coast or in the Northeast tend to have higher incomes independent of other factors. Since blacks and Hispanics are disproportionately located outside these areas when compared to the general population, location can help explain why these groups have quite low average incomes compared to the general population. Thus, racial income differentials would be reduced dramatically if we compared black and white families with the same educational attainment, same age of head of household, same family size, and same locality of residence.

Although women tend to have the same level of education as men, conservatives believe that female skill levels are substantially below male skill levels. Gary Becker (1964) takes for granted that women have a greater preference for child-rearing and household activities than men and thus have less of an incentive to pursue education as an investment in market skills. To illustrate this point, Becker draws an analogy between women and tourists:

> Women spend less time in the labor market than men and, therefore, have less incentive to invest in market skills; tourists spend little time in any one

area and have less incentive than residents of the area to invest in the knowledge of specific consumption opportunities. . . . A women wants her investment to be useful both as a housewife and as a participant in the labor force [while] a frequent traveler wants to be knowledgeable in many environments. (pp. 51–52)

Thus, the education women receive will be less specific and less skill-enhancing than the education men receive. Indeed, Becker suggests that a primary reason why women pursue college careers is to find high-income-earning husbands rather than career-oriented skills.

Competitive Markets

Conservatives assume that firms face strong competition for the products they sell and for the inputs they purchase. Assuming a fully employed economy so that potential employees have choices, firms are "wage takers"; they must pay the market wage for all those whom they wish to employ. They cannot hire at lower wage rates because all applicants can find alternative employment at the market wage. They have no reason to offer a higher wage because they can find all the workers they need at the market wage. In this environment, the choice facing firms is how many and which applicants to hire at the market wage. Let us now analyze how discriminatory preferences (attitudes) held by employers, employees, or customers influence the hiring practices of competitive firms.[2]

Employer Preferences. Suppose employers have discriminatory preferences, preferring certain individuals over equally qualified workers from other (nonpreferred) groups. These employers obtain psychic benefits—what economists call marginal utility—for each additional preferred worker hired. As long as the preferred workers are among the most productive applicants, hiring them will not conflict with productive efficiency. At some point, however, hiring a member of the preferred group will result in the rejection of a more productive applicant from the nonpreferred group.

When a firm chooses to discriminate, its production costs increase. If the firm can pass along these costs to its consumers, it will not experience a profit loss. If, however, the firm is selling its output in a highly competitive market, any production cost increases will reduce profits. A rational employer will discriminate as long as the psychic benefits derived from each additional preferred worker is larger than profit losses. If the incremental profit losses remain small and the incremental psychic benefits from each additional preferred worker remain large, there will be substantial employment discrimination. Conservatives contend, however, that costs will be too great for any individual firm to engage in substantial employment discrimination. Since profits are already at minimum acceptable levels in competitive industries, conservatives claim that firms that continue to use discriminatory hiring practices will be forced out. This is why conservatives contend that market forces are sufficient to discipline employers with discriminatory preferences.

Employee Preferences. Employers might choose to discriminate when they have employees who prefer not to work with certain other groups. For example, suppose men prefer not to work with women. In this case, individual firms may not be able to lower their production costs by choosing to hire some highly qualified female workers. The firm's gain in productivity might be more than offset by the resulting labor unrest and increased wage demands of male workers. Rather than having to pay male workers a premium to work with female workers, employers will discriminate against qualified female applicants.

Conservatives claim that even in this situation, discriminatory hiring could not persist in the long run. In many cases, when a group is excluded, it sets up its own professional organizations. Members of these alternative organizations often are hired to service their own group. This creates a dual system, providing organizational and financial support for individuals excluded from the dominant professional organization. This trained and experienced group presents an incentive to all employers. Eventually, some profit-seeking employers will decide to hire these qualified nonpreferred workers rather than less qualified preferred applicants.

The persistence of limited numbers of qualified applicants from nonpreferred groups also might result if the necessary training programs are discriminatory. Conservatives expect that in a free market system, alternative programs will be set up to train the excluded group members. Training barriers will persist only when there is interference with the free market, such as when government agencies provide funding only to discriminatory training programs.

The situation changes dramatically once there are a sufficient number of trained nonpreferred applicants. Preferred-group workers can no longer influence the hiring decision of employers, since they can be replaced. Firms that continue to discriminate will now be undersold by firms that hire qualified nonpreferred workers. Preferred-group members who wish to continue to work in a segregated environment must now work for below-average wage rates. Presumably there might be a sufficiently large wage reduction to compensate firms for refusing to hire more qualified nonpreferred applicants, and segregation could persist. Conservatives believe, however, that majority group workers are not willing to pay this price for their discriminatory attitudes so that they will separate their market behavior from their personal preferences.

Consumer Preferences. Suppose consumers have preferences for specific groups of workers. For example, what if majority consumers prefer being serviced by majority group workers. If these preferences are sufficient to compensate firms for the additional cost of hiring less productive majority workers, a restaurant that hired a technically efficient nonpreferred worker or a home repair company that hired a skilled repairman from a nonpreferred group would lose business and could not afford to hire in a nondiscriminatory manner. As before, individual firms are disciplined by the market, but in this case it is the market that has preferential values.

Baseball Hiring Practices

Conservatives often cite the changing pattern of employment in major league baseball as an example of the power of market forces to discipline employers. Professional baseball was organized during the 1870s. A decade later, Cap Anson, a future Hall of Famer, refused to allow his team to play against black players. In response, the major leagues became all-white. During the 1920s, with the popularity of Babe Ruth, baseball became the national pastime, and baseball attendance and incomes grew. The growth in popularity made it viable for blacks to form an alternative organization, the Negro Baseball League, which serviced primarily minority fans.

As the conservative model predicts, this alternative organization created incentives for all employers by providing a skilled and experienced black work force. Conscious of potential profits, some entrepreneurs wished to employ black players in the major leagues. Bill Veeck attempted to buy and improve a weaker team by stocking it with better black players. In 1944 he made an unsuccessful attempt to purchase the Philadelphia Phillies, but a few years later he was able to purchase the Cleveland Indians. At about the same time, Branch Rickey decided to integrate the Brooklyn Dodgers. In 1947 the Dodgers broke the color line in the National League, and the next year Cleveland broke it in the American League.

Table 2–2 summarizes the impact of integration on team performance. The average number of victories for each team during the years 1946 to 1949 is taken as a benchmark, since during this period integration had little impact on the competitiveness of teams. A team was considered to be integrated when it had a starting player who was black. As an alternative, we could measure integration by the total number of starting positions each team filled with black players during the entire period 1947 to 1959.[3] Using either of these criteria, teams fell into three groups: those that were rapidly and strongly integrated, those that were delayed and more modestly integrated, and those that had not really begun integration by 1959. For example, Cincinnati belonged to the middle group because it did not have its

Table 2–2
Integration of Baseball Teams, 1946–1959

| Team | Black Starters | | Average Wins | | | Average Wins | | |
	First Year	Number 1947–1959	1946–1950	1951–1959	Difference	1950–1954	1955–1959	Difference
Milw	1950	18	83.2	85.7	2.5	80.8	90.0	9.2
LA	1947	27	92.0	91.6	-0.4	95.8	86.8	-9.0
SF	1950	22	75.8	81.8	6.0	88.6	75.8	-12.8
Chi WS	1950	24	64.4	87.4	23.0	81.0	88.4	7.4
Clev	1948	25	85.2	90.2	5.0	96.2	84.6	-11.6
Average					7.2			- 3.2
StL	1958	2	88.8	77.7	-11.1	80.4	74.8	- 5.6
Phila	1957	1	73.8	75.1	1.3	81.8	71.6	-10.2
Wash	—	0	62.6	63.7	1.1	69.8	58.2	-11.6
Detr	—	0	87.4	71.4	-16.0	69.2	78.4	9.2
Bos	—	0	94.6	80.0	-14.6	82.0	80.8	- 1.2
NY	1959	2	94.6	94.1	- 0.5	98.6	92.4	6.2
Average					- 6.6			- 4.4
Pitts	1955	6	67.2	63.2	- 4.0	53.2	70.0	16.8
Cinc	1956	7	66.4	75.0	8.6	69.0	79.2	10.2
Chi Cub	1954	12	68.0	67.6	- 0.4	66.4	68.0	1.6
Balt	1955	5	59.2	63.8	4.6	56.4	70.0	13.6
KC	1954	8	68.8	63.6	- 5.2	62.2	62.6	0.4
Average					0.9			8.5

Source: Joseph Reichler, ed. The Baseball Encyclopedia, 7th ed. (New York: Macmillan, 1988).

first starting black player until 1956 and used black players to fill only six starting positions during the period 1947 to 1959.

According to the conservative model, integration should have improved team performance, since some black players who were better than some white players were available. Teams that continued to remain segregated would be less productive and not perform as well. This expectation is confirmed by the data in table 2–2. Teams in the first group averaged 7.2 more wins per year during 1950 through 1959 than during the benchmark years. Alternatively, teams that were not integrated by 1959 averaged 6.6 fewer wins yearly during the 1950s than during the benchmark years.

Let us now analyse those teams that only began to be integrated in the mid-1950s. For the 1950s as a whole, these teams fared virtually the same as during the benchmark years. However, when we compare performance during the last half of the decade to that during the first half, the results demonstrate that these teams strongly benefited from integration, as their yearly victories increased by 8.5.

One might ask why the pace of integration was relatively slow during this period. Why were there still a number of teams that had not integrated more than a decade after Jackie Robinson broke the color line? First, baseball was still dominated by owners who had made their fortunes in other activities. For them, baseball was a hobby. Moreover, player salaries were quite low, so winning and losing resulted in only small profit differences.

Second, owners might have been reluctant to change because they believed their fans would be unwilling to support an integrated team. Owners might have felt that maintaining segregation was a response to the desires of their consumers. If their teams were less competitive, fans would be more supportive than if they chose integration as a means of improving team performance. Conservatives would expect that these consumers would accustom themselves to integration only when they realized the costs of their actions—that is, that segregated teams would not be competitive.

The situation changed dramatically during the 1960s as a result of television coverage. Television revenues increased salaries and potential revenues to owners. This dramatically increased the gains from having a successful team and the losses from having an unsuccessful team. No longer could owners afford to treat their teams as personal hobbies. Owners could maintain their preferences in purely social activities, but they could no longer afford to act on them when employing ball players. As a result, by 1970 all teams were strongly integrated.[4]

Government Intervention and Discrimination

The previous section indicated why conservatives believe that there is very little discrimination in a laissez-faire economy. Today, however, the United

States does not have a laissez-faire economy, as both government production and government regulations have a substantial impact on the economy. This section details conservative assessments of the impact of government production and regulations on the amount of labor market discrimination.

Government Production

The conservative framework emphasizes that, to the extent firms have an economic incentive to be efficient, they will be nondiscriminatory. Since conservatives associate economic incentives with profits, they immediately assume that when there is little or no profit motive, there is no incentive to be nondiscriminatory. Since government or government-regulated industries usually have no profit motive, they may have no incentive to be efficient. They can base hiring decisions solely on political criteria. For this reason, conservatives claim that government and government-regulated industries are the most discriminatory employers.

Without a profit motive, regulated firms may have no reason to be antidiscriminatory and are free to hire on the basis of their own or majority workers' preferences. As evidence, conservative economist Thomas Sowell (1981) cites the record of employment in government-regulated industries during the first quarter of the twentieth century. During this period the railroads and utilities had virtually no black workers, whereas before federal regulations, blacks had significant employment in these industries, particularly on the railroads. Sowell also compares employment in the nonprofit sector to employment in private industry. In 1936 only three black PhD's in chemistry were employed by white universities, while private industry employed more than three hundred black chemists.

The conservatives' belief that government economic decisions are dominated by political rather than efficiency criteria is central to their explanation of the rapid growth of minority employment in government-regulated industries after the 1965 Civil Rights Act. Before the 1960s, minorities had little political power and government-regulated industries employed virtually no blacks. During the 1960s, minorities increased their political influence, while most whites were politically docile and complacent. In this environment, government officials decided to support the demands of the vocal minority rather than the dormant majority. Since efficiency was not a concern, government-regulated industries hired masses of blacks into white-collar and managerial positions, hiring both qualified and unqualified individuals.

Conservatives believe that what they term reverse discrimination against majority workers can be only temporary. Eventually, majority workers will discard their complacency and exert pressure on the government to give preferential treatment to them. For this reason, conservatives believe that blacks have made no long-term gains from government-regulated employment and that such regulations only weaken their position to rely on employers who have no incentive to be efficient and hence no incentive to hire on the basis of productive ability.

Discriminatory Attitudes versus Discriminatory Practices

It is important to note that the progressive reduction of labor market discrimination is totally independent of any changes in attitudes. Preferential attitudes remain, but the market makes it too costly for employers or employees to base their decisions on them. Conservatives envision a stable society in which majority group workers or employers will be highly discriminatory in their social behavior but nondiscriminatory in their market behavior.

Presumably, if the government changes attitudes through educational programs or enacts penalties for discriminatory behavior, firms will no longer hire in a discriminatory manner. But conservatives reject any policy that coerces individuals, not only because these policies are unnecessary but also because they make arbitrary judgments as to which values and behavior are unacceptable. These judgments allow government to manipulate attitudes, regardless of the desirability of objectives. Thus, Milton Friedman (1962) states,

> I believe strongly that the color of a man's skin . . . is no reason to treat him differently. . . . I deplore what seems to me the prejudice . . . of those whose tastes differ from mine in this respect. . . . But in a society based on free discussion, the appropriate recourse is for me to seek to change their views and their behavior, not to use coercive power to enforce my tastes and my attitudes on others. (p. 112)

Many conservatives are unwilling to support government antidiscrimination legislation even when it is in response to discrimination generated by consumer preferences. Conservatives like Friedman believe that it is arbitrary to characterize negatively consumer desires to purchase services from preferred suppliers. He notes that if we allow consumers to discriminate as to the music they will buy, why should we not allow them to discriminate as to the demographic characteristics of the musician performing the music? If we can discriminate against jazz, which causes jazz musicians to be financially harmed, why can't we discriminate against black home repairmen? Since in both cases discrimination financially harms particular suppliers, why should we say one form of discrimination is acceptable while the other is not? Thus, Friedman is even unwilling to accept the view that preferences for particular groups is unacceptable.

Gary Becker (1957) also rejects the view that government policies should attempt to influence preferential values. Becker certainly believes that competitive market pressures will encourage many white male–owned firms to expand their employment of black and female workers, but he does not believe that competitive pressures will be sufficient to eliminate the discrimination these groups face when seeking employment in white male–owned firms. Becker (1986) believes that labor market discrimination will be eliminated only when there are a sufficient number of black-owned firms that prefer black workers and female-owned firms that prefer female workers. Thus, Becker's concern is not that there is too much discrimination in labor markets but that the discrimination is too one-sided.

For conservatives, government legislation to change behavior is the hallmark of a totalitarian regime. Once we allow the government to decide which values are acceptable and which are not, individuals lost their basic liberties. Thus, Friedman (1962) claims that the civil rights laws passed in the United States during the 1960s were equivalent philosophically to the Nuremberg laws passed in Nazi Germany during the 1930s. Both sets of laws tried to legislate attitudes; one made it illegal to hire nonpreferred workers, while the other made it illegal not to hire them.

Government Regulations

According to liberals, certain legislation, including government child labor laws, compulsory education regulations, and industrial safety rules, will offset the disadvantages minorities face in the marketplace. In contrast, conservatives believe that these policies harm the disadvantaged.

Conservatives agree that government safety regulations have reduced the number of sweatshops, but they believe that this has been harmful to low-income (minority) households. Conservatives point out that this simply eliminates one option and whenever decision makers have fewer options, they are worse off. For example, Thomas Sowell (1981) contends that the sweatshop was an integral part of the upward mobility of Jews at the beginning of the twentieth century. These sweatshops gave Jews entry-level positions, allowed them to work long hours, which in turn allowed them to save money, and thus provided an indispensable opportunity that would not have existed if liberal reformers had been successful in eliminating the sweatshops.

According to conservatives, the fact that women often work for firms with more unstable employment and lower wages than firms that employ comparably skilled men does not reflect discrimination. Recall that conservatives believe that many women do not desire to work full-time year-round. Since conservatives believe that firms respond to the preferences of workers, they envision firms accommodating by reorganizing production in a more discontinuous fashion. Employers realize that if they organize production in a discontinuous fashion that results in layoffs, they will be providing a more attractive workplace for women, especially if the women qualify for unemployment compensation. Since these jobs with discontinuous employment are more attractive, female workers will accept lower pay. For this reason, Martin Feldstein (1973) claimed that both discontinuous employment and lower wages reflect a firm's adaptation to the preference of its female work force. This argument led the federal government to begin taxing unemployment compensation.[5]

Conservatives reject compulsory education because it reduces the choices available to youths. While for many further schooling is productive, for some it is a waste of valuable time. For many minority youths, compulsory schooling is counterproductive because it results in high truancy rates and general lack of discipline, behavioral traits that make it impossible to obtain jobs. If instead these youths were allowed to work at menial jobs, they would develop the proper behavioral traits of punctuality and low absenteeism. Thus, conservatives recommend ending compulsory education and changing child labor and minimum wage laws, enabling youths to be productively employed instead of having their improper behavioral traits reinforced in the school system.

In all these situations, conservatives contend that middle-class reformers are attempting to impose their values on society. Since reformers believe that schooling is good, they impose compulsory education even when it is harmful to the behavioral development of youths. Reformers reject certain working arrangements because these arrangements upset their sensibilities, even if they provide an indispensable opportunity for many. These regulations reinforce conservative fears that government policies are often attempts to impose values on society rather than meaningful attempts to help others.

Income Redistribution

Liberals believe that income inequality hinders black advancement and should be corrected by government policies. Conservatives believe that the primary obstacle to black advancement is internal inadequacies. Many conservatives contend that poor blacks are so present-oriented that they are unlikely to provide even meager support for their offspring. Banfield (1974) suggests,

> The women . . . are likely to have a succession of mates who contribute intermittently to [the household] but take little or no part in rearing the children. In managing the children, the mother (or aunt, or grandmother) is characteristically impulsive; once children have passed babyhood they are likely to be neglected or abused, and at best they never know what to expect. (p. 62)

From this perspective it follows that welfare programs are harmful. Once households become accustomed to these handouts, they develop a welfare dependency that is transmitted to their children. Charles Murray (1984) synthesizes the conservative view of the destructive nature of the welfare reforms initiated during the past few decades:

> For more than three centuries, the mainstream of Western social thought among intellectuals and the general public alike held that welfare was pernicious at bottom—"a bounty on indolence and vice." . . . The very existence of a welfare system was assumed to have the inherent, intrinsic, unavoidable effect of undermining the moral character of people. (p. 16).

Murray contends that this popular wisdom was rejected by civil rights activists, who claimed that black poverty was caused by white racism. These activists rejected policies that penalized the poor for dysfunctional behavior. Since this approach reinforced the predispositions of the poor, Murray believes that these social policies were responsible for a decline in the work ethic and rise in unwed pregnancies and female-headed households during the 1970s.

Conservatives consider minimum wage legislation to be one of the major obstacles to black advancement, since unemployment is generated by raising wage rates artificially. Conservatives contend that this unemployment would disproportionately be borne by minorities for two reasons. With an excess labor supply, firms could find a sufficient number of qualified white workers to hire, making discrimination virtually costless. Second, many minority youths, owing to their improper behavioral traits, are simply not worth the minimum wage rate and will not be hired. If the wage rate was allowed to decline to a level at which employers would hire these less productive workers, black youths would gain work experience and discipline. Thus, low wage rates enable the market to provide the discipline these youths require, while enforcement of the minimum wage dooms them to unemployment.

Historical Antecedents

The complete conservative model has now been presented. To overcome inequality, we must rely on the market rather than government interventionist policies, and we must eliminate internal deficiencies rather than external constraints. These views are not new but are patterned after those presented in earlier times. In particular, we find that the views expressed during the nineteenth century by Thomas Malthus and Booker T. Washington provide a basis for many of the more contemporary conservative views.

Malthus gained popularity through writings that emphasized the dysfunctional behavior of the lower classes, which was reinforced by liberal reform policies. Malthus believed that the overpopulation and present-oriented attitude of the lower classes resulted from parish charity. As evidence, Malthus (1966) noted, "Men marry from a prospect of parish provision with little or no chance of maintaining their independence. . . . [T]heir present wants employ their whole attention and they seldom think of the future. Even when they have an opportunity to save they seldom exercise it, spending [all the extra funds] on the ale houses" (p. 85). He believed that laborers would use income to support their families "instead of spending it in drunkenness and dissipation if they did not rely on parish assistance" (p. 87).

Malthus fought against reforms to improve health standards, such as better sewerage systems and compulsory vaccinations. He fought against attempts to lower the cost of food to the poor and against any policies that improved their health and welfare. Malthus feared that all these policies would allow the poor to maintain their present-oriented values and enable more of their children to survive. He believed that the poor would never change if they were helped by liberal reformers. For Malthus, child labor was the only possible way that these idlers could be transformed into productive individuals, and he was adamantly opposed to child labor reforms. For these reasons, many consider Malthus the forerunner of conservatives today who claim that liberal reforms create a welfare-dependent population.

Booker T. Washington gained wide acceptance when he became an advocate of conservative principles. In 1895 Washington was asked to prepare a speech for Atlanta's world exposition as a representative of black people. At the time, there was substantial unrest in the South. Many blacks were uniting with whites in the Populist movement against the southern elite for control of state governments. In this situation, Washington decided to discuss his views on the appropriate black strategy. Washington emphasized the economic advantages white capitalists would obtain by employing blacks and reminded whites of the long history of black faithfulness and diligence:

> As we have proved our loyalty to you in the past in nursing your children, watching by the sick-bed of your mothers and fathers, and often following them tear-dimmed to their graves, so in the future, in our humble way, we shall stand by you with a devotion that no foreigner can approach, ready to lay down our lives, if need be, in defence of yours, interlacing our industrial, commercial, civil and religious life with yours in a way that shall make the interest of both races one. (Washington 1963, 160)

Washington placed his faith in the market system, for he believed that "no race that has anything to contribute to the markets of the world is long in any degree ostracized" (p. 161).

Washington believed that it would be a mistake for blacks to rely on nonmarket forces, since "agitation [for] social equality is the extremest folly; . . . progress . . . will come to us [as a] result of severe and constant struggle rather than [by] artificial forcing" (p. 161). He also believed that part of the struggle was for blacks to become more disciplined and less present-oriented. He considered the Reconstruction era immediately after the Civil War to be an inappropriate preparation for an "ignorant and inexperienced" black population. Reconstruction, by offering blacks preferential treatment (reverse discrimination) increased their present-orientedness. Reconstruction enabled them to begin "at the top instead of at the bottom," to seek "a seat in Congress . . . [rather] than real estate or industrial skill" (p. 158). While recognizing the importance of legal rights, Washington claimed that "it is vastly more important that we be prepared for the exercise of these privileges" (p. 161).

Finally, Washington believed that it was possible for individuals to separate personal values from their economic decisions. Raising his hand, Washington proclaimed, "In all things that are purely social we can be as separate as the fingers, yet one as the hand in all things essential to mutual progress." For Washington, "[t]he opportunity to earn a dollar in a factory just now is worth infinitely more than the opportunity to spend a dollar in an opera house" (pp., 160–161). Thus, Washington signaled his willingness to accept Jim Crow laws, which in 1895 had not yet become a general or even legal policy in the South.

We find that in his speech Washington presents virtually all the aspects of the conservative view:

1. Markets will eventually discipline employers to hire in a nondiscriminatory manner.
2. Proper behavioral traits are critical for advancement.
3. Reliance on government is counterproductive because it reinforces dysfunctional behavior.
4. Internal inadequacies are significant obstacles to progress.
5. It is possible to separate personal attitudes from economic activities.

Conclusions

The conservative prescriptions for ending discrimination are quite clear: rely on the market and avoid government intervention. These recommendations follow logically from assumptions made concerning the workings of the economy and the role of economic incentives. First, competitive pressures imply that the major form of discrimination is the decision not to hire qualified members of nonpreferred groups. The ability to hire nonpreferred workers at differentially lower wages is not nearly as significant. Many liberals and radicals disagree. They believe that wage discrimination is significant and may even be more important than the employment discrimination conservatives emphasize. This is important because wage discrimination can be profitable and hence can persist in the long run even in competitive industries. Indeed, if discrimination is profitable, competitive pressures might intensify discriminatory employment practices.

Discrimination would benefit white male workers if they could convince employers to hire only them for the better jobs. Conservatives contend, however, that this pact between white male workers and employers would be undermined by market forces that would create a trained, experienced dual work force that could not be ignored by profit-seeking employers.

Conservatives equate discrimination against groups of products (jazz music, summer fruits, and so on) with discrimination against groups of individuals (Jewish entertainers, female accountants, and the like). They believe, however, that in general individuals can separate their personal preferences from their economic decisions. Just as importantly, conservatives fear government attempts to impose antidiscriminatory attitudes on individuals. Conservatives believe that once government begins to impose values, no matter how well intentioned, it is setting the stage for further intrusions into private lives. These intrusions reflect the policies of totalitarian regimes and should be opposed.

Conservatives also oppose government social and antidiscrimination programs, believing that not only are these programs unnecessary, but also that they can actually harm disadvantaged groups. Many conservatives emphasize that neither the black family nor the school system provides discipline and that the marketplace offers the only hope of salvation. While many will fail, the harsh discipline of the marketplace will save at least some. Although the marketplace can save some disadvantaged youths from their present-oriented and distorted values, conservatives believe that liberal programs perpetuate the false view that difficulties result from factors external to the individual. According to Edward Banfield (1974), this false view perpetuates income differences:

> Racial prejudice has long been declining . . . [but it] counts for little if the Negro *thinks* that white racism is as pervasive as ever; that his opportunities to improve his position by acquiring skills are at last fairly good counts for little if he *thinks* that "massive" government welfare, housing, and other programs—and *only* these—can help him. If he misperceives the situation he is likely to do things that are counterproductive. (p. 283)

This chapter has focused on three major conservative themes:

1. Labor market discrimination does not persist because competitive pressures force individuals to separate their attitudes from their market behavior.

2. Even if individuals continue to act on their discriminatory attitudes, it is inappropriate to use the government to change attitudes.

3. Even if discrimination persists, government social and antidiscrimination policies would make matters worse.

Since all three aspects of the conservative view are relatively independent of each other, it is possible that we may accept some hybrid of conservative views presented in this chapter and liberal views presented in the next chapter. For example, we may accept conservative criticisms of antidiscrimination programs, such as affirmative action, but reject conservative criticisms of certain government social programs. Or we might believe that competitive pressures are strong but also believe that government programs to reduce discriminatory attitudes can be helpful. For this reason, even for those who are inclined to accept the conservative thesis, the next chapters may be valuable in helping clarify which aspects of the conservative view they most strongly support and which may require modification.

Notes

1. Thomas Sowell (1981) has shown that even though the average income of Chinese American families is 22 percent above the national average, their income is below that of male-headed families once we standardize for education and number of workers in the household.

2. It is possible that labor market forces might result in a lower market wage rate for black workers relative to the market wage rate for white workers. This might make sense in situations where a competitive firm can hire from racially segmented labor markets. While this is the form some neoclassical models take (Becker 1957), this possibility would not change the analysis. Among all firms facing these racially differential market wage rates, a firm with a preference for white workers would still weigh the losses from hiring a less cost-effective white worker against psychic benefits.

3. This does not mean the number of different players who started; the same player is counted more than once if he was a starter in more than one year.

4. We have not assessed the impact of the profit motive on the hiring of black managers or administrators by baseball teams.

5. Feldstein (1973) overstates the value of unemployment compensation because he ignores the lost seniority, vacation pay, and other fringe benefits. Lloyd and Niemi (1979) find that when these losses are included, unemployment benefits are no longer as attractive, even for married women with working husbands.

References

Banfield, Edward. 1974. *The Unheavenly City Revisited*. Boston: Little, Brown.

Becker, Gary. 1957. *Economics of Discrimination*. Chicago: University of Chicago Press.

———. 1964. *Human Capital*. New York: Columbia University Press.

———. 1986. "Discussant." Paper presented at the Allied Social Science Meetings, New Orleans, 29 December.

Feldstein, Martin. 1973. "The Economics of the New Unemployment." *The Public Interest* 33:1–21.

Friedman, Milton. 1962. *Capitalism and Freedom*. Chicago: University of Chicago Press.

Lloyd, Cynthia, and Beth Niemi. 1979. *The Economics of Sex Differentials*. New York: Columbia University Press.

Malthus, Thomas. [1798] 1966. *First Essay on Population*. New York: Macmillan.

Murray, Charles. 1984. *Losing Ground: American Social Policy, 1950–1980*. New York: Basic Books.

Sowell, Thomas. 1981. *Markets and Minorities*. New York: Basic Books.

Washington, Booker T. 1963. *Up from Slavery*. Garden City, NY: Doubleday.

3
The Liberal View

onservatives contend that the market discourages discrimination by disciplining individuals; it is the government, through misguided policies, that intensifies problems. Alternatively, liberal economists argue that market forces, though often helpful, are not strong enough to counteract discrimination and that government policies are necessary. The first section of this chapter summarizes the evolution of liberal views, including those of Gunnar Myrdal. Myrdal's studies were the forerunner of theories based on the belief that without government intervention, there would be a vicious cycle in which problems, such as discrimination, would be self-perpetuated.

Liberals also believe that institutionalized procedures, such as the method of screening job applicants, often have an unintended discriminatory impact. In the second section of this chapter, I detail these and other examples of institutional discrimination. This section also discusses the impact that unequal income and unequal access to job information have on the education and earnings of disadvantaged groups. Finally, liberal views that emphasize the impact of skill and locational mismatches are discussed.

Development of the Liberal View

During the late 1930s, prodded by the unfolding dynamics of Nazism abroad and political events at home, the Carnegie Corporation of New York, which had previously been an important funder of the American eugenics movement, changed its approach. To develop a more sympathetic understanding of black Americans, the Carnegie Corporation funded major studies of American race relations coordinated by the Swedish economist Gunnar Myrdal. One focus of these studies was to determine the origins of the racist attitudes of white Americans.

Myrdal believed that the growth of discriminatory attitudes toward blacks was independent of perceptions of black inferiority. For Myrdal, racial attitudes become prevalent when individuals who support the American creed of equal opportunity seek a rationale for inequality of income and power:

> The race dogma is nearly the only way out for a people so moralistically equalitarian, if it is not prepared to live up to its faith. A nation less fervently

committed to democracy could, probably, live happily in a caste system with a somewhat less intensive belief in the biological inferiority of a subordinate group. *The need for race prejudice is, from this point of view, a need for defense on the part of the Americans against their own national Creed, against their own most cherished ideals.* And race prejudice is, in this sense, a function of equalitarianism. The former is a perversion of the latter. (Myrdal 1944, 89)

According to this viewpoint, when the Industrial Revolution began to change economic relationships, a new economic elite—the capitalists—justified new forms of inequality by claiming that workers were racially inferior. Not surprisingly, capitalists often adopted the views of the social Darwinists, who extended Malthus's theories in the latter part of the nineteenth century (Chase 1975).

Prior to the Myrdal study, theories of genetic inferiority were widely accepted by the upper classes and the intellectual community. These theories were primarily directed at immigrants from eastern and southern Europe and seemed to be reinforced by scientific findings concerning instincts and IQ testing. These genetic views were the basis of sterilization laws adopted by twenty-five states and national immigration legislation (Cherry 1976, 1980).

In response to these genetic views, which found their clearest organizational forms in the Ku Klux Klan (KKK) and American Eugenics Society, some liberals presented an alternative explanation for the plight of the immigrant. These liberals also believed that inferior traits were the major reason for the immigrants' low status, but they thought that these traits were not permanent (genetic) and that they could be remedied by sympathetic policies. These liberals, comprising the majority of Progressives, believed that settlement houses would educate the young to the virtues of the American way and proper unions would acculturate adult workers. In contrast, most of these liberals believed that the inferior traits blacks possessed were genetically determined and hence permanent. Liberals made a qualitative distinction between the causes of black inferiority and the causes of immigrant inferiority. They held out hope for immigrants but not for blacks.

An important example of this distinction made by many Progressives was the views of John R. Commons. Commons was an important labor economist and an influential member of the prestigious National Civic Federation. Commons emphasized that the inferiority of European immigrants was cultural, a product of centuries of serfdom and Catholicism. Immigrants could be culturally assimilated—that is, Americanized—only if the proper institutions were provided.

With respect to blacks, there were no such possibilities. Echoing proslavery views of a century earlier, Commons (1924) claimed that Negroes were "indolent and fickle" and "some form of compulsion" was necessary if they were to adopt the industrious life (p. 136). According to Commons, the situation of blacks in the South after Reconstruction was the result of a naive attempt to uplift them using education and democracy. He suggested that "the fearful collapse of the experiment is now recognized . . . as something that was inevitable [given] the nature of the race at that stage of development" (pp. 3–4).

Commons also believed that only races of the temperate zone contained traits of industry and ambition. Indeed, these immigrants would fiercely compete among themselves for scarce jobs, forcing wage rates below acceptable levels. Thus, unions were necessary to guarantee that wage rates immigrants received would not be undermined. Since blacks did not possess these characteristics, he said, they did not engage in destructive competition and had no need for unions. Not until the Myrdal study did liberals adopt the same attitude toward the inferior status of blacks as they had in explaining the inferior status of European immigrants thirty years earlier.

Myrdal accepted the view that blacks had inferior traits, but unlike the Malthusians, social Darwinists, and many Progressives, Myrdal believed that these traits stemmed from cultural factors that discrimination often reinforced. Myrdal (1944) reasoned that if people think blacks are inferior, they will restrict black employment and educational opportunities. Lacking education, blacks will indeed be less productive; lacking opportunity, they will not compete and instead will develop bad habits. If black skill levels remain low and blacks adapt in a dysfunctional manner, racial stereotypes will be reinforced and barriers to black opportunity strengthened. Thus, a vicious cycle develops, since racial stereotypes create dynamics that reinforce those stereotypes. Myrdal called this the cumulative process and reasoned that it was much stronger than any countervailing influences of the marketplace.

The Cumulative Process
and Women

Michael Piore (1977) has used a variant of Myrdal's cumulative process to explain the labor market behavior of women. Piore believes that many firms refuse to hire qualified female applicants because they believe women are not career-oriented. As a result, qualified women end up in low-wage, unstable jobs. Facing this situation, many women adapt. They realize it will be difficult to obtain jobs requiring a long-term commitment, so they decide it is not worth obtaining the educational background necessary to compete for career-oriented positions. Women shift to traditional female fields, which tend to have high rates of turnover. However rational women's actions are, they reinforce the stereotype that female applicants have little long-term attachment to the labor market.

Piore posits that over time, even qualified and well-motivated female workers can lose the proper behavioral traits necessary for career-oriented positions. They have poor attendance records and high turnover rates, which further reduce their chances of upward mobility. Piore even expects that many of these women give up altogether and seek welfare or illegal activities rather than pursue labor market activities. Thus, women who begin with the proper behavior traits for career-oriented employment often end up exhibiting the dysfunctional behavior conservatives highlight. As a result, the negative stereotype held by employers is reinforced, making it even more difficult for qualified women to have access to career-oriented employment.

In contrast with conservatives, liberals do not see this outcome simply as a matter of individual choice—the preferences of women. They believe that if the government discouraged discriminatory hiring practices, the cumulative process would be reversed. Once firms began to hire qualified women, these women would provide role models. Other women would become hopeful and again obtain the necessary training to qualify for career-oriented employment. Firms would begin to see many women with the necessary qualifications applying for positions and would be more willing to hire them. Eventually, the negative stereotype would disappear, and government enforcement of antidiscrimination regulations would become unnecessary.

Liberal Views on
the Black Family Structure

Myrdal's thesis is often used to explain the difference between black and white family structure. This difference is often cited as a major reason for the lower economic status of blacks. During the 1960s, data began to show a stark contrast between the percentages of black and white female-headed families. Liberals such as Daniel Moynihan (1965) claimed that the black nuclear family was destroyed by slavery, as black families were broken up by slave auctions and marriage among slaves was forbidden. Blacks adapted to this situation by not stressing nuclear families. This "legacy of slavery" continued after emancipation, with the result being a lack of effort on the part of blacks to maintain stable two-parent households and a failure to place any social stigma on unwed mothers. While this behavior was appropriate for a slave population, liberals claimed that it was dysfunctional in a free society.

After emancipation, racism intensified this dysfunctional behavior. By increasing black male unemployment, racism made it difficult for black men to earn a sufficient income to support a family. By not allowing black men dignity, American society made it more difficult for them to remain in a family structure and fulfill parental responsibilities. Many liberals agreed that this dysfunctional family structure had damaging effects on the attitudes and abilities of black youths. Summarizing this view, liberal economist Paul Samuelson (1970) states, "[I]f a black child comes from a broken home where no books line the shelves, and where one parent is hard-pressed to care for many children on a limited relief check, then, already at the age of six, the beginning student is under a handicap with respect to learning performance and educational achievement" (p. 788).

James Coleman (1966) and others have used Myrdal's cumulative thesis to explain why educational disparity grows with years of schooling. Within the school system, children are tracked according to perceived abilities from the earliest grades. Black inner-city youths, owing to the cultural disadvantages of child rearing in black female-headed households, are incorrectly perceived as being less intelligent and quickly tracked into the lowest groups.

In these lower-tracked groups, teachers develop a low expectation of their students and do not attempt to provide as much educational stimuli as possible. By discouraging learning and lowering educational goals, teachers prevent lower-tracked students from reducing their educational disadvantage. Indeed, these students are likely to become discouraged and no longer strive for excellence. Thus, this tracking system, while not necessarily racially motivated, has the effect of reinforcing the "vicious cycle of poverty" by destroying the ability of the educational system to compensate for cultural deficiencies.

Compensatory Educational Programs

If we accept the view that these deficiencies are not genetic but result from the dysfunctional black family structure, a wide variety of policies could be recommended. Whereas conservatives such as Banfield (1974) often recommend strict discipline, most liberals favor more sympathetic treatment. Arthur Okun (1977) notes,

> Even when the last-place entries do not exert their full effort, impoverishment is not necessarily the most effective way to get them to try harder in the future. We might learn something from primitive hunting societies that gave their slackers an equal share of the catch, but made them eat apart from the rest of the community. . . . Or our social rules might draw from our family rules, which only occasionally invoke material rewards and penalties. (p. 31)

Thus, even when liberals believe that individuals are responsible for their inferior lot, they usually recommend supportive programs. This viewpoint dominated the liberal rationale for the compensatory educational programs that were instituted during the late 1960s.

Compensatory educational policies were implemented at three levels—preschool, grade school, and college. The most widely funded preschool program was Head Start. It offered disadvantaged children access to federally funded nursery schools and developed reading readiness and other skills at an early age. At the grade school level, compensatory programs provided federally funded reading and math specialists who could work with students whose skills were assessed at below grade level. At the college level, compensatory programs justified admitting students who did not meet the traditionally required skill levels. These students would be placed in special programs in which additional skill development resources would be provided. These resources would enable disadvantaged students to make a transition after a limited amount of time into the college mainstream.

There is widespread support for these programs among liberals, who agree that funding per student should be high enough so that resources are not too widely dispersed. As Lloyd Ullman (1977) has noted, liberals differ in their views of how to increase funding. Some favor increasing total budgets, while others favor reducing the number of students in funded programs. Particularly with respect to college compensatory programs, many liberals argue that resources are wasted on students with significant skill deficiencies. These critics believe that improvement will be modest and that those students with significant skill deficiencies cannot be expected to improve enough to enter the college mainstream. This approach—labeled creaming—suggests that funds should be provided only for the least skill-deficient students in the disadvantaged group, as the most deficient are doomed to failure.

It may appear that restrictive compensatory programs that serve only the least deficient will provide only token access to entry-level occupations. However, even if only a few are initially aided by this policy, they become role models for others. As a result, female and black youths realize that it is possible to succeed, do not become discouraged in grade school, and do not develop significant skill deficiencies. The pool of college-bound minority and female students with sufficient skill levels grows, increasing the number successfully completing college programs with minimal compensatory support. Thus, the policy of creaming can provide sufficient role models so that dysfunctional adaptation is minimized and there is no need for more massive intervention.

Legislation against Discriminatory Actions

Capitalism is the first economic system that claims to be amoral. Feudalism before it and communism, which attempts to replace it, both enforce a set of moral values on society. Under capitalism, at least as envisioned by its conservative defenders, the government should never enforce moral values;

it should be responsible only for the protection of property rights. Conservatives minimize the dangers within an amoral society. They emphasize how the "invisible hand" operates through market forces to discipline decision makers so that socially desirable objectives are achieved. In contrast, liberals support attempts by the government to promote egalitarian and antidiscriminatory values.

Myrdal and his supporters understood that changing attitudes was a difficult process. When perceptions are deeply rooted and serve important functions, facts alone may not be sufficient to change individual behavior. In his influential work, *The Nature of Prejudice,* Gordon Allport (1954) notes, "This frequent segregation of knowledge from conduct is revealed in a few investigations that have tested both beliefs and attitudes. Intercultural instruction may have the power of correcting erroneous beliefs without appreciable altering attitudes. Children may, for example, learn the facts of Negro history without learning tolerance" (p. 485).

Allport believed, however, that it was likely that a consistent presentation of facts would overcome significant resistance. He thought that "in the long run, accurate information is probably an ally of improved human relations" (p. 485). He suggested that the most effective method of improving attitudes was through "film, novels and dreams . . . [which] induce identification with minority group members" (p. 488). For Allport, these milder presentations, being less threatening and confrontational, provided a beginning from which we could move gradually into "more realistic and informational levels of training" (p. 488). Thus, the treatment of blacks and women on television and ordinary school assignments may have a more important impact on white (male) attitudes than direct integration and presentations of factual material.

Institutional Discrimination

Individuals and institutions may use decision-making procedures that inadvertently discriminate and reinforce inequalities. For example, income differentials can cause unequal access to education even though the school system does not intend to discriminate; locational decisions of firms may have the unintended impact of reducing access to jobs. Similarly, when housing is segregated by income (race), all individuals do not have equal access to job information, as higher-income (white) households will tend to have greater access to job information through personal contacts than lower-income (black) households. Thus, employers will have more higher-income white applicants than if housing was distributed without regard to race or income. Also, employers attempting to reduce their screening costs might rely on group stereotypes rather than more individualized information when deciding which applicants to interview.

In none of these instances is discrimination consciously undertaken, but disadvantaged groups, having unequal access to education, job information, and the interviewing process, are nonetheless harmed. Though unintentional, these problems reinforce the "vicious cycle" of poverty.

Income Differentials
and Educational Attainment

Income constraints place heavy burdens on the allocation decisions of low-income households. Often they must "choose" to do without many necessities, such as education. In addition, children from low-income households often have explicit household responsibilities that take time away from school activities. This may involve responsibility for household activities (baby-sitting, shopping, and so on) or earning income. In either case, economists would argue that on average low-income students have a greater opportunity cost on their time than high-income students. Since their opportunity costs are greater, lower-income students rationally allocate less time to studying and school-related activities than equally motivated higher-income students.

At the college level, even the availability of low-cost public institutions does not necessarily equalize the economic cost of education to all students. Just as at the elementary and secondary school level, lower-income students have a greater opportunity cost on their time than comparable higher-income students. Even if family responsibilities are negligible, students still require income for their own support. This invariably requires lower-income students to work at least part-time while attending school and has often led to the sending of male but not female offspring to college.

The level of income required is influenced by whether the student can live at home while attending college. Historically, public colleges were located in rural areas. For example, none of the original campuses of the Big Ten or Big Eight colleges are located in the states' largest metropolitan areas. The original campus of the University of Illinois is not located in Chicago and the University of Missouri is not located in St. Louis or Kansas City. Thus, not only did lower-income students have to pay for room and board away from home, but it was usually difficult to find part-time employment in these rural communities. This implies that even the availability of low-cost public colleges did not necessarily place the lower-income student on an equal footing with more prosperous students.

Theoretically, low-income youths with appropriate abilities and motivation should be able to borrow money to finance their education. As long as the economic returns from schooling are greater than the interest rate, students will gain from borrowing rather than forgoing additional education.

The equalizing of economic costs can occur only if all students of equal promise can borrow at the same rates. Financial institutions, however, cannot accept expectations or probabilities of future income as sufficient collateral for loans. They require bank accounts or other tradable assets, which are normally held by upper-income but not lower-income households. Thus, students from lower-income households cannot borrow readily for education without government intervention.

It also appears that schools in poorer neighborhoods tend to have larger classes and weaker teachers. John Owen (1972a) found that within the same city, as the mean neighborhood income rose by 1 percent, class size decreased by 0.24 percent and the verbal ability of teachers rose by 0.11 percent. This inequality is even more glaring when comparisons are made between cities. Owen (1972b) found that for each 1 percent increase in the mean income of a city, there was a rise of 0.73 percent in real expenditures per student and a 1.20 percent increase in the verbal ability of teachers. Thus, students living in poorer neighborhoods in poorer cities have a double disadvantage.

If higher opportunity costs and lower-quality education were not sufficient to discourage educational attainment, Bennett Harrison (1977) found that for black inner-city youths, incomes are hardly affected by increases in educational attainment. He notes, "[A]s their education increases, blacks move into new occupations, but their earnings are hardly affected at all by anything short of a college degree, and there is no effect whatever on their chances of finding themselves without a job over the course of the year" (p. 262). Thus, independent of conscious discrimination by the educational system, we should expect low-income minority youths to have lower educational attainment than white youths, even when ability and motivation are held constant.[1]

During the 1970s, a number of policies were implemented in an attempt to compensate for the influence of family income on educational attainment. First, legislatures began funding state universities in larger urban areas. Second, court rulings forced states to change funding formulas so that per capita funding from wealthy and poor communities within each state would become more equal. Third, guaranteed student loans reduced the disadvantage low-income students faced when attempting to finance their education.

Differential Impact
of Incomplete Information

In the most simplified labor models, it is assumed that workers and firms act with complete information: Workers know the jobs that are available, and firms know the productivity of job seekers. In this situation, competitive firms would hire the best applicants for the jobs available, and workers would gain the maximum wage obtainable.

Economists have recently developed models in which information has a price; it is only "purchased" up to the point at which its benefits are at least as great as its costs. Neither firms nor workers rationally attempt to gain complete information concerning the labor market opportunities available. Workers find that some additional job information is not worth its cost, while firms find that some information on the productivity of applicants is not worth the additional personnel expenses. Liberals have argued that when workers and firms rationally decide to act on the basis of optimal rather than complete information, biases are generated.

Let us begin by analyzing how firms decide the optimal productivity information they should obtain. A firm benefits from additional productivity information if it translates into hiring a more profitable work force. A firm must weigh this increased profitability against the cost involved in seeking the additional information. After some point, it is likely that the benefits from additional information are insufficient to outweigh its cost. Even though the firm realizes additional information would probably result in hiring a somewhat more productive worker than otherwise, it knows that the added screening expenses would be even greater.

When a strong profit motive and wide productivity differentials among applicants are present, extensive screening will occur. This is the case with professional sports teams, especially since television revenues have transformed ownership from a hobby to a profit-making activity. Liberals believe, however, that in the vast majority of situations, productivity differentials among applicants are quite small and benefits from extensive screening are minimal.

Liberals suggest that the initial screening of applicants is often done with very little individual productivity information available. For firms with a large number of relatively equally qualified applicants, there is no reason to spend much time determining which applicants should be interviewed. These firms simply take a few minutes (seconds) to look over applications and select a promising group to interview. The employer realizes that such a superficial procedure will undoubtedly eliminate some job applicants who are slightly more productive than those selected for interviews. Since productivity differentials are perceived to be minor, however, this loss is not sufficient to warrant a more extensive (expensive) screening procedure.

There would be no discrimination if the job applicants victimized were random, but let us see why the screening method might cause the consistent victimization of individuals from disadvantaged groups. Suppose a firm considering college graduates for trainee positions decides that it has many equally qualified candidates. Looking at résumés, the firm can quickly identify each applicant's race, sex, and college attended. If the firm has enough applicants from better colleges, it is likely to say, "All things being equal, students from these colleges are likely to be more qualified than applicants who attended weaker colleges." Thus, the firm dismisses applicants from the weaker colleges, even though it realizes that weaker schools produce some qualified applicants. The firm has nothing against qualified graduates of weaker colleges. It simply reasons that the extra effort required to identify them is not worth the expense.

However unintentional, highly qualified graduates from weaker schools are discriminated against. Discrimination occurs because this screening method determines the selection for interviews on the basis of group characteristics rather than individual information. More generally, highly qualified applicants from any group that is perceived to have below-average productivity would be discriminated against by this superficial screening method.

Suppose employers believe that black and female applicants are typically less productive than their white male counterparts. If the firm has sufficient white male applicants, it will not interview black or female applicants. The firm will decide that although there are some black and female applicants who are slightly more productive than some white male applicants, it is not worth the added expense to identify them. The process by which individuals are discriminated against when firms use group characteristics to screen individuals is usually called statistical discrimination.

Statistical discrimination can occur indirectly. A firm hiring workers for on-the-job training may be primarily interested in selecting applicants who will stay an extended period of time. The firm does not want to invest training in individuals who will leave the firm quickly. Presumably, if the firm had a sufficient number of applicants who worked more than four years with their previous employer, it would not choose to interview applicants with more unstable work experience. Again, the firm reasons that although there are likely to be some qualified applicants among those with an unstable work record, it is too costly to identify them. This method of screening is likely to discriminate because of the nature of seniority systems, which operate on a "last hired, first fired" basis. Many minorities and women have unstable work records because they are hired last and fired first. Thus, even when firms do not use racial or gender stereotypes, they discriminate, since women and minorities are more likely to come from weaker schools and have more unstable work records than equally qualified white male applicants.

Financial and Occupational Effects

Many economists believe the job market is divided between good (primary) and bad (secondary) jobs. Good jobs have characteristics such as on-the-job training and promotions through well-organized internal labor markets. Bad jobs have little on-the-job training and minimum chance for promotions; they are dead-end jobs. Since on-the-job training is a significant aspect of primary-sector jobs, employment stability and behavioral traits are often more important than formal education and general skills. Both conservative and liberal economists agree that workers who do not possess the proper behavioral traits, such as low absenteeism and punctuality, will not be employed in the primary sector. Most liberals believe that many women and minority workers who possess the proper behavioral traits also will not find jobs in the primary sector as a result of statistical discrimination.

Facing discrimination in the primary sector, many qualified female and minority workers shift to secondary labor markets. As a result, secondary employers have a greater supply of workers and can reduce wages and standards for working conditions. Primary employers and majority workers also benefit from statistical discrimination. Since majority workers face less competition, more of them will gain primary employment than they would in the absence of statistical discrimination.

Primary employers may have to pay somewhat higher wages and employ somewhat less productive workers as a result of statistical discrimination, but the reduced screening costs more than compensate for the higher wages and productivity losses. Moreover, many primary employers also hire secondary workers. For them, the higher cost of primary employees will be offset by the resulting reduction in wages paid to secondary workers and their somewhat higher productivity.

Since primary workers, primary employers, and secondary employers benefit from statistical discrimination, there are identifiable forces opposed to change. Thus, rather than the market disciplining decision makers, statistical discrimination creates groups having a financial stake in its perpetuation.

Applicants and Their Search for Job Information

For job seekers, the cheapest source of job information is personal contacts, including neighbors and relatives and their acquaintances. Additional information can be obtained from newspaper advertisements and government employment offices. The most costly information is obtained from private employment agencies. A significant difference in the cost of job information would occur if one individual had few personal contacts and was forced to use private employment services, while another individual had extensive personal contacts. All things being equal, the individual with the lower cost of obtaining information would be better informed and hence more likely to obtain higher earnings.

The job information minorities receive from their search effort is likely to be less valuable than the job information received by their white counterparts. The fact that an individual is recommended by a personal contact might be sufficient reason to grant the person an interview. Those who obtain information from newspaper ads or government employment services do not have this advantage. This distinction is summed up in the adage "It's not what you know but who you know that counts."[2]

Low-income (minority) individuals tend to have fewer contacts than high-income (white) individuals of equal abilities and motivation. High-income (white) individuals tend to have many neighbors or relatives who have good jobs, own businesses, or are involved in their firm's hiring decisions. Low-income (minority) individuals, having few personal contacts, are forced to spend additional time and money to obtain job information. Even if the job information is as valuable as that obtained by their white counterparts, minorities might give up searching for employment sooner because it is more costly. They do not do so because they are less able or less motivated; they simply face greater expenses.

Affirmative Action

Affirmative action legislation is the major government attempt at counteracting the discriminatory features of the hiring process. Affirmative action assumes that discrimination results from employment decisions based on incomplete information. The role of the government is simply to encourage firms to hire all qualified applicants by forcing them to gather individualized productivity information.

Guidelines stipulate that all government agencies and private firms doing business with the government must publicly announce job openings at least forty-five days prior to the termination of acceptance of applications. This provision attempts to offset the information inequality disadvantaged workers face. More importantly, these employers must interview a minimum number of applicants from groups that tend to be victims of statistical discrimination.

It is important to remember the difference between affirmative action and quotas. Under affirmative action, there is no requirement to hire; employers are required only to interview female and minority applicants and make sure they have access to job information. Quotas are more drastic actions reserved for situations in which firms are not making good faith efforts to seek out and hire qualified female and minority applicants. For example, if a firm attempts to circumvent affirmative action guidelines by announcing job openings in papers that reached only the white community or, after interviewing applicants, uses discriminatory procedures to eliminate women from employment, the government can impose quotas. Thus, quotas are imposed only when it is demonstrated that the lack of female or minority employment reflects something more conscious than the unintentional effects of incomplete information.

Besides the government, some private groups have attempted to compensate for unequal access to information. Women's groups have attempted to set up networks to aid female job applicants for management positions. Female executives are encouraged to share as much information as possible with other women to offset the traditional networking done by men. In many areas, male networking is referred to as the old boy network, and entry into it has historically been critical to obtaining the most desirable jobs. Thus, the lack of personal contacts is at least partially offset by networks that direct job information to disadvantaged workers and provide low-cost productivity information to firms.

Skill and Locational Mismatches

Many individuals reject the view that groups are held back due to external pressures by noting that "when we came to America, we faced discrimination but were able to overcome it." In particular, these individuals often believe that internal inadequacies are responsible for the seemingly permanent economic problems minorities face. One response is to argue that the discrimination minorities face is more severe and their economic resources fewer than those of European immigrants at the turn of the century. Another response dominated the U.S. Riot Commission's assessment of black poverty. This presidential commission, which was created to study the causes of the urban rebellions of the late 1960s, noted,

> When the European immigrants were arriving in large numbers, America was becoming an urban-industrial society. To build its major cities and industries, America needed great pools of unskilled labor. Since World War II . . . America's urban-industrial society has matured: unskilled labor is far less essential than before, and blue-collar jobs of all kinds are decreasing in numbers and importance as sources of new employment; . . . The Negro, unlike the immigrant, found little opportunity in the city; he had arrived too late, and the unskilled labor he had to offer was no longer needed. (U.S. Riot Commission 1968, 278)

This commission, commonly known as the Kerner commission, avoided blaming either the victims (culture of poverty) or society (discrimination) for black economic problems; they were simply the result of technological change. To compensate for the higher skill levels required for entry-level positions, the Kerner commission recommended extensive job-training programs. Supposedly, once these skills were obtained, blacks would enter the employment mainstream and racial income disparities would diminish.

Job-training programs became the centerpiece of the liberal War on Poverty initiated during the Johnson administration. To an extent, these job-training programs complemented compensatory educational programs. Whereas the compensatory programs attempted to develop general skills, job-training programs attempted to develop specific job-related skills. Whereas the compensatory programs were attempts to increase white-collar skills, job-training programs were attempts to increase blue-collar skills.

The government's involvement in job-training programs was pragmatic; it sought upward mobility in ways that would not conflict with the interests of other groups. Thus, it did not aggressively institute training programs that would conflict with the objectives of many craft unions. This meant that in many of the construction trades, which had historically restricted membership, the government accepted union prerogatives. Job-training success also was impeded by the seeming irrelevance of many of the skills taught, and there were complaints that training programs did not use the latest equipment and the newest methods.

Many liberals discounted these complaints. They agreed with conservatives that the problems disadvantaged groups faced stemmed from their internal inadequacies. These liberals thought the actual technical skills developed were irrelevant; what was critical was the development of the proper behavioral traits of punctuality and low absenteeism. These liberals also recommended more restrictive programs that would train only the least deficient of the disadvantaged group. In contrast, those liberals who believed that external pressures, particularly discrimination, were dominant proposed costly training programs and a more aggressive approach to craft unions.

Job-training success also was impeded by the shifting of blue-collar jobs out of Northeastern and Midwestern urban areas. After World War II, technological changes decreased the viability of central city locations. First, trucking replaced the railroads as the major transportation mode. When firms delivered their output (and received their input) on railcars, central city locations were ideal. When trucking became dominant, traffic tie-ups made those locations too costly. Indeed, recognizing these costs, the federal government built a new interstate highway system so that travelers could bypass congested central city areas.

Second, new technologies emphasized assembly-line techniques that required one-level production. No longer could manufacturing firms use factory buildings in which they operated on a number of floors. High land costs made it too expensive to build one-level plants in urban centers, so manufacturing firms began to locate in industrial parks near the new interstate highways on the outskirts of urban areas. This intensified minority employment problems, as most minorities continued to live in the inner city.

Minorities with the proper behavioral requirements, education, and skills have difficulty obtaining employment due to these locational mismatches. Inner-city residents are likely to lack the financial ability to commute to suburban jobs. They are unlikely to own a car or to earn a sufficient income to justify the extensive commuting required, even if public transportation is available. Minorities also are less likely to have access to these jobs because they have fewer personal contacts working in suburban locations.

Liberals have offered a number of recommendations to offset locational mismatches. Some economists have favored government subsidies to transportation networks that would bring inner-city workers to suburban employment locations. These subsidies would be cost-effective if the added employment generated greater income tax revenues and government spending reductions. Other economists have favored subsidizing firms to relocate in targeted inner-city zones. This approach was even endorsed by President Reagan under the catchy name "Free Enterprise Zones."

Conclusions

This chapter has described the historic evolution of liberal views, their policy implications, and some of the ways they differ from conservative views. The basic liberal view begins with an assumption that disadvantaged groups have some internal inadequacies that become more damaging as a result of discrimination, technological change, and institutional impediments. Among liberals the relative weights placed on each of these factors varies. Some minimize the internal inadequacies and stress the external forces, while others reverse this emphasis. Direct action against discriminatory practices and affirmative action programs emphasize discrimination as the major obstacle to minority advancement. Compensatory educational and job-training programs tend to emphasize internal inadequacies. In particular, culture of poverty theories, which allege that cultural inadequacies are responsible for black poverty, lead to the position that internal deficiencies are the major obstacles.

As a middle position, some liberals emphasize the impact of locational changes on minority employment or the impact of low income on educational attainment. We found that education for minority youths is more costly and of lower quality than education for white youths. In addition, education has less economic value for minority youths than it has for equally skilled and motivated white youths. Even if black youths had no cultural deficiencies and were not victimized by an educational tracking system, they would likely have lower educational attainment than whites.

While all liberal views support government intervention, the differences in size and scope reflect the differences in views mentioned. Liberals who emphasize external pressures tend to favor more government intervention, even when it might be confrontational, while liberals who emphasize internal inadequacies tend to advocate more limited programs. For example, liberals differ as to the size and scope of job-training programs. In response to the limited success of many programs, the more aggressive liberals claim that existing programs have too little funding and do not respond aggressively enough to the discriminatory hiring practices of many craft unions. This group also complains that many programs teach students skills that are no longer marketable. The other group claims that because of internal inadequacies, manpower programs are capable of helping only the least deficient of the disadvantaged group. Moreover, this second group claims that the success of job-training programs is determined primarily by the behavioral traits developed rather than the specific skill mastered.

Both liberals and conservatives have always agreed that the internal inadequacies of minorities have a significant effect on their economic situation. Prior to World War II, conservatives believed that these differences were genetic and hence not subject to change. Today genetic (biological) theories are in disrepute, and many conservatives have shifted away from emphasizing the permanency of black inferiority. They accept the usefulness of some government programs and now tend to differ only slightly from those liberals who emphasize internal inadequacies.

Notes

1. Prior to the expansion of publicly funded colleges in urban areas, surveys consistently demonstrated the decisive influence of family income on educational attainment. For example, Samuel Bowles (1977) cites evidence that average-ability students from high-income households were much more likely to attend college than low-income students who scored in the highest-ability category.

2. Observers note that many well-paying blue-collar jobs, such as unionized positions for delivery truck drivers, are available to white males but not to women or blacks, since employment is based on personal contacts. Thus, white males who are not college graduates are much more likely to attain middle-class employment than comparably educated blacks or women.

References

Allport, Gordon. 1954. *The Nature of Prejudice.* Reading, MA: Addison-Wesley.

Banfield, Edward. 1974. *The Unheavenly City Revisited.* Boston: Little, Brown.

Bowles, Samuel. 1977. "Unequal Education and the Social Division of Labor." In *Problems in Political Economy: An Urban Perspective,* ed. David Gordon. Lexington, MA: D.C. Heath, 238–52.

Chase, Allan. 1975. *The Legacy of Malthus.* New York: Alfred A. Knopf.

Cherry, Robert. 1976. "Racial Thought in the Early Economics Profession." *Review of Social Economy* 33:147–62.

———. 1980. "Biology, Sociology, and Economics—An Historical Analysis." *Review of Social Economy* 37:140–51.

Coleman, James. 1966. *Equality of Educational Opportunity.* Washington, DC: U.S. Department of Health, Education, and Welfare.

Commons, John R. 1924. *Races and Immigrants in America*. New York: Macmillan.

Harrison, Bennett. 1977. "Education and Underemployment in the Urban Ghetto." In *Problems in Political Economy: An Urban Perspective*, ed. David Gordon. Lexington, MA: D.C. Heath, 252–61.

Moynihan, Daniel. 1965. *The Negro Family: The Case for National Action*. Washington DC: Office of Policy Planning and Research, U.S. Department of Labor.

Myrdal, Gunnar. 1944. *An American Dilemma: The Negro Problem and Modern Democracy*. New York: Harper and Row.

Okun, Arthur. 1977. "Equity and Efficiency: The Big Tradeoff." In *Problems in Political Economy: An Urban Perspective*, ed. David Gordon. Lexington, MA: D.C. Heath, 28–33.

Owen, John. 1972a. "The Distribution of Educational Resources in Large American Cities." *Journal of Human Resources* 7:26–38.

———. 1972b. "Toward a Public Employment Wage Theory: Some Econometric Evidence of Teacher Quality." *Industrial Labor Relations Review* 25:213–22.

Piore, Michael. 1977. "The Dual Labor Market." In *Problems in Political Economy: An Urban Perspective*, ed. David Gordon. Lexington, MA: D.C. Heath, 91–95.

Samuelson, Paul. 1970. *Economics*. 8th ed. New York: McGraw-Hill.

Ullman, Lloyd. 1977. "The Uses and Limits of Manpower Policy." In *Problems in Political Economy: An Urban Perspective*, ed. David Gordon. Lexington, MA: D.C. Heath, 113–19.

U.S. Riot Commission. 1968. *Report of the National Advisory Commission on Civil Disorders*. New York: E.P. Dunton.

4
The Radical View

Chapters 2 and 3 presented liberal and conservative theories of discrimination. While differing significantly, these two perspectives have broad areas of agreement that distinguish both from the radical view. In the first section of this chapter, I indicate why radical economists believe that the similarities between liberal and conservative theories of discrimination are far more important than their differences.

The next section details the major distinguishing aspects of the radical theory of discrimination. Unlike liberals and conservatives, radical economists believe that discrimination is profitable for all capitalists. Radicals, however, differ as to the degree to which specific groups of capitalists benefit from discrimination and its impact on the welfare of majority workers. Some radicals believe that the financial benefits of discrimination are broadly shared within the majority population—that is, both workers and elite benefit. Other radicals believe that the benefits go only to a small segment of the majority population—elite and certain sections of the upper-middle class.

The final section develops each of these conflicting radical views and their policy implications. In addition, an appendix highlights the different radical explanations for the support given to slavery by nonslaveholding southern whites during the antebellum period.

The Unity of Conservative and Liberal Views

Chapters 2 and 3 identified major differences between the liberal and conservative views. Without minimizing these differences, radicals contend that the underlying agreement between liberals and conservatives is far more important. Let us briefly summarize each of these areas of liberal–conservative agreement and how they differ with the radical view.

Discrimination and Secondary Labor Markets

Liberals believe that as a result of discrimination in primary labor markets, the supply of labor to secondary markets increases, enabling secondary employers to lower wages. Since conservatives do not believe that discrimination in primary labor markets is significant, they minimize the degree to which secondary employers benefit from discrimination. Liberals and conservatives differ in their views of the extent to which firms hiring secondary workers benefit from discrimination, but they agree that these benefits result from discrimination in primary labor markets.

In contrast, radicals believe that the existence of a reserve army of the unemployed in capitalist societies guarantees an excess supply of workers seeking employment in secondary labor markets. This reserve army is sometimes generated by natural market forces, such as automation or conscious government policies. Moreover, radicals claim that even if some secondary workers are able to find primary employment, new sources of labor will be introduced to replenish the reserve army. Thus, the exploitation of secondary workers is independent of the primary labor market and is a basic feature of capitalist societies.

Discrimination and Primary Labor Markets

Conservatives contend that there are wide productivity differentials among applicants in primary labor markets and that production costs will increase greatly if employers use discriminatory hiring practices. Liberals contend that productivity differences among applicants are so small that production costs will rise only slightly as a result of discriminatory hiring practices. Liberals and conservatives disagree about the extent to which discrimination causes primary-sector firms to incur higher costs, but they agree that these firms have no financial stake in its perpetuation.

In contrast, radicals believe that discrimination enables primary employers to benefit in a number of ways. Primary employers are able to employ secondary workers at lower wages, and inputs purchased from secondary employers also are cheaper. Moreover, radicals contend that even the primary workers hired are less expensive as a result of discrimination because primary employers can hire women, blacks, and other disadvantaged workers for lower-paid jobs within primary labor markets and also use secondary workers as a threat to primary workers.

Discrimination and Competitive Markets

Conservatives believe that competitive pressures make it impossible for discriminatory firms to pass along their higher costs to consumers; they must absorb these costs in order to maintain sales. Since profit margins in competitive industries are small, conservatives claim that the market will discipline owners to avoid using discriminatory hiring practices. Liberals believe that competition is not strong enough to force owners to absorb the full cost of discrimination.

While they disagree about the extent to which discrimination occurs, liberals and conservatives agree that whenever firms must compete against each other, labor market discrimination is reduced. If competition is beneficial, policies that increase competition should always benefit minority workers. In contrast, radicals contend that competition often forces weaker firms to superexploit the most defenseless workers.

Discrimination and Government Policies

Conservatives believe that the presence of wide productivity differentials and competitive markets fully discipline firms and thus antidiscrimination policies are not required. Liberals believe that the market does not discipline firms and government antidiscrimination policies are required.

While liberals favor government antidiscrimination laws, conservatives do not, but both groups agree that there is no reason to act directly against secondary employers. According to liberal economist Barbara Bergmann (1977), "[T]he discriminators and the beneficiaries of discrimination are for the most part different" (p. 168). Instead, antidiscrimination policies should focus on primary employers. Since liberals believe that primary employers have no financial stake in discrimination, they are confident that government affirmative action will be effective. According to liberals, once discrimination in primary labor markets ends, it will be impossible for secondary employers to continue to benefit from it.

In contrast, radicals are less hopeful that affirmative action programs can significantly reduce discrimination. First, radicals believe that primary firms benefit from discrimination and thus have an incentive to circumvent government antidiscrimination requirements. To reduce discrimination in primary labor markets, they argue, more aggressive policies, such as quotas, are necessary.

Second, radicals claim that even if these government policies are successful, they will have little impact on the wages and working conditions of secondary workers. Recall that radicals believe that the reserve army, not discrimination in primary markets, is responsible for the exploitation of secondary workers. Thus, they contend that even if government programs increase minority and female access to primary jobs, the vast number of minority and female workers remaining in secondary markets will be unaffected. Radicals believe that only policies with a direct effect on secondary labor markets can improve the wages and working conditions of low-wage workers.

Discrimination and
Educational Initiatives

Liberals consider educational initiatives that challenge discriminatory attitudes to be crucial to the success of government antidiscrimination policies. Since conservatives contend that the market will discipline employers to separate personal attitudes from employment decisions, they do not believe it is necessary to change personal beliefs. Indeed, they are primarily concerned with the potential danger of government imposition of values on society.

While they have different views on the appropriateness of attempts to change personal values, liberals and conservatives agree that discriminatory attitudes are generated by factors that have little to do with the workings of labor markets. Indeed, Myrdal (1944) believed that these attitudes were held most strongly by those forces (patrician class) who were most resistant to capitalism. Moreover, many liberals expect "racial prejudice in the population to express itself in economic terms more virulently under a socialist system . . . than a capitalist system" (Bergmann 1977, 169).

In contrast, radicals believe that discriminatory attitudes are reinforced by their profitability to members of the majority population. These attitudes rationalize exploitation. Beneficiaries promote racist ideas to convince others to support discriminatory practices. In addition, radicals contend that owners promote racist ideas to divide workers along ethnic and racial lines. These divisions make it easier for owners to exploit workers.

Discrimination and
Minority Behavior

Conservatives believe that minority workers have internal inadequacies causing them to exhibit dysfunctional behavior. Liberals agree that minority labor market problems often stem from dysfunctional behavior, but some believe that such behavior results from adaptation to external pressures rather than internal inadequacies.

Although they differ as to the source of this dysfunctional behavior, liberals and conservatives agree that this behavior is one reason for the persistence of income differentials. Radicals contend that this perspective essentially blames the victims for their situation. Antidiscrimination efforts are diverted to cultural conditioning of minority group members and to searching for the proper role models. Attacks against the forms discrimination takes are minimized, and it is the victims who are forced to change.

Radical Theories

The first section of this chapter summarized the distinguishing aspects of the radical theory of discrimination. This section develops more fully these radical views.

The Reserve Army

Radicals consider the existence of a reserve army of the unemployed to be a prerequisite for capitalist expansion. Radicals contend that U.S. capitalism developed only after immigration from Europe and China during the late nineteenth century generated an excess supply of industrial workers.

During the first half of the nineteenth century, technological advances created the basis for mass production of textiles. In New England, the only labor force available was young farm girls, an erratic and hard to discipline work force. For these reasons, the growth of the American textile industry was slow. All this changed with the immigration of Irish workers in the 1850s. Textile employment shifted from native-born women to Irish immigrants. Wages and working conditions deteriorated, while production and profits expanded.

During the post–World War II period, black rural migrants to urban areas, together with migrants, legal and otherwise, from the Caribbean Basin and Latin America, supplied the reserve army. More recently, radicals suggest that women and youths have become significant components of the reserve army.

Many radicals contend that the desire to maintain a reserve army has strongly influenced government welfare policies. Piven and Cloward (1971) found that welfare agencies in agricultural areas would automatically throw indigent workers off subsidies from planting through harvesting time. Government officials would use vagrancy laws to arrest and then subcontract able-bodied youths to farmers. In general, Piven and Cloward claim that welfare has always been made harsh and stigmatizing. Its purpose has been to force individuals into secondary labor markets by discouraging them from choosing welfare.

Herbert Gans (1967) has argued that if individuals could obtain decent welfare, they would not work at the dead-end, unsafe, dirty, low-paying jobs found in secondary labor markets. Gans's contentions are consistent with the manner in which the federal government assessed welfare reform proposals during the 1970s. Beginning in the 1960s, both liberal and conservative economists claimed that it would be more efficient and equitable for the government to institute a negative income tax system to replace welfare. Income transfers to the poor would be handled by the Internal Revenue Service. There would be no special welfare system and hence no stigma attached.

The federal government undertook extensive pilot programs to study alternative negative income tax proposals. Tax rates, maximum welfare payments, and the length of the study were varied. It was assumed that at least some current welfare recipients would seek part-time employment. Most studies focused on the impact of these policies on the working poor—households that had low-income jobs but were not currently collecting welfare. This clearly indicated that the government was most sensitive to the impact welfare reforms would have on those currently in the low-wage labor market. Since these studies found that there would be a significant labor market withdrawal by the working poor, negative income tax proposals were abandoned. They have been replaced by various workfare proposals designed to restrict and reduce income payments to welfare households.

Radicals contend that concerns for maintaining sources of cheap labor also affect macroemployment policies. According to Michael Piore (1978), as a result of business pressures, government officials usually claim that lowering unemployment is either impossible or in conflict with even more important objectives. During the post–World War II period, officials have often said that balancing the budget was the most important objective, even though government spending cuts and tax increases would initially reduce employment. Officials also have rejected expansionary policies because of a fear that they would generate too much inflation. More recently, natural unemployment rate theories have suggested that the lowest possible sustainable unemployment rate has risen to over 6 percent as a result of demographic changes in the labor market. Thus, once unemployment rates fall below 7 percent, government macroeconomic policies will simply generate large deficits or high inflation rates without permanently lowering unemployment.

Inadequacies of Liberal Policies

Liberals and radicals recommend different policies to raise wages in secondary markets. Liberals believe that policies increasing access to primary jobs are sufficient, while radicals contend that these policies are inadequate. As long as there is a reserve army, radicals expect that low wages for secondary workers will persist. As an example, radicals claim that liberal strategies have had no impact on the economic status of women.

Beginning in the 1960s, liberals claimed that all women would benefit from greater female access to primary jobs. While this liberal strategy was not completely successful, female employment in many high-wage occupations has increased dramatically. Despite these changes, the vast majority of females who did not graduate from college continue to earn low wages. As a result, the women's movement has begun to develop strategies that have a direct impact on secondary labor markets. One such strategy suggests that wages in secondary labor markets should be determined by comparable worth estimates rather than by unregulated market forces.

Benefits to Primary Employers

Not only do liberals misunderstand why secondary employers benefit from discrimination, but, radicals contend, they also incorrectly assess its impact on primary employers. Primary employers hire secondary workers to complement their primary work force—for example, legal secretaries to complement their lawyers or office staff to complement their managers. Owing to market discrimination, these secondary workers are hired at lower wages. Radicals believe that in many primary firms, this secondary work force is quite large. Thus, it is possible that discrimination, by lowering the wages of secondary workers hired, can more than offset the slightly higher wages these firms must pay their primary workers.

Radicals also believe that the overall costs of production are reduced through the impact of discrimination on the cost of inputs purchased. Many secondary firms are in highly competitive markets. They cannot profit from their lower labor costs because they must pass this cost savings on to their customers. Primary employers benefit if they buy inputs from these secondary employers. During the 1970s, U.S. automotive firms were unable to lower labor costs directly in their unionized plants. These firms began purchasing inputs from outside suppliers (known as outsourcing) rather than continuing to produce them directly in their unionized plants. These competitive suppliers hired secondary workers at low wages, passing along cost savings to the automotive corporations.

Radicals further contend that discrimination enables firms to reduce the wages paid to their primary workers in several ways. First, firms can develop secondary tracks in primary occupations. These tracks have lower starting salaries and less potential for advancement. Many female and black workers accept employment in these secondary tracks because their only alternative is employment in secondary labor markets.[1]

The ability of capitalists to place black workers in secondary tracks in primary labor markets was illustrated by the hiring practices of Henry Ford. Since all autoworkers are paid wages above the average for blue-collar workers, economists usually characterize all positions in the automobile industry as primary jobs. Within the auto plant, however, some jobs are somewhat better than others. During the 1920s and 1930s, Henry Ford was the only automobile manufacturer to employ black workers. In his River Rouge (Michigan) plant, the largest automobile assembly plant in the world, black workers comprised 12 percent of the work force, but they were not evenly distributed throughout the plant. Instead, they were overwhelmingly assigned to the least desirable positions, such as in the foundries. Even though Ford paid black workers less than white workers and gave them the worst jobs, they were grateful to him. Indeed, they were quite reluctant to support unionization efforts because they believed that Ford was their benefactor.

As a result of the exploitation blacks faced in secondary markets, Ford was able to lower his labor costs and at the same time obtain a grateful work force.

Radicals also contend that if low wages paid to secondary workers lower consumer prices, primary workers might reduce their wage demands. The struggle over the Corn Laws in England illustrates this relationship between consumer prices and wages. At the beginning of the nineteenth century, the British working class consumed domestic corn that cost substantially more than corn produced in the United States. Landowners favored restrictions on the importation of corn, but industrialists successfully fought for free trade, since lowering the cost of food staples would enable them to lower wages.

Today married women with children are a significant component of primary labor markets. Low wages in secondary markets influence the labor supply of these women. If child care and other services provided by secondary workers are expensive, women are more likely to take an extended leave from primary employment, lowering the labor supply and raising the wages firms must pay. Alternatively, if exploitation in the secondary market lowers these expenses, women might return to the primary labor force more quickly.

Radicals believe that the availability of cheap labor forces primary workers to lower their wage demands. Between 1860 and 1890, U.S. steel production increased from 12,000 net tons to 4,800,000 net tons per year. During this period, occupations in the steel industry were divided into two groups—skilled workers who performed activities requiring training and unskilled workers who performed heavy manual labor. The skilled steelworkers were members of the strongest union of its day. Steel mill owners, desiring more profits, wanted to weaken the power and earnings of their skilled work force, and with the wave of immigration in the last quarter of the nineteenth century, owners were able to seek their objective (Stone 1974).

In 1893 the owners were ready. The strongest union lodge was at Andrew Carnegie's Homestead (Pennsylvania) plant. He ordered the plant to be fenced in and platforms for sentinels to be constructed, then hired three hundred Pinkerton guards. At this point, Carnegie closed down the plant, laid off the entire work force, and announced that the plant would henceforth operate without a union. With the help of the state militia and federal government, Carnegie's planned destruction of the union was successful.

After reopening, Carnegie reorganized production. Some jobs that had been performed by skilled workers were eliminated by mechanization. Others were eliminated by dividing them into separate activities that could be performed by secondary workers. Thus, the presence of a reserve army enabled Carnegie to replace expensive skilled labor with lower-cost workers.

Today the internationalization of the labor process has enabled firms to replace high-wage American workers with cheaper foreign labor. Unionized plants are closed and replaced with nonunionized plants abroad. Many companies have convinced their unionized workers to accept lower wages and inferior working conditions. Thus, outsourcing in the automobile industry enables owners not only to obtain cheaper inputs but also to lower the wages of their unionized workers.

Competitive Forces and Discrimination

In contrast to conservatives and liberals, radicals associate intensified competition with increased exploitation. They note that many competitive industries contain two distinct types of firms: large-scale firms, which use the most advanced technology, and small-scale firms, which are technologically backward. In this situation, small-scale producers could not survive if they paid the same wages as their large-scale competitors. These small-scale producers search for new sources of exploitable labor so that lower labor costs can at least partially compensate for their technological backwardness. Although the exit of these small-scale firms diminishes competition, it also eliminates the most exploitive labor market conditions.

In nineteenth-century England, uneven development characterized the garment industry, as large-scale manufacturers competed against small-scale producers in the rural cottage industry. Marx (1967) noted that these small-scale producers could not utilize the newest technologies because they did not have the capital or the scale of operation. Instead, they sought out women, children, and others made destitute by unemployment. Marx considered workers in the domestic cottage industry to be the most exploited. He noted, "[B]ecause domestic industry must always compete with either the factory system, or with manufacturing in the same branch of production . . . [it] robs the workman of the conditions most essential to his labor, of space, light, and ventilation" (p. 462).

Marx did not believe, however, that superexploitation could fully compensate for the technological disadvantages small-scale producers faced. Eventually, he wrote, "[t]he cheapening of labor-power, by the sheer abuse of the labor of women and children, by the sheer robbery of every normal condition requisite for working and living, and by the sheer brutality of overwork and nightwork, meets at last with natural obstacles that cannot be overstepped" (p. 470). At this point, bankruptcy cannot be avoided, and with it comes the reduction of both competition and the superexploitation of the disadvantaged. For Marx, the elimination of competition was the principal reason for the decline in discrimination.

During the 1970s, uneven development again became a dominant feature of the garment industry. Small-scale firms in larger urban areas, under increasing competitive pressure from corporate production in the South and abroad, reverted back to sweatshop conditions, superexploiting undocumented foreign-born workers. Facilities became makeshift, unsafe, and unhealthy. But, as radicals point out, these conditions were often necessary for the survival of the firm and were not the result of greed. Fierce competition forced small-scale firms to intensify exploitation of the most defenseless workers.

Racist Ideologies

Radicals believe that racist ideologies have always been used by oppressors to justify their exploitation of others. During the nineteenth century, they were used to justify imperialist conquests abroad and the lack of social welfare at home. Social Darwinism was popularized by the largest capitalists, and survival of the fittest was their motto. Social Darwinism was a forerunner of the eugenics movement, which was based on the belief that the poor had defective genes and should be eliminated. Let us examine the impact these racist ideas had on government approaches to solving the problem of pellagra.

During the second half of the nineteenth century, corn became the basic food staple of poorer sections of the American working class. Because corn is deficient in many important vitamins, its widespread use as a food staple created a pellagra epidemic. By the beginning of the twentieth century, thousands of Americans were dying every year from this disease. Virtually all cases were among low-wage workers, with the vast majority located in the South.

Since the disease was not contagious and afflicted only the poor, the immediate response of the elite was that it must be genetic. Allan Chase (1977) shows how the elite quickly applied social Darwinist thinking to the problem. By 1915, however, there was seemingly irrefutable evidence that pellagra could be avoided by eating a more balanced diet. Joseph Goldberger, an employee of the Department of Agriculture, had studied the incidence of pellagra in state institutions. He found that it varied according to the diet inmates received. When Goldberger was able to change the inmates' diet, he reduced the incidence of pellagra. He presented this and other evidence in published papers.

Goldberger's findings conflicted with the genetic explanations being advanced by the economic elite. The elite hired Charles Davenport, a widely known eugenicist, to write a response. Davenport's genetic explanations were accepted by the medical profession and government health agencies. Pellagra continued to be a major problem for southern workers and continued to kill thousands each year through the 1930s. Davenport's theory was discarded only after scientific advances demonstrated that a niacin deficiency caused pellagra.

Radicals contend that the economic elite understood that Goldberger's findings implied that incomes should be raised so workers could afford to purchase a more balanced diet. But since raising wages would lower profits, it was far easier for capitalists to claim that bad genes, not bad diets, caused this deadly illness.

Behavioral Characteristics of Secondary Workers

During the 1960s, most major urban areas experienced some form of urban unrest. Ghetto rebellions, in which blacks destroyed property and engaged in other unlawful acts, were widespread. Both liberals and conservatives claimed that these actions reflected dysfunctional behavior rather than rational responses to oppression and inequities. Conservatives believed that these actions reflected personal and cultural patterns of the lower class, while liberals believed that they reflected dysfunctional adaptation to discriminatory barriers past and present.

In general, liberals believed that to a large extent riots resulted from the frustrations of inner-city residents caused by their inability to utilize institutional procedures. In a different context, Michael Piore (1977) suggests that these workers, living in an environment "where rewards and punishment are continually based on personal relationships . . . forget how to operate within [an] impersonal, institutional grievance procedure. . . . [They] are frustrated by the failure of the system to respond on a personal basis and their own inability to make it respond on an institutional basis" (p. 93).

While liberals did not feel that rioting was justified, they did believe that there were legitimate grievances. They recommended policies to reduce the pressures on minorities, which were summarized in the Kerner commission report (U.S. Riot Commission Report, 1968). In the conservative response, Edward Banfield (1974) characterized the inner-city upheavals as rioting mainly for fun and profit reflecting the inherently violent nature and present-oriented values of the lower classes.

According to Banfield, during the summer inner-city youths needed outlets for their violent tendencies. He claimed that in the past community institutions had created activities in which violent behavior could be released but that the middle-classification of community institutions, together with a more violence-prone black population, had eliminated the necessary safety valves. Thus, urban riots were rampages by violence-prone black youths. These riots quickly attracted criminal elements who engaged in forays for pillage. According to Banfield, riots provided fun for violence-prone black youths and profit for the criminal elements within the community.

Banfield suggested that liberals were responsible for the growth of rioting. First, by creating sympathy for rioters, liberals made it less likely that those apprehended would receive punishment. Second, liberal policies restricted the police. Every time police used force to restrain violent youths, liberals charged police brutality. Banfield proposed that inner-city violence could be reduced only by increasing the cost to rioters. As one example, he supported preventive detention, or the jailing of individuals who had not committed any crime but were deemed likely to do so.

Radicals rejected the conservative notion that the rioting simply reflected the ability of lower-class youths to manipulate bleeding-heart liberals for fun and profit. Radicals also rejected any liberal notion that rioting reflected the inadequacy of low-income workers to utilize institutional procedures such as civilian review boards, the court system, or the grievance process in the workplace.

In general, radicals have a different view of rebellious behavior. They contend that reforms can only be won when workers engage in militant actions. In the workplace, employees generally have little respect for company grievance procedures. Grievances often take years to be investigated, and even when rulings favor employees, they often are not enforced or are too narrowly defined to correct general problems. As a result, when workers have serious grievances, they initiate wildcat strikes. These work stoppages are illegal because contracts specify the grievance process as the appropriate channel through which workers can resolve differences. These more militant actions are often the only way to change company policy quickly and effectively, however.

Similarly, radicals believe that the ghetto rebellions of the 1960s were the most effective method of resolving societal grievances. They claim that institutional procedures (voting, court battles, petitioning governmental agencies, and so on) only divert attention and drain resources and energies. Radicals contend that once the elite was able to repress black militancy and direct civil rights protests into acceptable channels, reforms could no longer be won. Over the past decade, reformers have used these acceptable channels, but inner-city unemployment has increased, social services have deteriorated, and police violence has become more prevalent.

Distinctions among Radical Theories

All radical theories contend that primary and secondary capitalists benefit financially from discrimination, that a reserve army facilitates discrimination in secondary markets, and that competition causes the harshest forms of exploitation to occur in small-scale firms. Within this consensus, however, there are significant differences. Radical theories differ over the impact of discrimination on majority workers and which capitalists, small-scale or large-scale, are the major beneficiaries. According to traditional Marxists, primary capitalists are the major beneficiaries and, except for some upper-income groups, majority workers are harmed by discrimination. In contrast, neo-Marxists emphasize the economic benefits of discrimination to small-scale capitalists and believe that broad sections of majority workers benefit as well. This section details these differing radical views.

Primary and Secondary Workers

The relationship of primary workers to secondary workers is often complex. Earlier in this chapter, I discussed two ways American autoworkers have been affected by outsourcing. On the one hand, outsourcing has lowered the cost of automobile production by enabling firms to purchase certain inputs at a lower cost. This lower cost increases profit margins and automobile sales, thereby increasing the demand for American automobile workers. On the other hand, to the extent that outsourcing enables firms to shift production to suppliers so that they can substitute exploited secondary workers for unionized labor, it reduces the demand for American autoworkers. Depending on whether the output expansion or the substitution effect is stronger, the demand for and wages paid to American autoworkers can either increase or decrease. A simple numerical example will illustrate this point.

Let us assume that each unit of output requires eight American autoworkers along with other inputs purchased from suppliers. Given costs, U.S. automobile manufacturers set the prices at which they will sell 100,000 units. With this level of production, they will be hiring 800,000 American autoworkers. Now suppose the reserve army enables input suppliers to lower the wages they pay and, in turn, the prices they charge automobile manufacturers. With lower costs of inputs purchased from suppliers, U.S. automobile firms will lower their prices and increase their sales to 120,000. In this case, a reserve army will benefit American autoworkers because firms will now require 960,000 American autoworkers. Since secondary workers do not substitute for American workers, we could characterize their relationship as complementary.

Next, assume automobile manufacturers benefit from a reserve army not only by obtaining lower prices of inputs already purchased externally, but also by further shifting their production to secondary firms, thereby lowering to seven the number of American autoworkers required per unit output. In this case, although total production rises to 120,000, the number of American autoworkers hired rises to only 840,000. Here, most of the increased demand for autoworkers resulting from the output expansion has been offset by the substitution effect. Indeed, if the substitution effect was somewhat larger—for example, the direct labor requirement declined to six American autoworkers per unit output—the number of American autoworkers hired would decline despite increased production. In this situation, automobile manufacturers would likely be successful in their attempts to lower the wages and working conditions for their American workers.

Neo-Marxist Views

All radical models draw heavily on Marxist economics. Marx applied his methodology to a particular stage of capitalism, the competitive stage. Some radicals, often labeled neo-Marxists, believe that capitalism has passed into another stage, monopoly capitalism. They contend that once U.S. capitalism passed its competitive stage, primary capitalists—that is, large corporations—no longer had strong economic incentives to use racism to threaten the wages or working conditions of their primary workers.

Neo-Marxists contend that large sections of the white work force are in jobs that are not threatened by a low-wage work force and even those workers who could be replaced through outsourcing will not be. In particular, they contend that large-scale corporations, desiring the stability that business unions provide, are unwilling to upset labor relationships by aggressively shifting unionized jobs into the nonunionized secondary sector. Other neo-Marxists believe that corporations are reluctant to undermine unions because doing so would have a negative impact on labor morale and productivity. In this case, the output effect dominates and the American autoworkers benefit from the industry's indirect exploitation of secondary workers.

Although neo-Marxists tend to minimize the willingness of corporations to use racism to lower the wages of primary workers, they do believe there are some financial benefits. Harold Baron (1975) contends that when the economy contracts, capitalists can more easily lay off excess workers, since a racist society is more willing to accept higher unemployment if the unemployed are disproportionately black. When the economy expands, there is a ready labor supply that can be hired at the existing wage rate. In this way, the higher costs of a privileged white labor force are more than compensated for. Baron estimates, however, that "the gains from discrimination are at most 1–2 percent of total national wages . . . [so that] profits hardly seem to be of significant enough magnitude for corporate leadership to calculate it is sufficient grounds for maintaining the racial system with all its potential for social disruption and large costs for repression and welfare control" (p. 207).

More generally, neo-Marxists have argued that ideological and psychological factors have become most important during the monopoly stage of capitalism. Baron summarizes this position as follows: "Once White nationalism . . . [was] . . . grounded in a whole range of institutional and ideological forms, the special economic surplus extraction [profiteering] features of racial controls could drop to secondary importance and yet the overall system of racial subordination would remain intact. This process did occur in the twentieth century" (p. 191).

Paul Baran and Paul Sweezy (1965) emphasize how the insecurity of an individualistic capitalist system creates fears and anxieties: "The net result of all this is that each status group has a deeply-rooted psychological need to compensate for feelings of inferiority and contempt for those below. It thus happens that a special pariah group acts as a kind of lightning rod for the frustrations and hostilities of all the higher groups, the more so nearer they are the bottom" (pp. 270–71).

Some neo-Marxists contend that even when the threat of substitution enables firms to lower the wages of their primary workers, multiracial unity may not be the most effective strategy for majority workers. For example, Edna Bonacich (1975) claims that although multiracial unity might raise the wages of exploited workers only slightly, it would enable firms to hire them more easily for primary jobs. Thus, multiracial unity may actually make it easier for firms to substitute cheaper disadvantaged workers for at least some majority workers. Bonacich contends that in this situation the most effective strategy for majority workers is to intensify discrimination—that is, to make it more difficult for firms to substitute disadvantaged workers. In the extreme, this implies that majority workers would fight for a caste system, characterized by things such as Jim Crow laws, in order to protect themselves from having to compete against cheaper minority labor.

Thus, even when the elite desire a reduction in racism, they are confronted by the intransigency of white workers. Baran and Sweezy (1965) claim that when the Kennedy administration and Warren-led Supreme Court wished to reduce racism, they were ineffective because of the resistance of white workers.

Ray Franklin and Solomon Resnik (1973) offer another example of how the racism of white workers can circumvent corporate antiracist policies. They detail the testimony given at an industrial conference they attended during the late 1960s, reporting that many corporations claimed that their attempts to improve race relations were being thwarted by the actions of low-level supervisory personnel. These corporations were unable to control the racism of their foremen.

The neo-Marxist view, therefore, holds that white male workers are the major obstacle to changing discriminatory practices. These workers benefit financially by having jobs complementary to black or female workers and psychologically by having groups below them. Moreover, neo-Marxists contend that firms are unlikely to threaten white male workers with replacement by black or female workers and, even if they did, white male workers would benefit more by attempting to intensify racist and sexist employment restrictions than by uniting in a multiracial, nonsexist movement.

Although corporations may have a tenuous stake in the perpetuation of racism, neo-Marxists agree that small businesses clearly benefit. All neo-Marxists mention the gains to slumlords, ghetto shops that exploit their customers, and small manufacturers that superexploit their minority workers. Neo-Marxists tend to minimize the degree to which competition forces these small firms to pass along financial gains to their corporate customers. Thus, neo-Marxists tend to believe that, among capitalists, it is the small-scale ones who are the major financial beneficiaries of discrimination.

Traditional Marxist Views

Traditional Marxists (Reich 1981; Szymanski 1976) contend that most primary workers are harmed by chauvinist attitudes and practices. They believe that the neo-Marxist view minimizes the willingness of capitalists to use chauvinist attitudes to undercut the unity of workers who are fighting for better conditions on the job or fighting for government social spending programs. They also believe that the neo-Marxist view overstates the number of primary workers who do not have to fear being replaced by secondary workers. Assembly line techniques have made it easier for firms to break skilled functions down into their individual components. Computers and improved telecommunication systems have increased the ease with which firms can relocate to cheaper labor (nonunion) areas. Thus, particularly at the production level, more primary workers today are capable of being replaced by secondary workers than ever before.

Traditional Marxists note that many professionals provide government-funded social services to the poor. They are teachers, health professionals, and social workers. It is certainly possible that some of these workers would not have been hired if not for discrimination, but the wages and working conditions for the group as a whole may be harmed if racism facilitates social service funding cutbacks.

When discrimination lowers the funding of schooling, public transportation, and other urban services, this affects privileged majority workers as well. To avoid the drawbacks of an underfunded urban area, privileged primary workers can either buy private education for their children and remain in the city or buy large commuting costs and inflated property values by moving to the suburbs. Whatever they do, these privileged workers often pay more than the salary gains obtained from the exploitation of secondary workers. Only the very wealthy can easily buy their way out of the social costs of discrimination.

Radicals (Rosenberg 1988) cite recent changes in unemployment compensation as evidence that all workers are harmed by racist unemployment. Beginning in the 1970s, conservatives used racist and sexist stereotypes as evidence that unemployment compensation benefits were too high and subsidized individuals who did not seriously search for new employment. As a result of this campaign, the government began taxing unemployment compensation.

These stereotypes also buttressed claims that the official government measure of unemployment grossly overestimated the number of workers seeking employment. This enabled state governments to underfund unemployment compensation programs and cut benefits. As a result of these actions, the number of unemployed workers receiving unemployment compensation during the 1981–82 recession was much lower than the number that received compensation in any previous recession. Whereas during the 1975 recession, two-thirds of all unemployed workers collected unemployment compensation, during the 1981–82 recession only one-third collected compensation. Thus, radicals claimed racist and sexist ideologies facilitated government policies that lowered unemployment benefits to all workers.

Many neo-Marxists contend that even when primary workers are threatened with replacement, they do not gain from joining a united working-class movement. Instead, their most effective strategy is to support more discriminatory practices. Traditional Marxists agree that majority workers have made this choice many times, but they also believe that the choice of a discriminatory strategy has almost always been unsuccessful.

From the neo-Marxist perspective, an ideal arrangement for privileged workers would be as follows. Corporations would allow privileged workers to unionize and monopolize primary jobs. In return, privileged workers would allow corporations to hire nonunionized disadvantaged workers for secondary jobs. If privileged workers do not challenge the ability of companies to maintain a nonunionized secondary work force, however, the company will eventually attack their unionization rights.

At the beginning of this century, capitalists developed harsh responses to unionizing efforts by secondary workers. Capitalists claimed that these unionizing efforts reflected the cultural or genetic inferiority of the new immigrants. The American Federation of Labor (AFL) did not challenge these claims, as it was interested only in organizing native-born workers into skilled craft unions. Even when it became clear that unionizing efforts required the unity of primary and secondary workers, the AFL resisted. The AFL's nativist ideologies made it difficult to bring about the necessary unity. Indeed, just as Bonacich (1975) suggests, the AFL decided that it would be more effective to seek racist immigration restrictions than to encourage multiethnic unity.

For thirty years, the AFL chose a policy of exclusion over multiethnic unity. During that period, the nativist ideologies that enabled capitalists to attack unionizing efforts of immigrant workers also enabled them to attack unionizing efforts of native-born workers. When a racist immigration bill was finally enacted in 1924, it was a hollow victory for the AFL. By that time, capitalists had been so successful at union busting that the AFL barely existed.

Conclusions

This chapter identified distinctions among competing theories of discrimination. First, distinctions between radical and nonradical theories were enumerated. Critical to radical theories is the importance of the Marxist reserve army thesis. The first section of the chapter showed that these distinctions are much more substantial than the differences between the liberal and conservative viewpoints.

The next section detailed the radical viewpoint. Besides providing historical examples of capitalists' use of a reserve army for financial gain and the possibility that competitive forces intensify corporate discriminatory behavior, it presented radical assessments of the role of ideology in capitalist economies and of the rebellions of the poor. Unlike liberals or conservatives, radicals believe that racist and sexist ideologies are promoted by capitalists to serve their interests. We saw how capitalists promoted the view that pellagra was genetically determined, despite scientific evidence that showed otherwise, simply because this view was financially profitable. Radicals also have a more positive view of ghetto rebels than do nonradicals. Whereas conservatives and liberals believe the ghetto rebellions of the 1960s were inappropriate, radicals contend that these actions were warranted.[2]

We have found that primary employers benefit financially from discrimination. They gain by directly hiring large numbers of workers from secondary labor markets. They also gain by purchasing inputs from firms that employ secondary workers. These firms, often facing fierce competition, pass along cost savings to their customers. Radicals believe that discrimination facilitates the lowering of primary labor costs, as firms are able to employ a low-wage track within the primary labor force.

This chapter highlighted the important differences between traditional Marxist and neo-Marxist theories. According to the traditional Marxist viewpoint, if racist and other chauvinistic ideologies divide the working class so that all workers experience reduced employment, reduced protection at the workplace, and reduced social services, then it is likely that most majority workers are harmed. Even if they are fortunate enough to obtain privileged primary employment, these majority workers will be unable to obtain as much income, job security, or social benefits as they could if they were united with secondary workers in political or social movements. Without these movements, all sections of the working class are weakened and at the mercy of the elite. By contrast, neo-Marxists claim that large sections of white working-class people benefit from racial discrimination. In this case, race rather than class is the basis of unity.

Each viewpoint has its distinct assessment of particular historical events and issues. Subsequent chapters assess the impact of gender discrimination and show how the pattern of distinctions between various viewpoints parallels the pattern of distinctions concerning racial discrimination. In particular, these chapters examine the feminist analysis of patriarchy, which is quite consistent with the neo-Marxist viewpoint detailed in this chapter. Similarly, when the role of Jews in the economy and the relationship between blacks and American Jews is detailed, the contrasts between neo-Marxist and traditional Marxist views are relevant. Thus, the distinctions presented in this chapter will help us to identify distinctions between viewpoints when we analyze specific issues in later chapters.

Appendix: The Economics of Antebellum Slavery

To highlight the differences between various theories, let us identify different assessments of the impact of slavery during the antebellum period, 1830–1860.[3] Conservative views have often pictured this period as being rather benign, with plantation prosperity trickling down to slaves in the form of generous living conditions, widespread opportunity to become skilled workers, and general use of positive economic incentives rather than physical punishment to increase productivity.

More generally, conservative and some liberal economists have used competitive theory to argue that to the extent slavery was exploitive, it was consumers and slave traders, not plantation owners, who benefited. Individual cotton plantation owners were assumed to be small producers in a large competitive market. Within this framework, the price of cotton would be driven down until the typical plantation owner was making a minimum rate of profit. In this case, if slavery lowered the price of labor, this benefit would be passed along to consumers in the form of lower prices for cotton goods. Consistent with this viewpoint, Fogel and Engerman (1974) claim that the goods provided to slaves for their upkeep were quite close to the value of their productivity.

Fogel and Engerman do point out that, owing to the limited increase in the number of slaves during the antebellum period, the increased demand for cotton forced up the slave price. This higher price increased the supply of slaves available for cotton production for two reasons. First, it encouraged individuals who owned only one or two slaves, whom they used for domestic service rather than agricultural production, to sell them to cotton plantation owners. For these individuals, the benefits of slave-produced domestic services no longer outweighed the slaves' market value. Second, the increased price of slaves shifted the use of slaves away from less profitable agricultural production, such as indigo or sugar production. Thus, slave traders also profited from this increase. In all cases, however, the plantation owner is pictured as a competitive producer who provided for slaves fairly given the prices of slaves and cotton he faced.

Of course, radical and many liberal economists reject this idyllic view of slavery.[4] In particular, all radical views contend that plantation owners, rather than being passive agents, were the primary beneficiaries of slavery and used violence rather than economic incentives to maintain productivity. In this appendix, however, I focus primarily on the way various radical perspectives assess the impact of slavery on southern white men.[5]

Clearly, those white men who owned many slaves benefited financially from slavery. By the late antebellum period, this group represented less than 20 percent of southern white men. By 1850 the majority of southern whites were not slave owners. Let us look at how this group, most typified by the white yeoman, was affected by slavery. The white yeoman was a family farmer who relied exclusively on family labor. Having to sell produce at the same price as the plantation, this small-scale producer was in direct competition with slave labor. In this situation, the yeoman could not maintain a higher standard of living than the plantation owner provided his slaves. Often the inefficiency of small-scale production would force the yeoman to accept a lower standard of living than slaves on large-scale, technically superior plantations.[6]

From this perspective, it appears that the majority of southern white men were adversely affected financially by the presence of slavery. Evidence indicates, however, that the institution of slavery was strongly supported by the overwhelming majority of southern whites, including the yeomen. Let us look at how each of the radical viewpoints attempts to explain this support.

Edna Bonacich (1975) agrees that slavery was harmful to the white yeoman. She contends that given their inability to compete against the plantation system, yeomen were forced uphill to inferior land, they were forced out of commercial production, and many were forced to migrate west. Bonacich claims, however, that the yeomen still had economic incentives to continue to support the slave system in the South. According to Bonacich, free blacks in the South were even more of a threat to the standard of living of whites than were slaves. Free blacks were employed in a broader array of trades, including manufacturing and urban construction, than was possible for slave labor. Thus, for whites the freeing of blacks would further undercut their standard of living. Instead, Bonacich claims, southern whites sought relief by increasing the restrictions placed on slave labor in order to limit as much as possible areas of competition.

The views of Harold Baron (1975) provide another explanation for the persistence of support for slavery. Baron contends that even when material benefits disappear, cultural and psychological benefits are often sufficient to allow policies to be perpetuated. Southern slavery was not simply an instrument to rationalize exploitation. It also provided the foundation for a distinct way of life. Defenders of slavery argued that slavery enabled southerners to avoid the competitive materialistic pattern of life they associated with capitalism.[7] They asserted that the South was able to maintain a more genteel, cultured, asthetic way of life as a result of slavery. This view was shared even by those who did not own slaves. Moreover, just as Baron visualizes, slavery provided a group below poor whites. Even though these whites were poor, they had the dignity of being a member of the superior race. For many whites, the benefits were worth far more than the material losses resulting from economic competition with slave labor.

Traditional Marxists provide a somewhat different explanation. First, they point out that a large group of yeomen was somewhat ambivalent toward slavery. This group of poorer up-country whites would at times be willing to forge unity with black sharecroppers after the Civil War, both during Reconstruction when they were labeled scalawags and later during the Populist era when they sought control of southern state legislatures. While black–white unity between these two groups of farmers was broken, the attempts at unity indicate that the view that all groups of southern whites strongly and consistently supported the oppresion of blacks can be questioned.

Second, traditional Marxists point out that there was extensive employment of white labor in support of the slave system. Whites worked as overseers, law enforcement officers, slave traders, slave catchers, and so on. These whites had a strong financial stake in the continuation of slavery. In addition, many whites who had one or two slaves still saw slavery as a benefit even though their slaves were not sufficient to allow them to maintain competitive production. Many of these whites hoped that savings would enable them to buy additional slaves so that they could become competitive. Even if this possibility was unrealistic, these whites could still benefit from the continuance of slavery by selling their slaves to larger plantations. This would provide them with start-up capital for another farm if they migrated outside the South or to purchase a business in an urban area. Most importantly, because a large number of whites benefited from slavery either through their work or their ownership of one or two slaves, virtually all families had a close relative who benefited from slavery. In this case, to be against slavery was to be against a system that benefited brothers, sisters, sons, and daughters.

Traditional Marxists argue that only when the benefits from the oppression of southern blacks were substantially reduced—when poorer whites and richer whites became more distinct cultures—was it possible to forge a multiracial movement of white and black farmers. Only after the Civil War, then, do we find examples of multiracial unity occurring.

Notes

1. Kingson (1988) reports on the growing "mommy track" within elite law firms. Increasingly, women working in these firms are locked in a dead-end track with no chance for partnership. Even though these women work a forty-hour week, the firms to not consider that sufficient for advancement.

2. Reflecting this radical view, Harvard Law School professor Derrick Bell said, "You don't . . . applaud the riots of the '60s. But black folks got more change as a result of riots, than they did as a result of litigation" (McCarthy 1987, 24).

3. This period had some distinctive characteristics: After 1808 it became illegal to import slaves into the United States, making slave labor relatively scarce; the demand for cotton textiles grew dramatically, increasing the profitability of cotton production; and until the Civil War, owing to limited importation of Egyptian and Indian cotton, the United States was the predominant supplier of cotton to Europe. Thus, the antebellum period was the most favorable period in which to analyze U.S. slavery. It avoids the harshness of the eighteenth-century slave trade and the impact that a depressed cotton market would have had on the treatment of slaves.

4. For an extensive critique of Fogel and Engerman, see David et al. (1976).

5. For a discussion of the impact of slavery on southern white women, see chapter 9 of this book.

6. This position assumes that the consumption of the plantation owner was not great enough to alter the analysis. More importantly, it assumes that the productivity of slave labor was equivalent to the labor of the yeoman family. While Fogel and Engerman (1974) believe that slave labor was actually more productive than free agricultural labor, Eugene Genovese (1966) argues that slave labor was not as productive because slaves engaged in sabotage as a protest to their captivity. As evidence, Genovese cites statistics on capital implements used by plantations. He finds that because of destruction, plantations purchased heavier equipment than necessary and purchased it more frequently than the yeomen.

7. Slavery's defenders often pointed to the harshness of the industrialization process then taking place in England. They claimed that slavery protected the weakest individuals from the exploitation of the marketplace. Whereas child labor was widespread in England, with family dissolution typical, southerners thought slavery minimized the brutalization of children and the breakup of families. For a collection of proslavery views, see McKitrick (1963).

References

Banfield, Edward. 1974. *The Unheavenly City Revisited*. Boston: Little, Brown.
Baran, Paul, and Paul Sweezy. 1965. *Monopoly Capital*. New York: Monthly Review Press.

Baron, Harold. 1975. "Racial Domination in Advanced Capitalism: A Theory of Nationalism and Divisions in the Labor Market." In *Labor Market Segmentation,* ed. Richard Edwards, Michael Reich, and David Gordon. Lexington, MA: D.C. Heath, 173–216.

Bergmann, Barbara. 1977. "Can Discrimination Be Ended?" In *Problems in Political Economy: An Urban Perspective,* ed. David Gordon. Lexington, MA: D.C. Heath, 161–65.

Bonacich, Edna. 1975. "Abolition, the Extension of Slavery, and the Position of Free Blacks." *American Journal of Sociology* 81:601–27.

Chase, Allan. 1977. *The Legacy of Malthus.* New York: Alfred A. Knopf.

David, Paul, et al. 1976. *Reckoning with Slavery.* New York: Oxford University Press.

Fogel, Robert, and Stanley Engerman. 1974. *Time on the Cross: The Economics of American Negro Slavery.* Boston: Little, Brown.

Franklin, Raymond, and Solomon Resnik. 1973. *The Political Economy of Racism.* New York: Random House.

Gans, Herbert. 1967. "Income Grants and 'Dirty' Work." *The Public Interest* 6:110–13.

Genovese, Eugene. 1966. *The Political Economy of Slavery.* London: MacGibbon and Kee.

Kingson, Jennifer. 1988. "Women in the Law Say Path Is Limited by 'Mommy Track.' " *New York Times,* 8 August, A1.

Marx, Karl. 1967. *Capital.* Vol. 1. New York: International Publishers.

McCarthy, Sheryl. 1987. "Frustration Fuels Protest, Experts Say." *New York Newsday,* 24 December, 19, 32.

McKitrick, Eric, ed. 1963. *Slavery Defended: The Views of the Old South.* New York: Columbia University Press.

Myrdal, Gunnar. 1944. *An American Dilemma: The Negro Problem and Modern Democracy.* New York: Harper and Row.

Piore, Michael. 1977. "The Dual Labor Market." In *Problems in Political Economy: An Urban Perspective,* ed. David Gordon. Lexington, MA: D.C. Heath, 91–95.

———. 1978. "Unemployment and Inflation: An Alternative View." *Challenge* 21:24–31.

Piven, Frances, and Richard Cloward. 1971. *Regulating the Poor.* New York: W. W. Norton.

Reich, Michael. 1981. *Racial Inequality.* Princeton, NJ: Princeton University Press.

Rosenberg, Sam. 1988. "Restructuring the Labor Force: The Role of Government Policies." In *The Imperited Economy: Through the Safety Net,* ed. Robert Cherry, et al. New York: Union for Radical Political Economics, 27–38.

Stone, Kathy. 1974. "The Origins of Job Structures in the Steel Industry." *Review of Radical Political Economy* 6:61–97.

Szymanski, Albert. 1976. "Racial Discrimination and White Gain." *American Sociological Review* 41:403–14.

U.S. Riot Commission. 1968. *Report of the National Advisory Commission on Civil Disorders.* New York: E. P. Dunton.

5
The Impact of
Racial Discrimination

Chapters 2, 3 and 4 presented alternative theories of discrimination. Conservatives contend that the large gap in earnings between groups reflects productivity differences. Once these differences are accounted for, only small income differences result from discrimination. Moreover, conservatives contend that competitive pressures discourage discrimination. As a result, they suggest that black–white income ratios should increase continuously. In the first section of this chapter, I summarize empirical studies that assess these conservative contentions. I include studies that estimate the extent to which productivity differences explain black–white income differences. (Similar studies assessing female–male income differences are presented in chapter 8.) This section also includes various assessments of the impact of 1960s civil rights legislation on black–white income ratios.

In the second section, I describe competing explanations for fluctuations in the support among whites for civil rights legislation. In particular, this section details differences among radicals as to the actions of whites and the reasons why multiracial unity among workers was not sustained after World War II. The section concludes with a summary of empirical attempts to estimate which sections of the white population benefit from racial discrimination and which are harmed by it.

The Black–White Income Ratio

This section evaluates competing interpretations of changes in various measures of post–World War II black–white income ratios. It begins with some general statistics and is followed by liberal, conservative, and radical assessments.

Background Data

Table 5–1 presents black–white ratios using two income measures, family income and male income. There are two reasons why most economists do not use family income for comparison purposes. First, the proportion of female-headed households has increased more rapidly for blacks than for

Table 5–1
Ratios of Nonwhite to White Median Incomes, 1970–1986

| Year | Black Family | White Family | Black–White Ratio | All Male Workers* | | Nonwhite–White Ratio | Full-Time Year-Round Male Workers | | Nonwhite–White Ratio |
				Nonwhite	White		Nonwhite	White	
1970	$ 6,279	$10,236	61.3	$ 4,220	$ 7,011	60.2	$ 6,638	$ 9,447	70.3
1972	6,864	11,549	59.4	4,811	7,814	61.5	7,576	10,918	69.4
1974	8,004	13,408	59.7	5,689	8,854	64.3	9,320	12,399	75.2
1976	9,242	15,537	59.5	6,216	9,937	62.6	10,478	14,272	73.4
1978	10,879	18,363	59.2	7,297	11,453	63.7	12,943	16,360	79.1
1980	12,674	21,904	57.9	8,354	13,328	62.7	14,727	19,720	74.7
1982	13,598	24,603	55.3	9,493	14,748	64.4	16,710	22,232	75.2
1984	15,432	27,686	55.7	10,394	16,467	63.1	18,294	24,826	73.7
1986	17,604	30,809	57.1	11,528	18,060	63.4	20,219	26,617	76.0

Source: U.S. Department of Commerce, Bureau of the Census, "Income of Families and Persons in the United States, 1986," P-60, no. 159.
*Includes only workers with nonzero incomes.

whites. Since female-headed households tend to have lower incomes, this would cause the black–white family income ratio to decline independent of changes in labor market discrimination. Second, there has been a dramatic increase in the income of black women compared to that of white women as a result of occupational shifts. Black women are no longer significantly employed as low-wage agricultural or domestic workers. This occupational shift would increase the black–white family ratio independent of changes in the level of discrimination. Thus, structural changes rather than changes in labor market discrimination may have dominated changes in the black–white family income ratio.

Numerous studies attempt to adjust the black–white male income ratio for factors that influence productivity, such as age, place of residence, and educational attainment. Black males tend to be younger, have less formal education, and be more likely to live in low-income areas than white males. Thus, each of these variables can be expected to explain at least part of the black–white male income gap. Summarizing these studies, Glen Cain (1985) found that on average adjustments for skill differences explain half the black–white income gap. For example, with an observed black–white ratio of 60 percent, after standardizing for skill differences, the adjusted black–white ratio rises to 80 percent. These results were found in studies comparing the median income among all black male workers to the median income among all white male workers. Table 5–1 indicates that the earnings gap is much smaller when only full-time year-round male workers are compared. Similarly, Corcoran and Duncan (1979) found that if the comparison was restricted to male heads of household who worked more than five hundred hours during the year, the observed black–white ratio was 77 percent. Not surprisingly, after further adjustments for education, training, and tenure with current employer, they estimated that the black–white ratio would be 89 percent for comparable males.

Liberal Viewpoints

Liberals contend that, in the absence of antidiscrimination policies, the black–white income gap would not have declined significantly during the post–World War II period. They note that prior to 1960s civil rights legislation, there was no sustained improvement (Masters 1975). Conservative economists James Smith and Finis Welch (1986) found that there was a dramatic increase in the black–white income ratio between 1940 and 1980. Their data also indicate that little of this improvement occurred during the 1950s. Table 5–2 reproduces a portion of Smith and Welch's findings. For a number of levels of education, the black–white income ratio did not increase between 1950 and 1960. For example, among high school graduates, the income ratio remained at 66 percent. For those levels of education where income ratios

Table 5–2
Black–White Income Ratios by Education, 1940–1980

Years of Education	1940	1950	1960	1970	1980
0–7	54.5	63.6	67.0	73.9	82.5
8–11	58.7	70.9	70.1	78.8	74.8
12	56.5	66.5	66.2	72.2	78.8
13–15	47.4	55.8	62.9	75.0	79.8
16+	48.7	50.4	60.2	73.0	76.2

Source: Smith and Welch 1986.

increased, more detailed data presented later in this section demonstrate that these gains were not the result of lessening labor market discrimination.

Beginning in 1964, the observed black–white income ratio increased substantially. Stanley Masters (1975) estimates that civil rights legislation was responsible for a 9 percentage point increase in the black–white male income ratio between 1963 and 1971. In the late 1970s, liberal economists were confident that improvements would continue. Barbara Bergmann (1977) claims, "I would like cautiously to suggest that this movement in the ratio represents the first fruits of the agitation of the 1960s in favor of a better deal for black citizens" (p. 162). But table 5–1 indicates that these liberal expectations are overly optimistic. After 1974 no further improvement was observed in the black–white income ratio. Liberal economists differ as to the reasons why the closing of the gap between blacks and whites appears to have stopped, but most tend to believe that substantial labor market discrimination remains, and they all favor continued reliance on federal civil rights legislation.

Conservative Viewpoints

Conservative economists reject liberal claims that civil rights legislation was responsible for the decade-long increase in the black–white income ratio beginning in 1964. They contend that the closing of the earnings gap reflects the improved quality of black education, which was independent of civil rights legislation. According to Welch (1973), the rate of return to education increased more rapidly for blacks than for whites during the 1950s, reaching parity in the early 1960s. Smith and Welch (1986) also question the role of civil rights legislation because enforcement did not begin until the 1970s. Thus, improvements between 1964 and 1970 could not be due to legislation.

The work by Smith and Welch, both separately and jointly, represents the major evidence in support of conservative claims that improvement continued through 1980 until there was no longer an earnings gap between comparably skilled workers. Welch (1981) estimates that for recent college graduates, the black–white income ratio was 98 percent during the early 1970s. Smith (1984) found that for male college graduates, ages twenty-five to thirty-four, the black–white income ratio increased from 62 percent in 1960, to 77 percent in 1970, and to 89 percent in 1980. As a result, Smith and Welch believe that continued affirmative action initiatives are unwarranted.

The use of time-series data, adjusted for levels of education and age, has been a major emphasis of the joint work of Smith and Welch. They contend that studies that either ignore age or use only cross-sectional data (data at one point in time) reach incorrect conclusions. The hypothetical black–white income ratios presented in table 5–3 illustrate the issues involved.

Suppose we had data for only one year, 1970. If we look down that column in table 5–3, the black–white income ratio decreases with age, from 80 percent for college graduates ages twenty-five to thirty-four (born 1936 to 1945) to 60 percent for college graduates ages fifty-five to sixty-four (born 1906 to 1915). Studies by Lazear (1979) and Hoffman (1979), suggest that differential rates of promotion and on-the-job training are responsible for the lower income ratio for older workers. Even though recent black college graduates may have income close to that of their white counterparts, the data seem to imply that the gap will grow as these individuals age—that is, their salary increases will be less than those received by white college graduates.

With only one year's data, we are not really observing a specific group of workers to find out how their incomes changed as they aged. In 1970 college graduates ages twenty-five to thirty-four were different individuals from those ages thirty-five to forty-four. Our ability to forecast income ratios as individual workers age assumes that the ratio for workers who were twenty-five to thirty-four years old in 1970 will be the same in 1980 as the

Table 5–3
Hypothetical Black–White Income Ratios for College Graduates, 1940–1980

Birth Cohort	1940	1950	1960	1970	1980
1946–1955					90
1936–1945				80	80
1926–1935			70	70	70
1916–1925		70	70	70	70
1906–1915	60	60	60	60	
1896–1905	50	50	50		
1886–1895	40	40			
1876–1885	30				
All graduates	45	55	62.5	70	77.5

ratio for workers thirty-five to forty-four years old in 1970. Conservatives reject this assumption. They contend that each new group of workers experiences less discrimination than older workers. In this case, the lower income ratio of older workers reflects the effects of past discrimination. The hypothetical data in table 5–3 illustrate this. By reading across each horizontal row, we can observe the income ratio for each individual birth cohort as members of the cohort age. The numbers are selected so that for each birth cohort there is no change in income ratios as they age. This indicates that the incomes of black and white workers grow at the same rate as they age.

Smith and Welch (1986) contend that their estimates are relatively consistent, with constant ratios along each horizontal row. For this reason, they claim that the declining income ratio with age groups found in cross-sectional studies does not reflect discriminatory promotion rates or discriminatory access to on-the-job training. Instead, it reflects the lower levels of discrimination faced by younger workers.

Table 5–3 also can clarify whether labor market discrimination lessened during the 1950s. Earlier in this section, I suggested that even though the black–white income ratio for college graduates increased from 50 percent in 1950 to 60 percent in 1960, this did not necessarily prove that discrimination lessened during the decade. In table 5–3, the work force each year comprises four birth cohorts, each ten-year grouping of those between twenty-five and sixty-four years old. For simplicity, let us assume that there is an equal number of workers in each of the four groupings so that the black–white income ratio for all college graduates in any year is the simple average of the ratio for each of the four birth cohorts.

These calculated income ratios for all college graduates in each year are listed at the bottom of table 5–3. Just as in table 5–2, they indicate that in each successive year, the black–white income ratio for college graduates increased. But let us look more closely at the increase between 1950 and 1960. Numbers were selected so that the discrimination recent black college graduates faced when they entered the labor market during 1951 to 1960 was the same as that faced by those black college graduates who entered the labor market a decade earlier. Both groups had yearly incomes that were 70 percent of those of their white counterparts. Thus, there was no decline in discrimination during the 1950s. The income ratio for all college graduates rose, however, because the birth cohort that retired in the 1950s—those born between 1886–1895—had faced severe discrimination, having incomes that were only 40 percent of their white counterparts. It is exactly this situation that explains why in table 5–2 the black–white income ratio rose in the 1950s. Smith and Welch's data (1986) indicate that for every educational level, recent entrants in 1960 had the same (if not lower) income ratios as entrants ten years earlier.

Liberal and Radical Responses

There are a number of liberal and radical responses to conservative claims. First, liberals note that Smith and Welch's findings (1986) estimate income ratios by comparing usual weekly wages rather than yearly incomes. It is well documented that black workers suffer disproportionate unemployment, so they have fewer weeks of work per year than comparable white workers. Thus, this assumption raises income ratios, just as the elimination of part-time workers does in the Corcoran and Duncan study (1979). This impact is clearly visible when we compare Smith and Welch's (1986) findings to those presented earlier by Smith (1984). In his earlier work, Smith used essentially the same data set but calculated income ratios using yearly income. Table 5–4 compares the ratios for workers ages twenty-five to thirty-four for each income measure. For virtually every year and every educational level, income ratios are substantially higher when weekly wage comparisons are made.

Liberals claim that discrimination affects not only the wages blacks receive but also the types of jobs. Blacks are more likely to be employed at jobs that have unstable employment patterns and are more likely to be laid off than comparable white workers. Thus, a shorter number of weeks worked per year and more part-time employment is not a matter of choice but part of the impact of discrimination in the labor market. For this reason, liberals contend that it is inappropriate to use only full-time workers or usual weekly wages to assess the relative labor market experience of black and white workers.

Second, liberals suggest that the gains experienced by recent black college graduates may be greater than those for black workers with less education. Smith's (1984) findings indicate that for young black workers with

Table 5–4
Comparison of Black–White Income Ratios for Workers Ages 25 to 34 When Yearly versus Weekly Wages Are Used, 1940–1980

Years of Education	1940		1950		1960		1970		1980	
	Week	Year	Week	Year	Week	Year	Week	Year	Week	Year
16+	64.8	49.6	68.4	63.4	69.4	62.5	84.7	76.7	87.8	88.5*
12	70.4	55.7	82.3	68.7	72.8	65.1	80.9	74.6	83.0	75.1
8–11	68.2	57.8	75.6	68.4	70.9	65.9	83.9	72.8	87.1	73.2
Average difference	13.4		8.6		6.5		8.5		7.0*	

Sources: Weekly wage comparisons in Smith and Welch 1986. Yearly income comparisons in Smith 1984.
*Smith (1984) uses Current Population Survey data for 1980, which yields higher ratios than census data. This is most glaring for college graduates. Reich (1988) retabulated 1980 figures with census data. For college graduates, his estimate, using Smith's procedure, is 79.9. When this is included, the average difference for 1980 is 9.9.

a high school degree or less, yearly incomes are still only three-quarters those of comparable white workers. Since affirmative action policies have focused primarily on college graduates, this implies that government antidiscrimination policies are effective and more regulations are required so that there can be a reduction of discrimination against less educated black workers.

Third, table 5–4 indicates that when yearly income was used, there was no lessening of labor market discrimination during the 1970s. For recent labor market entrants with a high school degree or less, yearly income ratios did not change between 1970 and 1980. It does appear that for college graduates there was a substantial improvement, as the yearly income ratio increased from 77 percent to 89 percent. But Smith changed data bases between 1970 and 1980, shifting from the U.S. census to Current Population Surveys. If the 1980 figures are recalculated using census data, the gain for recent graduates is less than 3 percent (Reich 1988).

Finally, even among liberals who accept Smith and Welch's contention that discrimination for black college graduates has ended, there is a belief that civil rights legislation was responsible. For example, Richard Freeman (1973) also found that recent black college graduates had incomes approaching those of white college graduates. But Freeman rejects conservative claims that these results indicate that improved educational quality was responsible for the growing black–white parity. Echoing the Myrdal hypothesis (Myrdal 1944), Freeman suggests that as a result of civil rights legislation, employers became more willing to hire qualified black applicants. In response, more black youths sought the educational credentials needed for advancement. Thus, antidiscrimination legislation was a precondition for black advances.

Radicals often support liberal criticisms of conservative contentions, but they contend that liberals overestimate the degree to which civil rights legislation was responsible for improvements during the 1960s. For example, Michael Reich (1988) contends that the increase in the black–white income ratio between 1964 and 1974 primarily reflects the ongoing migration of blacks from areas of high discrimination (the rural South) to areas of lower discrimination. He notes that unadjusted black–white income ratios in the Northeast, Midwest, and West have been unchanged since the mid-1950s; only in the South did the ratio increase from 38 percent in 1960, to 52 percent in 1970, and to 59 percent in 1980. Indeed, the unadjusted black–white income ratio in the urban non-South actually declined continuously between 1959 and 1979.

William Darity (1980) offers another explanation for the increase in the black–white income ratio. He contends that the decline in the rate of black male labor force participation during this period reflects involuntary unemployment and should not be excluded from an analysis of black–white income gaps. Darity found that when he included these potential workers, the black–white income ratio was unchanged between 1964 and 1974. Peter

Gottschalk and Sheldon Danziger (1986) note that when only males with income are included, the black–white ratio increases from 43 percent to 69 percent between 1939 and 1979, but if those with zero income are included, the increase is only from 44 percent to 60 percent.[1]

Evaluation of Affirmative Action Programs

Many conservatives (see, for example, Smith and Welch 1986) dismiss affirmative action as meaningless, having little lasting impact on employment decisions. Other conservatives contend that affirmative action programs generate reverse discrimination. While blacks may benefit initially from these policies, conservatives believe that they will be harmed in the long run. Thomas Sowell (1981) claims that affirmative action programs legitimize the right of employers to substitute political for economic criteria in hiring. Since whites are the majority, eventually they will use their political power to shape the political criteria in their favor. Charles Murray (1984) also contends that affirmative action programs harm blacks and women. According to Murray, as a result of affirmative action requirements,

> a young black social scientist . . . is hired as one of the senior staff for a research grant that must have a black in a senior position. He is not expected to prepare questionnaire items or wrestle with computer printouts or even write the first draft of the analysis. He is given people to do all that *for* him. He is not forced to serve his apprenticeship and, unless he has exceptional determination, he forever remains a black with a degree sociology instead of developing into a sociologist. (p. 91)

In contrast, supporters (Leonard 1984a) contend that the impact of affirmative action guidelines has been modest and that these guidelines have not resulted in reverse discrimination. For example, Randall Ebert and Joe Stone (1985) studied the impact of affirmative action guidelines on government professional employment in Oregon and New York. They found that differences between male and female promotion rates were much smaller after the institution of guidelines. Ebert and Stone also found, however, that women still had substantially lower promotion rates than comparable men.

Jonathan Leonard (1984b) believes that gains for blacks and women have been small because the government does not significantly penalize firms that do not comply. He notes that the likelihood of a firm being reviewed was small—only 11 percent for nondefense contractors and 24 percent for defense contractors. Moreover, he found that firms that hired more blacks were more likely to be reviewed than those whose black employment lagged. For less than 4 percent of those firms reviewed is there a show cause determination, and more than half of those were for blatant paperwork deficiencies. In 1974 average back pay awards were only $63 per beneficiary in the small number of successful suits. Between 1974 and 1980, awards fell drastically. Finally, between 1970 and 1980, only twenty-six firms lost the right to compete for government contracts as a result of their noncompliance.

Radical Assessment of Black Gains

We have found that there is substantial disagreement between liberals, who believe that there has been modest improvement as a result of civil rights legislation, and conservatives, who believe that improvement has been extensive and has resulted from the rising quality of black education. Radicals believe that liberals overstate black gains, but the main distinction between liberals and radicals is their contrasting explanations of gains. Liberals emphasize using the courts and legislative lobbying, which allows them to identify and cultivate sympathetic politicians. In contrast, radicals emphasize the importance of the multiracial unity of workers and the use of militant confrontational actions. In particular, radicals claim that the alliance of black and white workers was responsible for black gains in the 1940s and that the militancy of ghetto residents and civil rights activists was responsible for black gains in the 1960s. This section details these radical contentions, indicating the differences between traditional Marxist and neo-Marxist interpretations.

Birth of a Multiracial Labor Movement

During the first quarter of the twentieth century, there was a rapid rise of militant trade unionism. At the same time, elite theorists publicized the view that newer immigrants came from an inferior racial stock and that labor militancy reflected the criminal antidemocratic tendencies of inferior immigrant workers rather than responses to legitimate grievances. Wide acceptance of these ideas enabled capitalists to brutally suppress the demands of workers.

The response of organized labor only strengthened racism. Samuel Gompers, leader of the AFL, promoted segregated unions, which enabled capitalists to use black workers as strikebreakers. Moreover, Gompers used racist notions to convince native white workers that they had more to gain by allying with capitalists to restrict immigration than by allying with immigrants (and blacks) to win more rights for all workers.

Gompers's efforts to restrict immigration dominated his agenda for twenty-five years. Between 1896 and 1917, immigration restriction laws passed different bodies of Congress thirty-one times but were vetoed by four different presidents (Fairchild 1917). Finally, in 1923 Congress enacted a comprehensive immigration restriction law. Patterned after recommendations from the American Eugenics Society, this bill dramatically curtailed immigration from eastern and southern Europe. This was a hollow victory for organized labor, however, as the racial and ethnic divisions Gompers promoted had so weakened labor that there were few unions left in 1924 to benefit from the immigration restriction bill.

In the 1930s, a totally different labor movement developed. Led by communists, a number of mass-organizing activities fundamentally weakened racism in the South. Hugh Murray (1969) documents how communist initiatives enabled the Scottsboro trial, in which nine black youths were accused of raping two white women in Mississippi, to galvanize nationwide protests against the lack of legal rights for southern blacks. Cayton and Mitchell (1939) and Williams (1969) describe how multiracial unity was stressed in the organizing drives of the United Mine Workers in Alabama and the Textile Workers' Union in North Carolina. Hoffman (1969) contends that this environment helped build multiracial unemployment councils and sharecroppers' unions in the South. Chalmers (1987) claims that not only did this lead to the decimation of the KKK, but it also forced the KKK to spend all its remaining energies on stopping unions rather than on preserving white supremacy.

Multiracial unity also developed in the North. In 1919 racial and ethnic divisions within the working class undermined the unionizing efforts of 365,000 steelworkers. Learning from that experience, the Steel Workers' Organizing Committee placed special emphasis on overcoming the racist attitudes of many steelworkers and encouraging blacks to join the union in its 1936 organizing drive (Cayton and Mitchell 1939). The National Negro Congress was established that same year. Its objective was to promote multiracial working-class unity in order to facilitate black advancement. It was instrumental in the successful struggles for unionization in many industries in which blacks made up a significant part of the work force.

When the AFL balked at endorsing the antidiscriminatory policies of the newly organized unions, dissidents formed the Congress of Industrial Organizations (CIO). The CIO not only supported egalitarianism within the union movement, but it also supported progressive social legislation, such as minimum wage requirements and unemployment insurance, which were popular within the black community. To cement the relationship, the CIO donated funds to black institutions and encouraged black union officials to participate in black organizations. The stance of the CIO even forced the AFL to eliminate some of its racist practices.

Radicals contend that this growing antiracist sentiment was responsible for the dramatic increase in the black–white income ratio during the 1940s. Radicals are well aware that, as a result of World War II, millions of black and white migrants to urban areas found employment in the growing defense industry. Fusfeld and Bates (1984) document the dramatic black population increase in urban areas, especially on the West Coast, but they reject the view that the black–white income ratio increased simply because of the general increase in the demand for labor: "The vital contribution of the CIO unions was . . . the[ir] insistence that blacks be granted access to skilled jobs. In the absence of this pressure, blacks would have been much less likely to move up from the lowest-paying, dirtiest, most dangerous jobs that they had traditionally entered en mass during periods of labor shortage" (p. 73).

Some liberals might suggest that antidiscrimination legislation was responsible for the unprecedented gains made by black workers during the war years. In 1941 President Roosevelt issued Executive Order 8802, which required all defense contractors to hire workers regardless of race, creed, or color. It also required vocational training programs to be nondiscriminatory. Fusfeld and Bates (1984) point out, however, that the executive order was often ignored. Even when shortages of vitally needed skills such as welding were identified, blacks were neither trained nor hired. Ralph Dalfiume (1969) documents the largely ineffective protest made by black workers against unfair labor practices in defense plants and training programs. Thus, most observers contend that Roosevelt's executive order played a minor role at best in the struggle against discriminatory practices.

Radicals also reject the view that the increased quality of black education was responsible for gains during the 1940s. Until 1950 the majority of black Americans lived in the rural South and attended segregated schools. Bates and Fusfeld (1984) document the lack of funding provided to southern black schools. As an example, they cite school expenditures in Macon County, Georgia. In 1934 expenditures per schoolchild were $47.10 for whites and $1.82 for blacks, a 25.9 to 1 ratio. Thus, any migration out of the South would have automatically raised the quality of education received. These changes would not have influenced productivity and earnings immediately, however, and cannot explain the rapid increase in these during the 1940s, even though Robert Weaver (1946) claims that this increase "represented more industrial and occupational diversification for Negroes than had occurred in the seventy-five preceding years" (p. 82).

Origins of the
Civil Rights Movement

Radicals contend that the multiracial unity formed in the 1930s and 1940s had a decisive impact on the development of the movement for civil rights in the 1960s. Fusfeld and Bates (1984) emphasize the role played by the

CIO-organized Highlander School in Tennessee. This school was founded in the 1930s by left-wing union activists to encourage disenfranchised blacks and whites to exercise their democratic rights as Americans. Rosa Parks, initiator of the Montgomery boycott in 1956, attended the Highlander School. Parks later said, "I gained there the strength to persevere in my work for freedom, not just for Blacks but for all oppressed people" (Adams 1975, 122). Dr. Martin Luther King, Jr., was a frequent participant at Highlander, and many of the future leaders of the Student Nonviolent Coordinating Committee (SNCC), including Stokley Carmichael, attended Highlander during the 1950s.

Traditional Marxists contend that many whites became convinced that it was in their interest to oppose discrimination. This created support within the white community for civil rights, making it harder to isolate black activists who initiated and led militant actions. Thus, the multiracial movement built during the Depression was responsible for the leadership of and support given to the 1960s civil rights movement.

Radicals contend that many of the liberal actions often cited as crucial to the formation of the civil rights movement were really responses to this already formed multiracial movement. Indeed, radicals claim that many of these liberal activities were attempts to to divert activities rather than genuine attempts to further the advancement of blacks. Liberals often cite the Myrdal study (Myrdal 1944) as the first serious attempt to undermine racism. When we assess its role in light of the multiracial movement, however, the report may well have had objectives other than simply undermining racism.

Prior to the Myrdal study, unionizing efforts were convincing many people that racism was fundamentally economic in nature, with white workers losing and capitalists gaining. Also, the lack of legal concessions weakened the effectiveness of lobbying by the National Association for the Advancement of Colored People (NAACP). Many blacks were becoming increasingly antagonistic toward the NAACP. In contrast, St. Clair Drake and Horace Cayton (1945) note the growing popularity of the Communist party among blacks. From the liberal perspective, these attitudes were dangerous and had to be countered. Radicals contend that this was the primary objective of the Myrdal study.

The Myrdal study attacks racism and theories of genetic inferiority, but much of the study attempts to counter the radical views that many felt had become dangerous. Myrdal continuously tells his readers that racism is not financially motivated. He suggests that, through the cumulative process, the low income of blacks has resulted from cultural inferiority. Myrdal also goes to great lengths to convince readers that the NAACP was the most effective channel for antiracist protests. Myrdal's assault on economic explanations of racial discrimination created a favorable intellectual climate for Gordon

Allport's influential study, *The Nature of Prejudice* (1954). This work develops the thesis that racist attitudes are purely psychologically motivated.

At the same time that these liberal theories were being widely circulated, a number of important events occurred. The most famous was the 1948 Democratic party platform, which opposed racial segregation. This action, initiated by Hubert Humphrey, has always been considered a courageous, principled stand. In light of the already formed multiracial movement, however, this action might have been a pragmatic and necessary action to forestall mass defection of urban workers to the third party candidacy of Henry Wallace. Remember that Truman was expected to lose before this platform was adopted, and despite the bolting of southern Dixiecrats, he gained enough support to win.

All the liberal initiatives, including the desegregation of the armed forces and later the 1954 Supreme Court school desegregation ruling, were related directly to the outlook of Myrdal and Allport. First, none of the initiatives attacked labor market discrimination. Second, these actions were attempts to convince antiracists to rely on legislative and legal strategies rather than continuing a labor-oriented multiracial approach.

At the same time liberals began supporting these initiatives, they began attacking the more radical approach. Using cold war rationales, liberal forces did not allow radicals to participate in the post–World War II union organizing drive in the South. Without these activists, who had the most experience and deepest commitment, the organizing drive was doomed and quickly abandoned. Liberals then purged communists from CIO unions and replaced them with leaders who had little commitment to fighting racism and building multiracial unity. With the purging of radical leadership, differences between the CIO and AFL became negligible, making merger in 1955 possible. The CIO no longer even protested the presence of discriminatory unions within its midst. Thus, the civil rights movement of the 1960s occurred despite the actions of liberal organizations. The ideas and institutions created by radical activists in the 1930s were strong enough to provide the foundation for a militant civil rights movement despite attempts by liberals to undermine and divert it.

Alternative Radical Interpretations

Both traditional and neo-Marxists agree with the general outline of events described above. Both believe that left-wing forces were instrumental in cementing multiracial unity, which benefited both black and white workers, and they both believe that liberal forces shifted civil rights emphasis to legalistic approaches. But they have contrasting interpretations of the actions of whites and the reasons why multiracial unity was not sustained after World War II.

Traditional Marxists contend that white workers began to support multiracial unity when they realized that capitalists were able to use a divide-and-conquer strategy to undermine unions. White workers realized that having a white-only work force made it easy for firms to use blacks as strikebreakers. Multiracial organizations grew because many whites became convinced that only through unity could worker struggles be successful.

Traditional Marxists contend that the weakening of multiracial unity was primarily the result of the elimination of communists and other left-wing activists from leadership in the union movement. Without this leadership, union organizing in the South was doomed, its support for progressive social legislation waned, and its willingness to accommodate the racist practices of the AFL increased. Crucial to the traditional Marxist view is the belief that these union policy changes were fundamentally against the interests of white workers—that is, the workers were sold out by the new leadership.

Neo-Marxists have a different assessment of the changing patterns of race relations. From the neo-Marxist perspective, white workers always favored consigning blacks to the lower end of the job structure but had to support multiracial unity in the 1930s to meet this objective. William Wilson (1980) contends that after World War I, many firms sought to make better use of black labor and that they desired permanent black employees rather than those hired only during times of severe labor shortages or labor unrest. Due to the weakening position of white workers, firms were able for the first time to maintain racially integrated work forces. This often meant relegating black workers to the lowest, most difficult jobs available.

Neo-Marxists contend, however, that capitalists did not choose this job allocation because it enabled them to threaten white workers who had better-paying jobs. Wilson cites David Brody, who claimed that firms were constrained in their use of black workers because "company officials feared the reaction of white employees" (p. 141). Wilson also cites Donald Young, who claimed that some firms feared that too aggressive an approach to the hiring of blacks would cause firms to lose white patrons (p. 142).

During the Depression, a number of owners were prominent supporters of the employment and welfare of blacks. Bonacich (1976) cites the actions of Homer Ferguson, who substantially increased black employment in the Newport News (Virginia) shipyard. Henry Ford not only hired many blacks, but also gave generously to black institutions. The National Urban League and black colleges also received broad capitalist financial support. As a result, many black leaders decided that black workers could gain more by allying with owners than by siding with white workers. Spero and Harris (1968) note that Marcus Garvey was one leader who took a procompany, antiunion position.

According to neo-Marxists, white unionists began to support multiracial unity only when they feared firms would eventually break the white monopoly of better-paying jobs. They reasoned that only through building unions in which all power would remain in the hands of white male leaders would they be able to maintain the privileges white male workers monopolized.

Given the racist policies of trade unions, most black workers considered white owners their allies. In this situation, white unionists realized that communists and other left-wing activists were indispensable, as they had the credibility and rhetoric that could overcome black resistance to unionization. Thus, white unionists tolerated left-wing rhetoric that preached equality and progressive social legislation because it was expedient.

Once unions were solidified in the 1940s, white unionists no longer had any need for left-wing activists. First, white unionists reach an accommodation with capitalists. White union leaders agreed to support the foreign policy objectives of capitalists and to refrain from entering politics independently—that is, from forming a labor party. In return, capitalists helped weed out left-wing activists and allow white unionists to solidify their monopoly on better-paying jobs. Once white unionists gained control, they abandoned their commitment to racial equality and reinstituted racist practices, thereby reversing many of the gains made during the 1940s.

Neo-Marxists contend that it was inevitable that the employment situation of black workers would worsen during the 1950s. Edna Bonacich (1976) suggests that even if racist practices did not increase, black unemployment would have increased relative to white unemployment. She claims that the rising cost of labor forced capitalists to shift production away from unionized labor. Companies moved production either overseas or to rural areas, or they automated. Bonacich believes that layoffs were not necessarily racially biased but that blacks were employed disproportionately in areas most vulnerable to these shifts.

Harold Baron (1975) suggests that the institutionalizing of blacks in marginal, unstable jobs benefited both white capitalists and white workers. White capitalists benefited because they could easily adjust their labor force to the changing demand—that is, they could lay off black workers during economic recessions and hire them back during economic expansions. White workers benefited because companies were less resistant to guaranteeing them stable employment and generous benefits. Thus, the post–World War II labor–management accord was not in the interest of black workers, and benefits to the participants were at black workers' expense.

Evaluating the meager gains made during the 1960s, many neo-Marxists emphasize the power of white workers to block civil rights legislation. Baran and Sweezy (1965), Harold Baron (1975), and Franklin and Resnik (1973) all suggest that capitalists were often genuinely motivated to lessen labor market discrimination but were unsuccessful because of white worker resistance. This implies that it was white elite, not white working-class, support that aided civil rights reforms during the 1960s.

The neo-Marxist viewpoint can be questioned. During the 1940s, multiracial unity accelerated black upward mobility into previously segregated jobs and undermined many areas in which white workers had previously had a monopoly. This is consistent with the traditional Marxist view that multiracial unity provided a foundation for all workers to benefit rather than the neo-Marxist view that it was a tactic enabling white workers to reinstitute their monopoly of higher-paying jobs.

Second, if white unionists believed that communist activists had outlived their usefulness, union elections would have led to a more conservative leadership. In most unions, however, communists were ousted from leadership positions through government intimidation and legislation. In some cases, only Mafia influence was sufficient to end left-wing support among white workers. This indicates that union members had a deeper appreciation of the goals and actions of communists than the neo-Marxist viewpoint allows.

Even if white workers actively supported a shift to racist policies after World War II, traditional Marxists question claims that the workers benefited. Traditional Marxists contend that these policies weakened unions and working-class organizations and resulted in low wages, less job protection, and lower government social spending. Thus, whatever their perceptions, most white workers were harmed.

Traditional Marxists also point out that white workers benefited greatly from the 1960s civil rights movement. The white working class benefited from the massive expansion of social services, and all workers benefited from the renewed commitment to full employment stimulated by antiracist protests. In addition, the antiracist movement opened the way for other oppressed groups to protest against their unfair treatment. As James Q. Wilson (1965) reluctantly admits, "The nonpolitical strategies developed by the Negro for gaining bargaining power—sit-ins, the protest march, and passive resistance—have already been adopted by whites. . . . This spillover of civil rights tactics . . . has probably been one of the most important consequences of increased Negro militancy" (p. 973).

Empirical Evidence

Thus far, this section has identified disagreements among radicals as to which group of whites—workers or capitalists—benefit from discrimination against nonwhites. Michael Reich (1981) developed econometric tests of the competing hypotheses. Reich estimated the degree of discrimination, income of whites, unionization rates, and per capita social spending in each of the forty-eight largest metropolitan areas. He hypothesized that those areas with the highest levels of discrimination would benefit white capitalists at the expense of white workers. Profits would be higher and white wages would be lower. Reich also hypothesized that areas with the highest levels of racism would have the lowest levels of unionization and per capita social spending.

Reich assumed that the unadjusted black–white family income ratio was an accurate proxy for the degree of discrimination in each urban area—the higher the ratio, the less discrimination. As a proxy for capitalist income, Reich used the income share going to the richest 1 percent of households. Reich found that there was a strong statistically significant relationship between the two variables—the higher the income ratio (and hence the lower the discrimination), the less income went to the richest 1 percent of households. This outcome is consistent with radical views but inconsistent with liberal or conservative views.

Reich also tested whether broad sections of the white population benefited from increased discrimination. He estimated the degree of income inequality within the white population. Reich argued that if large sections of the white population benefited financially from discrimination, we should expect income among whites to be more equal in more discriminatory as opposed to less discriminatory areas. He found, however, that there was a positive correlation between the level of discrimination and the degree of income inequality among whites. This is consistent with the traditional Marxist view that white workers are harmed financially by increased discrimination.[2]

According to the traditional Marxist viewpoint, white workers are harmed because discriminatory attitudes weaken unity within the working class. Since this weakened unity should reduce the political as well as the economic power of workers, Reich hypothesized that discrimination would influence unionization rates and per capita social spending patterns. Reich found that there was a negative correlation between the level of discrimination and the unionization rate—that is, areas with more discrimination had lower levels of unionization. He also found a negative correlation between the level of discrimination and per capita social spending. Areas with more discrimination had lower levels of government expenditures on social programs.

Many studies (see, for example, Thompson and Mattila 1968) have found that income distribution is influenced by the industrial composition of firms and educational attainment of workers. For example, areas with a large durable goods industry tend to have a more equal income distribution than areas with more light industry and white-collar employment. Similarly, the more equal the level of education among workers, the more equal the distribution of income should be regardless of the level of discrimination or industrial composition. Reich found that even after including these and other controlling factors, the correlations between discrimination and each of the dependent variables were unchanged.[3]

Finally, Reich notes that his results might be sensitive to regional differences between the South and non-South. Of the eleven areas with the lowest black–white income ratios, nine were in the South. To test whether his results were influenced by regional differences, Reich eliminated all southern areas. His new results were remarkably similar to his results when southern metropolitan areas were included. Reich concludes,

> Despite the dramatic civil rights developments of the decade, the consider-able urban migration of blacks, the rapid growth of southern cities, and the tighter labor markets in 1969 (which might have diminished racial divisions between black and white workers), the 1960 results are replicated with 1970 data; racial discrimination in metropolitan areas continued to benefit rich whites and to hurt most white as well as black workers. (p. 157)

A number of critics have suggested that there are serious methodological problems with Reich's study. Some critics focus on the black–white family income ratio, the principal proxy variable for discrimination Reich used. Reich was well aware that this variable is influenced by the higher propor-tion of female-headed households among blacks and numerous other factors, including educational attainment. But he contends that it would be a mistake to adjust black–white income ratios for these factors, since he believes that black–white educational and marital differences are just as much indicators of discrimination as are narrow measures of labor market discrimination.

Wayne Villemez (1978) claims that the Index of Net Differences is a more accurate measure of local discrimination. Using this alternative meas-ure, he reestimated the relationships both Reich (1981) and Szymanski (1976) tested. Villemez found that when this alternative proxy measure is used, white workers are shown to benefit from discrimination. Szymanski (1978) demonstrated, however, that Villemez's results were based on an incorrect application of his alternative measure.

E.M. Beck (1980) also claims that Reich's model was faulty and led to incorrect conclusions. Beck used the Index of Dissimilarity as his measure of discrimination and national time series rather than metropolitan area cross-sectional data. He found that during the period 1947 to 1974, union-ization rates fell, while racial income inequality lessened. He contends that this demonstrates that the unions increased racial income inequality. More detailed studies by numerous economists (see, for example, Ashenfelter 1972; Leigh 1978) have assessed the impact of unionization on racial inequality, and virtually all have found that the unions increased equality.

Neo-Marxist economist Steven Shulman also has found fault with Reich's findings. Shulman (1984) notes that Reich does not show directly that white workers had lower incomes as a result of discrimination, only that there was more income inequality among whites. Growing inequality is possible, even if the income of white workers rises, as long as the income of wealthy whites rises even faster.

More importantly, Shulman suggests that racism primarily affects the probability of unemployment. He believes that as racism increases, the probability of a white worker experiencing unemployment decreases. Thus, Shulman contends that even if the wages received by white workers are decreased slightly by racism, the workers benefit, as their lower wages are more than compensated for by the reduced likelihood that white workers will experience unemployment. Since Reich's study did not incorporate the impact of racism on unemployment rates, Shulman contends that Reich's assertion that white workers are harmed by discrimination "is problematical" (p. 51).

Conclusions

The first section of the chapter indicated how sensitive assessments of black–white ratios are to the statistics used. Black–white ratios rise if data eliminate underemployed, less educated, or older workers. This section also indicated that the timing of black gains has been disputed. Conservatives believe that gains were relatively continuous through 1980, while nonconservatives contend that gains were limited to spurts during the 1940s and late 1960s. Finally, although many conservatives do not claim that civil rights legislation promoted reverse discrimination, they do dismiss this legislation as ineffective and contend that educational advances have been the primary reason for black gains.

In contrast with conservatives, both liberal and radical economists believe that civil rights legislation has been helpful, but the groups differ in their assessments. Liberals emphasize judicial victories over segregated schooling, while radicals claim that the multiracial movement begun in the 1930s was responsible for black gains. While all radicals agree that this multiracial movement was beneficial, neo-Marxists and traditional Marxists have different explanations for its breakdown. Whereas traditional Marxists emphasize political repression, neo-Marxists claim that white workers decided they could benefit more from an alliance with capitalists than from continued multiracial unity.

This chapter also discussed Michael Reich's data, which appears to demonstrate that white workers are harmed by discrimination. Reich (1981) found that discrimination lowers social spending and unionization rates, while it increases the incomes of the wealthy and the inequality among white households. These findings are consistent with traditional Marxist claims that white workers benefit from multiracial unity. The chapter ended by noting that nonradicals and neo-Marxists have found inadequacies in Reich's study that they believe undermine traditional Marxist contentions.

Notes

1. Even conservative economists Butler and Heckman (1978) believe that reductions in the rate of black labor force participation explain at least part of the increase in the black–white income ratio during this period. Indeed, Smith (1981) also admits that some compensation may be justifiable.

2. Al Szymanski (1976) replicated Reich's 1977 study. Symanski used statewide rather than metropolitan area data. He found that capitalists benefited from racism, while white workers were harmed by it.

3. Reich also explored the possibility that the size of the black population rather than the degree of discrimination explained each of the dependent variables. Many economists contend that blacks are crowded into secondary job markets, thereby lowering their wages relative to white workers. If the proportion of blacks in the labor force increases, earnings in low-wage sectors will decline relative to earnings in high-wage sectors, as will the black–white income ratio. In this case, changes in the proportion of blacks in the labor force will directly influence the black–white income ratio. Unlike Glen Cain (1985), Reich believes that his econometric results demonstrate decisively that this crowding hypothesis is incorrect.

References

Adams, Frank. 1975. *Unearthing the Seeds of Fire: The Idea of Highlander.* Winston-Salem, NC: John F. Blair.

Allport, Gordon. 1954. *The Nature of Prejudice.* Reading, MA: Addison-Wesley.

Ashenfelter, Orley. 1972. "Racial Discrimination and Trade Unions." *Journal of Political Economy* 80:435–64.

Baran, Paul, and Paul Sweezy. 1965. *Monopoly Capital.* New York: Monthly Review Press.

Baron, Harold. 1975. "Racial Domination in Advanced Capitalism: A Theory of Nationalism and Divisions in the Labor Market." In *Labor Market Segmentation,* ed. Richard Edwards, Michael Reich, and David Gordon. Lexington, MA: D.C. Heath, 173–216.

Beck, E.M. 1980. "Labor Unionism and Racial Income Inequality." *American Journal of Sociology* 85:791–814.

Bergmann, Barbara. 1977. "Can Discrimination Be Ended?" In *Problems in Political Economy: An Urban Perspective,* ed. David Gordon. Lexington, MA: D.C. Heath, 161–65.

Bonacich, Edna. 1976. "Advanced Capitalism and Black–White Relations in the United States: A Split Labor Market Interpretation." *American Sociological Review* 41:34–51.

Butler, William, and James J. Heckman. 1978. "The Impact of the Government on the Labor Market Status of Black Americans: A Critical Review of Literature and New Evidence." In *Equal Rights and Industrial Relations,* ed. Leonard S. Hausman et al. Madison, WI: Industrial Relations Research Association.

Cain, Glen. 1985. "The Economic Analysis of Labor Market Discrimination: A Survey." Institute for Research on Poverty, University of Wisconsin–Madison.

Cayton, Horace, and George Mitchell. 1939. *Black Workers and the New Unions.* Chapel Hill, NC: University of North Carolina Press.

Chalmers, David. 1987. *Hooded Americanism.* Durham, NC: Duke University Press.

Corcoran, Mary, and Greg J. Duncan. 1979. "Work History, Labor Force Attachment, and Earnings Differences between the Races and Sexes." *Journal of Human Resources* 14:497–520.

Dalfiume, Ralph. 1969. "The 'Forgotten Years' of Negro Revolution." In *The Negro in Depression and War,* ed. Bernard Sternsher. New York: Schocken, 298–311.

Darity, William G. 1980. "Illusion of Black Economic Progress." *Review of Black Political Economy* 10:355–79.

Drake, St. Clair, and Horace Cayton. 1945. *Black Metropolis.* New York: Harcourt and Brace.

Ebert, Randall, and Joe Stone. 1985. "Male–Female Differences in Promotions: EEO in Public Education." *Journal of Human Resources* 20:504–21.

Fairchild, Henry. 1917. "Literacy Tests." *Quarterly Journal of Economics* 31:447–51.

Franklin, Raymond, and Solomon Resnik. 1973. *The Political Economy of Racism.* New York: Random House.

Freeman, Richard B. 1973. "Decline of Labor Market Discrimination and Economic Analysis." *American Economics Review* 63:280–86.

Fusfeld, Daniel, and Timothy Bates. 1984. *The Political Economy of the Urban Ghetto.* Carbondale IL: Southern Illinois University Press.

Gottschalk, Peter, and Sheldon Danziger. 1986. "Earnings Inequality, the Spatial Concentration of Poverty, and the Underclass." Paper presented at the Allied Social Science Association Meetings, New Orleans, 29 December 29.

Hoffman, Erwin. 1969. "The Genesis of the Modern Movement." In *The Negro in Depression and War,* ed. Bernard Sternsher. New York: Schocken, 193–215.

Hoffman, Saul. 1979. "Black–White Life Cycle Earnings Differences and the Vintage Hypothesis: A Longitudinal Analysis." *American Economics Review* 69:855–67.

Lazear, Edward. 1979. "The Narrowing of the Black–White Wage Gap Is Illusionary." *American Economics Review* 69:553–564.

Leigh, Duane. 1978. "Racial Discrimination and Labor Unions: Evidence from the NLS Sample of Middle-Aged Men." *Journal of Human Resources* 13:227–41.

Leonard, Jonathan. 1984a. "Anti-Discrimination or Reverse Discrimination?" *Journal of Human Resources* 19:143–61.

———. 1984b. "What Are Promises Worth: The Impact of Affirmative Action Goals." *Journal of Human Resources* 20:3–20.

Masters, Stanley H. 1975. *Black–White Income Differentials.* New York: Academic Press.

Murray, Charles. 1984. *Losing Ground: American Social Policy, 1950–1980.* New York: Basic Books.

Murray, Hugh. 1969. "The NAACP Versus the Communist Party." In *The Negro in Depression and War,* ed. Bernard Sternsher. New York: Schocken, 267–80.

Myrdal, Gunnar. 1944. *An American Dilemma: The Negro Problem and Modern Democracy.* New York: Harper and Row.

Reich, Michael. 1977. "Theories of Racism." In *Problems in Political Economy: An Urban Perspective,* ed. David Gordon. Lexington, MA: D.C. Heath, 183–87.

———. 1981. *Racial Inequality.* Princeton, NJ: Princeton University Press.

———. 1988. "Postwar Racial Income Differences: Trends and Theories." In *The Three Worlds of Labor Economics,* ed. Garth Mangum and Peter Philips. White Plains, NY: M.E. Sharpe, 125–47.

Shulman, Steven. 1984. "The Politics of Race." *Monthly Review* 35:49–53.

Smith, James P. 1981. "Comment." *Review of Black Political Economy* 4:384–90.

———. 1984. "Race and Human Capital. *American Economics Review* 74:685–98.

Smith, James P., and Finis Welch. 1986. *Closing the Gap: Forty Years of Economic Progress for Blacks.* Santa Monica, CA: Rand Corporation.

Sowell, Thomas. 1981. *Markets and Minorities.* New York: Basic Books.

Spero, Sterling, and Harris, Abram. 1968. The Black Worker. New York: Atheneum.

Szymanski, Albert. 1976. "Racial Discrimination and White Gain." *American Sociological Review* 41:403–14.

———. 1978. "White Workers' Loss from Racial Discrimination: Reply to Villemez." *American Sociological Review* 43:776–82

Thompson, Wilbur, and John Mattila. 1968. "Toward an Econometric Model of Urban Development." In *Issues in Urban Economics,* ed. Harvey Perloff and Lowdon Wingo. Baltimore: Johns Hopkins Press.

Villemez, Wayne. 1978. "Black Subordination and White Economic Well-Being." *American Sociological Review* 43:772–76.

Weaver, Robert. 1946. *Negro Labor: A National Problem.* New York: Harcourt and Brace.

Welch, Finis. 1973. "Black–White Differences in Returns to Schooling." *American Economics Review* 63:893–907.

———. 1981. "Affirmative Action and Its Enforcement." *American Economics Review* 71S:127–33.

Williams, John. 1969. "Struggles of the Thirties in the South." In *Negro in Depression and War,* ed. Bernard Sternsher. New York: Schocken, 166–80.

Wilson, James Q. 1965. "The Negro in Politics." *Daedalus* 94:972–77.

Wilson, William J. 1980. *The Declining Significance of Race.* Chicago: University of Chicago Press.

6
Black Youth Employment Problems

D espite extensive civil rights legislation, unemployment rates for black males ages sixteen to nineteen and twenty to twenty-four have remained over 30 percent and over 20 percent respectively. This is more than double the rates for comparably aged white males. Between 1969 and 1977, black male labor force participation rates fell dramatically and continued to decline thereafter. In contrast, the labor force participation rates for white male youths increased between 1969 and 1977 and fell only modestly thereafter. As a result, since 1969 there has been a striking change in black, but not white, youth employment rates (the percentage of youths employed). Table 6–1 indicates that employment rates for black male teenagers were only one-half those for white male teenagers in 1986. For males ages twenty to twenty-four, the black employment rate was only three-quarters that of the white rate.

Economists disagree as to the seriousness of the employment problems, the role government policies have played, and the reasons for the black–white employment differential. Conservatives tend to believe that more accurate measures would indicate that black youth employment problems are not very serious, affecting only a small percentage of the black youth population. Moreover, conservatives contend that to the extent problems exist, they reflect the internal inadequacies of black youths, compounded by the adverse effects of government antipoverty policies, including welfare and minimum wage legislation. The first two sections of this chapter develop these contentions.

Liberals reject conservative beliefs that internal inadequacies and problems created by government policies are responsible for the persistence of low employment rates among young black males. Instead, liberals emphasize external factors such as declining employment opportunities due to a weakening of economic growth and increasing labor market imbalances. They also note that discrimination continues to affect black workers adversely. The third section of this chapter details liberal criticisms of conservative contentions, while the fourth section presents liberal explanations for the persistence of black youth employment problems.

Radicals believe more strongly than liberals that discrimination decisively influences black youth employment rates. Liberals tend to believe that capitalists have no financial stake in the perpetuation of discriminatory hiring practices. In contrast, radicals believe that capitalists have a strong eco-

Table 6–1
Black and White Male Employment Rates, 1969–1986

Age	Black Employment Rate				White Employment Rate				Black–White Ratio			
	1969	*1977*	*1984*	*1986*	*1969*	*1977*	*1984*	*1986*	*1969*	*1977*	*1984*	*1986*
16–17	28.4	18.9	15.1	17.6	42.7	44.3	37.7	39.7	0.67	0.43	0.40	0.44
18–19	51.1	36.9	32.5	36.2	61.8	65.2	60.2	60.1	0.83	0.57	0.58	0.61
20–24	77.3	61.2	58.1	61.3	78.8	80.5	78.0	79.3	0.98	0.76	0.75	0.77

Source: U.S. Department of Labor, Bureau of Labor Statistics, *Employment and Earnings*, 1969, 1977, 1984, 1986.

nomic stake in its perpetuation. Moreover, radicals contend that changes in labor markets during the post–World War II period have led firms to rely increasingly on racial discrimination, worsening the position of black youths. The final section of the chapter presents these radical views.

Conservative Viewpoints

Conservatives believe that an accurate assessment of the labor market experience of young black males indicates that only a small segment of this population has serious employment problems. In addition, to the extent that young black males experience difficulties, conservatives claim it is due to their own inadequacies rather than discrimination. This section details both of these conservative contentions.

Limited Employment Problems

Many economists do not believe that the official unemployment rate is an accurate measure of the labor market difficulties experienced by youths. Wachter and Kim (1982) constructed an adjusted unemployment rate by assuming that military service and school attendance were equivalent to employment. In this case, the only unemployment counted was that of out-of-school youths who were engaged in an active job search. These adjustments dramatically lowered measured unemployment rates. Whereas the official unemployment rates (1978) for black youths ages sixteen to seventeen, eighteen to nineteen, and twenty to twenty-four were 40.7 percent, 30.9 percent, and 20.1 percent respectively, the adjusted rates were only 7.8 percent, 14.2 percent, and 13.6 percent respectively.

Not only does it appear that rates are quite low once they are adjusted for military enlistment and school attendance, but it also appears that problems may be serious for only a small percentage of youths. Martin Feldstein and David Ellwood (1982) found that for youths as a whole, unemployment was a momentary occurrence if it occurred at all. They found that sustained unemployment, defined as more than twenty-six weeks, was experienced by only 8 percent of the youth population, or a group of about 250,000 youths.

Feldstein and Ellwood also minimize the seriousness of the high percentage of youths who are neither in school nor in the labor force. They reject the notion that these youths are discouraged workers—individuals who do not seek employment due to a lack of available jobs. They cite the doubling of youth employment during the summer months as an indication of the large demand for youth employment. Moreover, Feldstein and Ellwood note that surveys indicate that the vast majority of the out-of-school, out-of-work population live with parents and thus have little pressure to seek employment.

Feldstein and Ellwood contend that much of the youth racial unemployment differential is due to educational and family income differences rather than racial discrimination. Black youths tend to have less income and live in poorer households than white youths. If black youths had the same education and came from households with the same family income as white youths, Feldstein and Ellwood estimate that more than half the racial unemployment differential would be eliminated.

Internal Inadequacies

Conservatives contend that black labor market failures reflect internal inadequacies. Summarizing this perspective, Glenn Loury (1985) notes, "The next frontier for the black community is to grapple with the internal problems which lower class blacks now face" (p. 14). As evidence that cultural factors strongly influence labor market outcomes, Datcher-Loury and Loury (1986) and Freeman (1986a) cite evidence that there is a positive correlation between church attendance and productive time (school, work, or household activities). Freeman also found that family environment played a significant role in determining the productive activity of young black males. The more parents work, the more time youths will spend at productive activities. These studies yielded results consistent with the culture of poverty thesis—that is, growing up in poor households, black youths develop dysfunctional attitudes that increase their likelihood of remaining poor.

Many conservatives claim that black unemployment reflects voluntary choice rather than a lack of jobs. They contend that black youths set too high a reservation wage (the lowest wage at which they will work). Kip Viscusi (1986) found that for a large proportion of inner-city youths, criminal activity was an acceptable alternative. Harry Holzer (1986) contends that "outside income generated by illegal activities (and other sources) for young blacks with low skill levels may be an important source of their relatively high reservation wage" (p. 51).

Christopher Jencks (1987) associates this high reservation wage with rising expectations. He claims that in the 1960s, blacks believed that their inability to obtain good jobs was due solely to discrimination. Blacks thought that once discrimination was illegal, they would obtain these jobs, so they were unwilling to take lower-paying jobs. Similarly, Elijah Anderson (1980) suggests that black youths, having developed a new consciousness and set of expectations as a result of the civil rights movement, now shun low-status jobs that were once associated with racial degradation.

Data from researchers (Clark and Summers 1982; Leighton and Mincer 1982) consistently indicate that black youths are much more likely to be fired or laid off than white youths. According to liberals, black youths tend to have higher termination rates as a result of discrimination or lack of seniority. In contrast, conservatives believe that the source is internal inadequacies that undermine work ethics. Some conservatives cite government data indicating that black youths have a higher rate of absenteeism than white youths. Walter Williams (1981) claims that these inadequacies make black youths much less productive than white youths, and hence they are more likely to be laid off.

Conservative Policy Recommendations

Conservatives believe that internal inadequacies are responsible for the adverse economic situation of black youths. Even if these behavioral deficiencies result from a maladaption to discrimination, "the responsibility for the behavior of black youngsters lies squarely on the shoulders of the black community itself" (Loury 1985, 12). This section summarizes conservative critiques of government programs that affect minority youths, including welfare and minimum wage legislation. It concludes with a summary of conservative policy recommendations.

Welfare Programs

Conservatives generally believe that welfare programs have had an adverse effect on black youth employment rates. Freeman (1986a) and Lerman (1986) found that black youths growing up in a welfare household were much more likely to have employment difficulties than comparably educated black youths growing up in a working family, even after holding income and family structure constant. Charles Murray (1984) claims that welfare raised black reservation wage rates by funding "social programs [which] reinforced the ethic that certain jobs are too demeaning to ask people to do" (p. 201).

Murray believes that welfare generates significant work disincentives. He reviews federally funded negative income tax (NIT) studies to determine the impact on labor supplies (hours of work) if the government were to increase guaranteed welfare payments. He takes as representative the Seattle–Denver NIT results, which estimated a 40 percent decline in the youth labor supply. Murray considers this most damaging because these youths are at a "critical age in their lives: about to enter into responsibilities of marriage and just establishing themselves in the labor force" (p. 151).

Minimum Wage Legislation

Minimum wage legislation is the most widely used explanation for youth unemployment rates. A higher minimum wage raises labor costs, forcing firms to raise prices. When consumers reduce their demand, firms must cut their production and labor demand. Firms also might reduce their labor demand when it becomes cost-effective to automate production. Minimum wage critics generally believe that these disemployment effects create hardship for a large enough segment of the low-wage work force that they outweigh the benefits received by those fortunate enough to keep their jobs.

Since many believe that black youths are the least productive workers, it follows that they should experience a disproportionate share of the layoffs that result. Summarizing this position, Baumol and Blinder (1979) state, "[D]espite all the legislation adopted to improve the position of black people, [the minimum wage law], which, though apparently designed to protect low-skilled workers, is in fact a crippling impediment to any attempt to improve job opportunities for blacks" (p. 510).

Alternative Policy Proposals

As expected, conservatives recommend a drastic cutback in antidiscrimination legislation, welfare eligibility, and minimum wage coverage. They also recommend reducing compulsory education requirements and enacting a subminimum wage for youths.

Currently, all youngsters under sixteen years of age must attend school and cannot work full-time. Many conservatives consider these restrictions harmful. They reason that for many, extended compulsory school reinforces negative behavior. Being placed in the lowest track and often performing at well below grade level, these youngsters develop a low self-esteem. As a result, they develop bad habits, including high truancy, and reject learning situations.

Once these traits are developed, they carry over into employment situations. Having unstable school attendance, these youngsters will likely have unstable work attendance. Having given up attempting to learn in school, they will have difficulty learning on the job. To avoid encouraging these negative traits to develop, many conservatives (see, for example, Sowell 1981) recommend the termination of compulsory education and employment restrictions at age fourteen. They contend that early employment can give youngsters the self-discipline and self-respect that further compulsory education undermines.

Conservatives favor a subminimum wage rate for youngsters between sixteen and nineteen years old. For example, suppose the subminimum for teenagers was set at 80 percent of the adult minimum wage rate. If the adult rate was $3.60 an hour, then the teenage rate would be $2.88 an hour. Conservatives believe that at these lower wages, firms would be more likely to hire inner-city black youths. Conservatives contend that, although the wages may be low, these jobs would enable black youths to develop the discipline and self-respect they need for future success.

To demonstrate the long-term benefits from low-wage steady employment, Thomas Sowell (1981) cites the turn-of-the-century sweatshops. Although these sweatshops paid very low wages, Sowell claims that they provided stable employment with substantial on-the-job training for an illiterate immigrant population.[1] Sowell hypothesizes that if there had been minimum wage and other restrictive government legislation then, these immigrants would not have been employed and would never have developed the skills necessary to attain middle-class incomes.

Criticisms of Conservative Views

Liberal and radical economists disagree with conservative evaluations and policy recommendations. They reject the claim that black youth employment problems are not serious and the emphasis on internal inadequacies. Many also believe that minimum wage legislation has been more effective than the conservative analysis suggests. Finally, liberal and radical economists reject conservative policy proposals. This section details these criticisms of conservative views.

Black Youth Employment Difficulties

Data in the previous section indicate that a significant part of the decline in black youth employment during the 1970s reflected increasing school attendance and military enlistment. Liberal and radical economists do not agree with Feldstein and Ellwood (1982) that employment problems are severe only for a small percentage of black youths. Using the same data set, Freeman and Medoff (1982) point out that 21 percent of out-of-school black men ages twenty to twenty-four had no work experience in the previous year. This was more than double the white rate (7.2 percent) and almost double the black rate seven years earlier (12.8 percent).

Although Feldstein and Ellwood emphasize that unemployment is concentrated among high school dropouts who live in poor households and minimize the significance of the large out-of-school, out-of-work youth population, their data indicate otherwise. Almost 30 percent of black high school graduates ages twenty to twenty-four were out of the labor force in 1978. Also, unemployment and labor force participation rates were the same for black youths living in low-income and middle-income households. Thus, for black youths, gaining a high school degree or being fortunate enough to live in a middle-income household did not eliminate severe employment problems.

The short spells of youth unemployment that Feldstein and Ellwood

(1982) document reflect their measurement technique. They consider an unemployment spell to end if either the individual finds employment or drops out of the labor force. Since more than one-half of the unemployment spells of in-school youths end within a month due to exit from the labor force, it is not surprising that measured unemployment spells were short. Clark and Summers (1982) contend that these movements out of the labor force reflect an inability to find employment. Thus, the appropriate measure is the duration of joblessness—that is, how long youths spend between jobs. They found that for high school graduates, the average duration of joblessness was more than six months and for high school dropouts almost ten months.

Clark and Summers also suggest that black youths have much more difficulty finding employment than white youths and that black youths have a lower probability of gaining employment whether or not they are officially unemployed in the labor force. Ballen and Freeman (1986) believe that this is a result of hiring criteria. They claim that firms are sensitive to spotty work records in black youth applicants but not in white youth applicants.

Dysfunctional Behavior

Conservatives believe that black youths have severe internal inadequacies, including poor work ethics, a high reservation wage, and high absenteeism. Liberals believe that black youths exhibit behavioral problems because of a maladaption to discriminatory barriers and these problems have little impact on the size of racial employment differentials. More importantly, liberals question the validity of conservative assertions that black youths have more behavioral problems than white youths.

Even if black youths have a higher reservation wage, it is likely an outgrowth of the migration process. Michael Piore (1979) argues that rural migrants to urban areas willingly accepted the lowest-rung jobs because these jobs still represented upward mobility. For their children, however, these jobs do not represent mobility and will be rejected. Thus, independent of race, Piore conjectures that all second-generation migrants will reject low-wage, dead-end employment. It is only because black youths have not had the opportunity for upward mobility that they experience employment problems.

Even if criminal activities adversely affect black youths, conservatives overstate their importance. Data tabulated by Richard Freeman (1986b) indicate that the employment rate differential between those who did and those who did not commit crimes was entirely the result of the lack of employment of a small group comprising those who had spent time in jail the previous year. The legal employment record of the other 84 percent who committed crimes was virtually the same as that of youths who reported they had not committed crimes. Second, even if all of the adverse effects of criminal behavior on black employment are eliminated, Freeman (1986b) estimates that the unemployment rate among inner-city black youths would decline from 50 percent to 37 percent, leaving it still far above that of white youths.

Critics also question conservative claims that black youths have higher reservation wage rates than white youths. Some studies (Wachter and Kim 1982; Borus 1982; Culp and Dunson 1986) have found that the wage rates at which black youths will accept employment are the same as, if not lower than, the rates at which white youths will accept employment. Since the actual wages paid to black youths are below those paid to white youths, researchers characterize blacks as having a higher reservation wage relative to earnings. While black youths may be unrealistic in attempting to earn wages similar to those earned by white youths, this hardly supports conservative claims that blacks reject jobs offers that whites are willing to accept.

While black youths have higher rates of absenteeism than white youths, Allen (1981) found that the differences could be accounted for by differences in job characteristics. Black youths have a disproportionate share of the dead-end jobs that everyone quits. If black and white youths were employed at jobs with the same characteristics, there would be no difference between their rates of absenteeism. Ferguson and Filer (1986) also found that job characteristics "play a decisive role in predicting employee behavior" (p. 264). Jackson and Montgomery (1986) found that even among youths, black workers have less job tenure than white workers and this has a significant impact on job-loss rates. These studies indicate that black youths are not very different than white youths. If you give them decent jobs, they will behave just as responsibly.

Welfare Policy

Even if living in welfare households is associated with lower employment rates, Samuel Myers (1986) claims that the relationship is far more complex than conservatives believe. Myers notes that the percentage of black youths ages eighteen to twenty-four who are living at home is double that of comparably aged white youths. For Myers, black youths who are unable to find jobs are forced to remain at home, often in a welfare household. Thus, he believes, the correlation between unemployment and living in a welfare household reflects deficient job opportunities.

Critics believe that conservatives overstate the impact of welfare on work ethics. Between 1950 and 1970, John Cogan (1982) found that teenage employment rates rose from 26 percent to 27 percent in the North but declined from 55 percent to 27 percent in the South. This occurred despite the fact that the Aid to Families with Dependent Children (AFDC) participation rate increased three times faster in the North than in the South. Critics also contend that the results from NIT studies that Murray (1984) emphasizes are misleading, since the vast majority of labor supply withdrawals were by youths in school who presumably were now able to spend more time on their education. Myers (1986) also found that an increase in welfare recipiency had little effect on black–white earnings ratios, causing him to claim, "These results . . . dim any hopes of finding major new explanations for wage inequality in the phenomenon of welfare participation" (p. 440).

Minimum Wage Legislation

Many economists believe that the minimum wage does not have a negative impact on black youth employment. First, these proponents (see, for example, Cherry 1985) note that if the labor demand decline resulted in most workers experiencing either a modest decline in the hours of employment per week or weeks worked per year, they would still benefit because fewer hours per year of work would be more than offset by the higher hourly wage. A numerical example will illustrate these points.

At the current minimum wage of $3.35 an hour, individuals working full-time year-round (2,080 hours per year) have yearly earnings of $6,968. If the minimum wage was raised to $4 an hour, they would have a higher yearly income as long as they worked at least 1,742 hours per year (the equivalent of slightly less than forty-four weeks). Thus, even if workers were laid off, as long as their unemployment was less than two months, they would have both more income and more nonmarket time. Given the small labor demand elasticity and the high turnover in many low-wage jobs, this outcome is quite plausible. Indeed, even if people suffered somewhat greater unemployment, their situations would still be improved if they valued the gained nonmarket time more than the lost income.

Proponents also reject any notions that black youths are the least productive members of the low-wage work force. Interestingly, there is little evidence that black-youth employment suffers disproportionately from the minimum wage. Brown, Gilroy, and Kohn (1982) found that as many studies indicate that black youths experience a smaller disemployment effect than white youths as indicate that this effect is greater among blacks. They conclude that any contention that black youths are differentially affected "must rest on theoretical rather than empirical grounds" (p. 508).

Responses to Conservative
Policy Recommendations

Liberal and radical economists generally reject recommendations to relax compulsory education requirements and institute a subminimum wage. As a result of increased use of sophisticated technologies, entry-level jobs require greater literacy than they did fifty years ago. No longer is brute strength and hard work sufficient for gainful employment in upwardly mobile occupations. Schooling has become more important, not less. Moreover, if youngsters expect to leave school at fourteen, they will give up on school even before the fifth grade and are likely to be given up on by their teachers.

Critics of conservative views reject claims that a subminimum wage would create a large number of additional jobs. Bernard Anderson (1981) notes that few firms take advantage of current provisions that make it possible to hire youths at subminimum wage levels. If firms are not currently willing to utilize subminimum wage provisions, it is unlikely that a broader subminimum wage would have any significant effect on jobs available to youths.

Even if the jobs generated were significant, they might have little impact on the employment of inner-city black youths. Since all youths would be subject to the lower subminimum rate, the vast majority of jobs generated might go to white youths, especially those living in suburban areas. Finally, studies estimate that a subminimum wage would cause a considerable redistribution of employment, as many adult female low-wage workers would lose their job to teenagers. Thus, youth employment gains would primarily be at the expense of adult workers.[2]

Liberal Views on Black Youth Unemployment

This section summarizes liberal explanations emphasizing influences external to black youths. These factors include the overall strength of aggregate demand, the changing composition of the labor force, changing locational patterns, and discriminatory barriers.

According to Clark and Summers (1982), "The teenage unemployment problem is not the lack of desire to hold jobs, but the inability to find work" (p. 227). In a study of job advertisements, they found that for most low-wage jobs requiring no skills or previous experience, employers were swamped with applications. Focusing on the worst jobs advertised in the Sunday paper, they found an average of fifteen to twenty responses within two days of an ad's placement.

During the 1970s, the job market for teenagers deteriorated for two reasons—a less robust economy and an overcrowding of youths and women in low-wage markets. Clark and Summers found that teenage employment was especially sensitive to the overall state of the economy. They estimated that for each one-point decrease in the prime-age male unemployment rate—an indicator of the general vitality of the economy—there would be a 4.5 percentage-point increase in the teenage employment rate; for black teenagers the increase would be 6.3 percentage points. They note that between 1969 and 1976, when the aggregate unemployment rate rose from 3.6 percent to 7.7 percent, "The proportion of 16–19 year olds suffering more than six months unemployment rose fourfold. For black youths the same figure increased by almost six times" (p. 226).

During the 1970s, there was a dramatic increase in the labor force participation rates of teenagers and adult women. The result was an overcrowding of applicants in low-wage labor markets. Not surprisingly, real wages for low-wage workers declined. Dooley and Gottschalk (1985) found that the percentage of male workers earning low wages increased from 15.4 percent in 1969 to 21.0 percent in 1977. White youths were able to maintain employment in the face of these adverse labor market conditions by adjusting their wage demands downward. Freeman and Wise (1982) believe that the reduction in the gap between white and black youth wage rates "contributed to the deterioration in the black versus white [youth] employment rate" (p. 10).

Many investigators (see, for example, Clark and Summers 1982) have found that low-wage jobs are filled through personal contacts rather than through public advertising. Businesses often hire by asking relatives, neighbors, or current employees to identify applicants. Using these informal networks lowers screening costs. Moreover, employers are more confident when relying on trusted recommendations than on an applicant pool generated by advertisements. Hiring through informal networks is advantageous to white youths because there are a disproportionate number of white-owned firms. This differential access to information is magnified by segregated housing, schooling, and social arrangements.

After World War II, the large black migration to northern urban areas began. Previously, most blacks lived in southern rural areas. Even when the farm work done was minimal, they were considered employed. Because of this disguised rural unemployment, the official measure of black youth unemployment increased simply by their shifting from a rural to an urban environment. Indeed, John Cogan (1982) estimates that the entire growth in black youth unemployment rates between 1950 and 1970 can be explained by the decline in the number of agricultural jobs available to southern youths.

By 1970 manufacturing jobs began moving out of the central city as a result of rising land and transportation costs. William Wilson (1987) notes that between 1970 and 1985, Chicago lost more than half its blue-collar employment opportunities. Many liberal economists contend that black employment is lower the farther firms are located away from black residential areas. Commuting costs—both time and money—make it unrealistic for black youths to consider employment at firms that are far from their homes. In this case, the movement of low-wage manufacturing and service sector jobs away from the central business district could explain the increasing employment difficulties inner-city black youths have been experiencing.[3]

Wilson (1986) suggests an additional reason why ghetto residents have lower employment rates. He claims that with the increasing ability of middle-class blacks to live outside the inner city, black urban ghettos contain only poor blacks. Wilson believes that this reduces the role models and middle-class culture available to inner-city black youths. Thus, not only are jobs more difficult to obtain, but inner-city blacks are less likely to develop and maintain the proper behavioral traits necessary for permanent employment.

Radical Views on Black Youth Unemployment

Radicals believe that liberal critiques of conservative views are extremely useful, as they undermine negative racial stereotypes. Radicals also believe that liberal explanations understate the importance of combatting discriminatory practices. Even when research (Culp and Dunson 1986; Clark and Summers 1982) documents the consistent racist nature of employment practices, liberals reject emphasizing antidiscrimination legislation. Since liberals believe that racism is not in the interest of capitalists, they view these practices as anomalies or atavisms. In contrast, radicals believe that racism is a fundamental aspect of a capitalism and as such must be directly addressed.

Radicals contend that racism persists because it serves the financial and political interests of capitalists. Racism enables capitalists to maintain an underemployed work force, which radicals refer to as an industrial reserve army. This group can be underpaid and overworked either directly or through subcontracting. It can be used as a threat against better-paid white workers. Radicals also believe that racism allows the government to reduce social spending by dividing the working class. It encourages white workers to blame blacks for inadequate living conditions and public services.

These differences in perspective are reflected in the differences between liberal and radical evaluations of training programs and the spatial mismatch theory. Liberals believe that training programs are important and that the suburbanization of employment opportunities has been responsible for increased black employment difficulties. Thus, when conservatives cite studies that training programs have had little impact on black earnings or that the spatial location of jobs has little influence on black employment, liberals are quick to claim that these studies are faulty.[4] In contrast, radicals do not strongly question conservative evaluations of training programs or the impact of locational changes. For example, Piore (1977) believes that training programs tend to be undermined by the resistance of opponents who benefit from the continuation of racist employment practices. Harrison (1977) found that black unemployment rates were not influenced by residential location, as blacks residing in the inner city had the same unemployment rates as those living in the suburbs. These findings buttress radical contentions that only policies that confront discrimination directly can overcome black youth employment difficulties.

Radicals also believe that U.S. capitalism required increased racism after World War II. Until the 1930s, European immigrants provided U.S. capitalism with an industrial reserve army. Their integration into American society created potential labor shortages, but the subsequent migration of rural blacks out of agriculture provided capitalism with a new industrial reserve army.

Political considerations also adversely affected black workers (Cherry 1977). After World War II, there was a concerted effort to purge communist influence from unions. Communists had gained considerable influence as a result of their leadership in union organizing and relief efforts during the Depression. After the Taft-Hartley Act made it illegal for communists to be union officials, many firms gave their workers generous contracts to convince them that they could win more with anticommunist leadership than with communist leadership.

These developments intensified racism in two ways. First, it was communists who had fought for multiracial unity within the union movement. They had convinced many white workers that all workers gain through unity. This made distinctions between the CIO and the AFL clear. With the elimination of communists, the new leaders of the CIO convinced white members that there was more to be gained by uniting with the racist AFL than by maintaining unity with black workers. Thus, the elimination of communists resulted in the weakening of racial unity and the increased willingness of union leaders to adopt racist strategies (Fusfeld and Bates 1984).

Second, firms wished to minimize the concessions given to unions. Many unionized firms began to shift portions of production to the nonunion sector or to move their production away from high-wage urban areas. While a modest segment of white unionized workers benefited, these policies generated greater inequality among blue-collar workers. Although black workers gained access to manufacturing jobs, they dominated the expanding low-wage tier (Bonacich 1976).

National black–white income data disguised this intensification of racism. As long as blacks were moving out of agriculture, low-wage manufacturing employment was an improvement and the national black–white income ratio rose modestly through 1970. In urban areas and within occupations, however, the black–white income ratio was unchanged despite dramatic improvements in the education and skills of black workers compared to their white counterparts.

Until the 1970s, the U.S. capitalist system was the unchallenged world industrial power. If black workers had to run faster just to stay in place prior to the 1970s, it is not surprising that, with increased international competition and worldwide economic stagnation, their position would deteriorate. Growing international competition resulted in excess industrial capacity worldwide. As a result, racism has become an important way to rationalize growing unemployment. World competition also made it too costly to provide decent social services. Again, racism serves the needs of capitalists by convincing whites that blacks are responsible for the reduced quality of urban services. Finally, by splitting the working class, racism made it easier for capitalists to cut the wages of all workers and to attack unions. Thus, radicals contend that capitalism, rather than the structural factors liberals emphasize, is responsible for the growth in racist practices and attitudes.

Conclusions

This chapter has assessed various explanations for the declining black youth employment rate. Conservatives minimize the significance of this decline and reject external explanations. Liberals point to the growing joblessness of young black high school graduates and the difficulties caused by discontinuous work records. They also emphasize that structural factors, including the suburban location of manufacturing jobs, have weakened the ability of inner-city youths to obtain decent employment. Radicals suggest that liberals overstate the importance of structural factors and understate the importance of financially motivated racism in explaining black youth employment problems.

Just as the introductory chapters emphasized, conservatives stress individual choice based on cultural factors, liberals stress structural factors, and radicals stress capitalism's need for a reserve army. Whereas liberals look favorably at the possibilities of government instituting helpful policies, others reject this approach—conservatives because they think government programs promote internal shortcomings and radicals because they believe government will not voluntarily undertake policies that counter profitability.

As chapter 5 indicated, empirical evidence does not necessarily distinguish between correct and incorrect views. Do black youths refuse jobs because they would rather live at home, or do they live at home because no jobs are available? Do black youths give up looking for jobs because they have little interest in finding them or because they become discouraged? Do black youths have a higher rate of absenteeism because of the jobs they have, or do they have those jobs because they lack the proper behavioral traits (such as low absenteeism) necessary to obtain better jobs?

Black youth unemployment brings out the most extreme positions: Are these youths so dysfunctional that they cannot take advantage of the benefits capitalism offers them, or are they the victims of an exploitive racist society that feeds on those least able to defend themselves? Is capitalism beneficent or exploitive? This chapter has presented some information on which you can make your own judgments.

Notes

1. Roger Waldinger (1984) makes a similar argument in describing more recent garment firms in New York City: "[W]orkers acquire those managerial and productive skills which permit them to move into entrepreneurial positions. For workers employed in [these] firms, the opportunity to acquire these skills compensates for the low wages. . . . Thus, the small immigrant firm, despite its image as a 'sweatshop,' serves as a ladder for immigrant social mobility" (p. 71).

2. As an alternative, some economists have proposed government subsidies to employers who hire inner-city youths. Dave O'Neill (1982), however, found targeted wage subsidy programs to be quite costly with little employment benefits. Indeed, in a controlled experiment, Gary Burtless (1985) found that firms were more willing to hire unsubsidized youths than the targeted population. He speculated that the subsidies had a stigmatizing effect, as employers feared that the targeted workers were damaged goods.

3. While a study by Ellwood (1986) seems to indicate that the spatial location of jobs does not explain black–white employment differences in Chicago, Wilson (1987) states, "It strains credulity to believe that the suburbanization of blue-collar jobs has not had devastating consequences for the work experiences of inner-city minorities" (p. 16).

4. For the controversy over the extent to which training programs have been effective in raising earnings, see Bloom (1984); Cavin and Maynard (1985); and Dickerson, Johnson, and West (1986).

References

Allen, S.G. 1981. "Compensation, Safety, and Absenteeism." *Industrial and Labor Relations Review* 34:207–18.

Anderson, Bernard. 1981. "A Partial Dissent: Fiddling with the Economy is Not Enough." In *The Fairmont Papers,* ed. Bernard Anderson et al.. San Francisco: Institute for Contemporary Studies, 47–51.

Anderson, Elijah. 1980. "Some Observations on Black Youth Unemployment." In *Youth Employment and Public Policy,* ed. Bernard Anderson and Isabel Sawhill. Englewood Cliffs, NJ: Prentice-Hall, 37–46.

Ballen, John, and Richard Freeman. 1986. "Transitions between Employment and Unemployment." In *The Black Youth Employment Crisis,* ed. Richard Freeman and Harry Holzer. Chicago: University of Chicago Press, 23–74.

Baumol, William, and Robert Blinder. 1979. *Economics.* New York: Harcourt and Brace.

Bloom, Howard S. 1984. "Estimating the Effects of Job-Training Programs Using Longitudinal Data: Ashenfelter's Findings Reconsidered." *Journal of Human Resources* 19:544–56.

Bonacich, Edna. 1976. "Advanced Capitalism and Black/White Relations in the United States: A Split Labor Market Interpretation." *American Sociological Review* 41:34–51.

Borus, Michael. 1982. "Willingness to Work among Youth." *Journal of Human Resources* 17:581–93.

Brown, C., C. Gilroy, and A. Kohn. 1982. "The Effects of Minimum Wage on Employment and Unemployment." *Journal of Economic Literature* 20:487–528.

Burtless, Gary. 1985. "Are Targeted Wage Subsidies Harmful? Evidence from a Wage Voucher Experiment." *Industrial and Labor Relations Review* 39:105–14.

Cavin, Edward, and Rebecca Maynard. 1985. "Short-term Indicators of Employment Program Performance." *Journal of Human Resources* 20:331–45.

Cherry, Robert. 1977. "Theories of Racism." In *Problems in Political Economy: An Urban Perspective,* ed. David Gordon. Lexington, MA: D.C. Heath, 170–83.

———. 1985. "Textbook Treatments of Minimum Wage Legislation." *Review of Black Political Economy* 13:25–38.

Clark, Kim, and Lawrence Summers. 1982. "The Dynamics of Youth Unemployment." In *The Youth Labor Market Problem,* ed. Richard Freeman and David Wise. Chicago: University of Chicago Press, 199–230.

Cogan, John. 1982. "The Decline in Black Teenage Employment: 1950–70." *American Economics Review* 72:521–38.

Culp, Jerome, and Bruce Dunson. 1986. "Brothers of a Different Color: A Preliminary Look at Employment Treatment of White and Black Youth." In *The Black Youth Employment Crisis,* ed. Richard Freeman and Harry Holzer. Chicago: University of Chicago Press, 233–60.

Datcher-Loury, Linda, and Glenn Loury. 1986. "The Effects of Attitudes and Aspirations on the Labor Supply of Young Men." In *The Black Youth Employment Crisis,* ed. Richard Freeman and Harry Holzer. Chicago: University of Chicago Press, 377–402.

Dickerson, Katherine, Terry Johnson, and Richard West. 1986. "An Analysis of the Impact of CETA on Participants' Earnings." *Journal of Human Resources* 21:64–91.

Dooley, Martin, and Peter Gottschalk. 1985. "The Increasing Proportion of Men with Low Earnings in the United States." *Demography* 22:25–34.

Ellwood, David. 1986. "The Spatial Mismatch Hypothesis: Are There Teenage Jobs Missing in the Ghetto?" In *The Black Youth Employment Crisis,* ed. Richard Freeman and Harry Holzer. Chicago: University of Chicago Press, 147–90.

Feldstein, Martin, and David Ellwood. 1982. "Teenage Unemployment: What Is the Problem?" In *The Youth Labor Market Problem,* ed. Richard Freeman and David Wise. Chicago: University of Chicago Press, 17–34.

Ferguson, Ronald, and Randall Filer. 1986. "Do Better Jobs Make Better Workers? Absenteeism from Work among Inner-City Black Youth." In *The Black Youth Employment Crisis,* ed. Richard Freeman and Harry Holzer. Chicago: University of Chicago Press, 261–98.

Freeman, Richard. 1986a. "Who Escapes? The Relation of Churchgoing and Other Background Factors to the Socioeconomic Performance of Black Youths from Inner-City Poverty Tracts." In *The Black Youth Employment Crisis,* ed. Richard Freeman and Harry Holzer. Chicago: University of Chicago Press, 353–76.

———. 1986b. "The Relation of Criminal Activity to Black Youth Employment."

Paper presented at Allied Social Science Association Meetings, New Orleans, 28 December.

Freeman, Richard, and James Medoff. 1982. "Why Does the Rate of Youth Labor Force Activity Differ across Surveys?" In *The Youth Labor Market Problem*, ed. Richard Freeman and David Wise. Chicago: University of Chicago Press, 75–114.

Freeman, Richard, and David Wise. 1982. "The Youth Labor Market Problem: Its Nature, Causes, and Consequences." In *The Youth Labor Market Problem*, ed. Richard Freeman and David Wise. Chicago: University of Chicago Press, 3–20.

Fusfeld, Daniel, and Timothy Bates. 1984. *The Political Economy of the Urban Ghetto*. Carbondale, IL: Southern Illinois University Press.

Harrison, Bennett. 1977. "Education and Underemployment in the Urban Ghetto." In *Problems in Political Economy: An Urban Perspective*, ed. David Gordon. Lexington, MA: D.C. Heath, 252–63.

Holzer, Harry. 1986. "Black Youth Nonemployment: Duration and Job Search." In *The Black Youth Employment Crisis*, ed. Richard Freeman and Harry Holzer. Chicago: University of Chicago Press, 23–70.

Jackson, Peter, and Edward Montgomery. 1986. "Layoffs, Discharges, and Youth Unemployment." In *The Black Youth Employment Crisis*, ed. Richard Freeman and Harry Holzer. Chicago: University of Chicago Press, 115–41.

Jencks, Christopher. 1987. "Genes and Crime." *New York Review of Books,* 12 February, 33–41.

Leighton, Linda, and Jacob Mincer. 1982. "Labor Turnover and Youth Unemployment." In *The Youth Labor Market Problem*, ed. Richard Freeman and David Wise. Chicago: University of Chicago Press, 235–67.

Lerman, Robert. 1986. "Do Welfare Programs Affect the Schooling and Work Patterns of Young Black Men?" In *The Black Youth Employment Crisis*, ed. Richard Freeman and Harry Holzer. Chicago: University of Chicago Press, 403–38.

Loury, Glenn. 1985. "The Moral Quandary of the Black Community." *The Public Interest* 79:9–23.

Murray, Charles. 1984. *Losing Ground: American Social Policy, 1950–1980*. New York: Basic Books.

Myers, Samuel. 1986. "Comment." In *The Black Youth Employment Crisis*, ed. Richard Freeman and Harry Holzer. Chicago: University of Chicago Press, 438–41.

O'Neill, Dave. 1982. "Employment Tax Credit Programs: The Effects of Socioeconomic Targeting Provisions." *Journal of Human Resources* 17:449–59.

Piore, Michael. 1977. "The Dual Labor Market." In *Problems in Political Economy: An Urban Perspective*, ed. David Gordon. Lexington, MA: D.C. Heath, 91–95.

———. 1979. *Birds of Passage*. New York: Cambridge University Press.

Sowell, Thomas. 1981. *Markets and Minorities*. New York: Basic Books.

Viscusi, Kip. 1986. "Market Incentives for Criminal Behavior." In *The Black Youth Employment Crisis*, ed. Richard Freeman and Harry Holzer. Chicago: University of Chicago Press, 301–46.

Wachter, Michael, and Choongsoo Kim. 1982. "Time Series Changes in Youth Joblessness." In *The Youth Labor Market Problem,* ed. Richard Freeman and David Wise. Chicago: University of Chicago Press, 155–85.

Waldinger, Roger. 1984. "Ethnic Enterprise in New York Garment Industry." *Social Problems* 32:60–71.

Williams, Walter. 1981. "A Culprit Is a Culprit." In *The Fairmont Papers,* ed. Bernard Anderson et al. San Francisco: Institute for Contemporary Studies, 51–53.

Wilson, William. 1986. "Social Policy and Minority Groups." Paper presented at the Poverty and Social Policy Conference sponsored by the Institute for Research on Poverty, Washington, D.C., 5–7 November.

———. 1987. "The Obligation to Work and the Availability of Jobs." *Focus* 10:14–18.

7
The Impact of
Social Welfare Programs

Between 1960 and 1970 the percentage of population living in poverty declined dramatically, fueling the belief that in another decade poverty would be virtually eliminated. Poverty rates did not decline further, however, and even increased during the recession of the early 1980s. Whereas poverty rates had fallen to 11 percent in 1969, they peaked at 15 percent in 1983; rates for black households were 26 percent in 1969 but 33 percent in 1983.[1]

During this period, the number of female-headed households, especially among blacks, soared. Between 1970 and 1985, the share of two-parent households among blacks declined from 64 percent to 40 percent, while the share among white households declined but was still at almost 80 percent. The black–white difference is even more dramatic if we look at the share of all households that are female headed. Among blacks, 42 percent of all households are female headed, while the figure is only 12 percent for whites.

Data also seem to indicate that there has been a dramatic rise in out-of-wedlock births, especially within the black community. In 1980 48.3 percent of all black children born were out of wedlock, compared to 26.3 percent in 1965. The increased number of out-of-wedlock births is most striking among black teenagers. The percent of out-of-wedlock births to black women ages fifteen to nineteen rose from 49.2 percent in 1965 to 82.1 percent in 1980.

During this period, aid to the poor from government social programs grew in relation to the level of aid provided by private charities. Liberals and conservatives have contrasting assessments of the impact of these government programs, especially on family structure within the black community. The first section of this chapter details the conservative view that federal programs, by reducing work incentives and undermining individual initiative, have been responsible for rising poverty rates and the growth of female-headed households and out-of-wedlock births.

The second section begins the presentation of liberal criticisms of conservative views. According to liberals, appropriate measures of poverty rates, economic growth, and welfare dependency seriously undermine conservative claims. The next section presents the liberal response to conservative claims that welfare programs have encouraged changes in family structure and discouraged work effort. Liberals suggest that cuts in welfare have created increased hardship without significantly changing the incentives to work. In the past, most liberals considered conservative proposals to require welfare recipients to work punitive. Recently, however, some liberals have supported reforms that include work requirements for welfare recipients. The fourth section of the chapter presents these workfare proposals and indicates how they differ from previous conservative proposals. This section also assesses the most successful of the state welfare reform initiatives, Massachusetts's Employment and Training program.

The final section of the chapter summarizes leftist explanations of the growing support for welfare reform proposals. It indicates that political and economic considerations rather than changes in the size of the welfare population may be the most important reasons for these proposals. This section also discusses the possibility that a minimum wage increase is central to the success of these welfare reform proposals.

Conservative Assessment of Social Programs

Conservatives claim that government social welfare programs have such large disincentives to proper behavior that they are counterproductive. Similar to the attempts of Malthus to reduce parish charity, today many conservatives claim that we must eliminate welfare and other income transfers to the poor. The evidence emphasized by the new Malthusians has been summarized by Charles Murray (1984).

Murray (1984) presents data on the growth in public aid (welfare plus food stamp payments). He contends that the inability of this "surging rise" of social spending to reduce poverty rates was due to the rising number of individuals who had pretransfer incomes below the poverty line (p. 64). In 1950, it has been estimated that 33 percent of the population lived in households with pretransfer income below the poverty line. This latent poverty rate fell to 21 percent in 1965, but after bottoming out at 18.2 percent in 1968, Murray indicates that it began to increase, reaching 21.9 percent in 1980.

Murray and others claim that growing latent poverty rates among the nonaged are due to the growth in female-headed households. He estimates that the poverty rate would have declined by one-third if the percentage of female-headed households had remained at the 1965 level. Using a somewhat different definition of poverty, James Smith and Finis Welch (1986) estimate that if the percentage of black female-headed households had remained unchanged, the black poverty rate in 1980 would have been 23 percent rather than 29 percent.

Murray rejects the argument that higher poverty rates are the result of a weakening economy. He notes that the 3.2 percent growth rate during the 1970s "was noticeably higher than the 2.7 percent growth rate during the Eisenhower years" and after controlling for population growth and inflation was "only a little less rapid than . . . in the booming sixties" (Murray 1984, 59). He even believes that growth figures underestimate the bouyancy of the economy during the 1970s.

Murray claims that many who would ordinarily have chosen work and marriage found their way onto welfare. These individuals chose the short-run incentives offered by the welfare system and became trapped in long-term poverty. In support of his contention, Murray reviews federally funded NIT studies to determine the impact on labor supplies (hours of work) if the government were to increase guaranteed welfare payments. He takes as representative the Seattle–Denver NIT results, which estimated that husbands and wives reduced their labor supplies by 9 percent and 20 percent respectively.

In addition, Murray contends that liberal-inspired welfare programs have eroded distinctions among the poor, as well as the status of the hardworking deserving poor. This homogenization of the poor has undermined moral incentives to maintain independence and self-sufficiency. Murray considers the institution of means-tested programs as the paramount example of this process. These programs have given transfers to individuals solely on the basis of income, while judgments on the worthiness of the recipient were totally ignored. As a result, Murray (1984) contends, "Virtually all low-income persons became welfare recipients (remember that by 1980 Food Stamps alone counted more than 21,000,000 recipients). Pride in independence was compromised, and with it a certain degree of pressure on the younger generation to make good on the family tradition" (p. 184–85).

Measurement Issues

Conservatives claim that during the 1970s increased welfare dependency resulted from the increased generosity of government transfer programs even though an expending economy was capable of employing all those willing to work. This section details liberal responses to these contentions. Liberals claim that more appropriate measures would indicate that welfare payments became less generous, welfare dependency was quite limited, and it became increasingly difficult for households to escape poverty through work.

Poverty Rates, Employment, and Welfare

Murray (1984) claims that the growing generosity of government transfer programs explains the rising poverty rate. While it is true that total transfer payments grew during the 1970s, this is a poor measure to use to judge the economic benefits to individual households. More relevant would be the transfers available to female-headed households with no market income—that is, the welfare guarantee. Table 7–1 indicates that the welfare guarantee declined by 22 percent between 1972 and 1984. Thus, it would appear that welfare became less generous, totally undermining Murray's thesis.

Liberals suggest that rising poverty rates reflect declining economic performance and falling real wage rates. During the 1970s, unemployment rates rose steadily. Blank and Blinder (1986) note the hardship created by the weakening economy: "Our estimates . . . suggest that the substandard economic performance of the 1973–83 decade . . . raised the poverty count by 4.5 percentage points" (p. 207).

Table 7–1 documents the decline in real wage rates in low-wage labor markets during the 1970s. In 1968 an individual working full-time year-round at a minimum wage job would have earned 92.7 percent of the income necessary to escape from poverty. If she had a job paying the average salary for retail and wholesale workers, she would have earned 18.2 percent more than the poverty income. By 1980 those employed full-time year-round at a minimum wage job earned only 76.7 percent of the income necessary to escape poverty, while those employed in retail and wholesale trade barely earned enough to escape poverty. Ellwood and Summers (1986) note, "[I]n real terms median family income in 1980 was no higher than it was in 1969.

Table 7–1
Ratios of Full-Time Year-Round Income to Poverty Budget, 1960–1984*

Year	Minimum Wage Employment	Mean Wage of Wholesale/Retail	Mean Wage of Manufacturing	Welfare Guarantee
1960	68.8	105.3	143.1	63.4
1964	82.1	113.8	156.9	62.4
1968	92.7	118.2	166.5	67.8
1972	77.8	120.3	174.9	84.0
1976	82.3	111.4	173.9	82.6
1980	76.7	101.2	165.4	70.8
1984	65.7	112.9	173.9	65.8

Sources: Weekly wage data: U.S. Department of Labor, Bureau of Labor Statistics, *Employment and Earnings*. Welfare guarantees: U.S. Congress, Committee on Ways and Means, *Background Material and Data on Programs within the Jurisdiction of the Committee on Ways and Means* (1985). Poverty budget and minimum wage: Social Security Administration, *Social Security Bulletin, Annual Statistical Supplement, 1984–85* (Washington: U.S. Government Printing Office, 1986), 68.

*Full-time year-round income was computed as follows:

For workers at minimum wage, wage rate multiplied by 2,080 hours.

For workers in wholesale/retail, weekly wage multiplied by 52 weeks.

For workers in manufacturing, weekly wage multiplied by 52 weeks.

For welfare guarantee, the weighted average of state's AFDC and food stamp benefit level for a family of four with no income.

. . . Since average families have no more than they did almost fifteen years ago, it should come as no surprise that poor families are not much better off either" (p. 82).

The Myth of
Welfare Dependency

Liberals believe that conservatives overstate the growth in the number of households using the welfare system. Maurice McDonald (1985) notes that in 1979 less than 40 percent of the households eligible received food stamps. Using data collected by the University of Michigan on five thousand representative households, Richard Coe (1982) rejects Malthusian contentions that federal policies have created a massive welfare-dependent population. Coe assesses the share of those people, by length of time on welfare, who received some portion or a majority of their income from welfare. Table 7–2 indicates that in the ten-year period between 1969 and 1978, 25.2 percent of all households received some form of welfare transfers. He defines short-term recipients as those who received welfare in at most two years; intermediate recipients as those who received welfare in three to seven years; and long-term recipients as those who received welfare in at least eight years. Coe found that only 17.5 percent of welfare recipients, or 4.4 percent of the entire population, lived in long-term recipient households; almost half of all individuals who lived in households that had at some time received income transfers did so during only one or two years.[2] This indicates that during the 1970s, long-term utilization was the exception rather than the rule among welfare recipients.

Coe believes that even these figures overstate the size of the welfare-dependent population, as only long-term users who received the majority of

Table 7–2
Distribution of Welfare Recipients by Length of Time a Recipient, 1969–1978

Length of Time on Welfare	Percentage of All Welfare Recipients	Percentage of Entire Population
Short-term (1–3 years)	48.8	12.3
Intermediate-term (4–7 years)	33.7	8.5
Long-term (8–10 years)	17.5	4.4
All recipients	100.0	25.2

Source: Coe 1982.

their income from welfare should be included. Table 7–3 indicates that only 34.4 percent of those who ever received welfare received more than half their income in at least one year from welfare. This indicates that the typical welfare household is receiving income to supplement market earnings rather than the majority of their income from government transfer programs.

Coe notes that even among those households that at some point received the majority of their income from government transfer programs, long-term dependency was the exception to the rule. Table 7–3 indicates that only 22.3 percent of those households received the majority of their income from transfer programs in at least eight of the ten years. This group represents only 7.7 percent of those individuals who ever received welfare and only 1.9 percent of the entire population.

Welfare Dependency and Black Women

Many observers agree that most welfare recipients are short-term users, but they will contend that the problem is principally one of black welfare dependency. Describing this viewpoint, Barbara Jones (1986) notes,

> The prevailing wisdom is that all or most black women who head families are dependent upon welfare for support, have virtually no job skills or work experience and that the growth in number of female-headed families is due to the steady increase in teenage pregnancies and increased birth rates among young black women. Together, these notions, which are usually projected without documentation, suggest that the source of the economic problems, and thus their solution, lie with the women themselves. (p. 1)

Table 7–3
Distribution of Population Dependent on Welfare Income by Length of Time Dependent, 1969–1978

Length of Time Dependent	Percentage of Population Ever Dependent	Percentage of All Welfare Recipients	Percentage of Entire Population
Short-term (1–3 years)	38.1	13.1	3.3
Intermediate-term (4–7 years)	39.6	13.6	3.5
Long-term (8–10 years)	22.3	7.7	1.9
Ever dependent	100.0	34.4	8.7

Source: Coe 1982.

Jones rejects these stereotypes. She notes that contrary to the myth of large families, in 1985 half of all black female-headed families had no children or one child. More importantly, Jones points to the high labor force participation rate among black female household heads. In 1984 almost 50 percent of all black mothers who headed households worked full-time; more than 60 percent worked at some point during the year. Even 36 percent of poverty level black female heads of household worked, and 8.6 percent of them worked full-time year-round.

Coe (1982) also found the stereotype to be inconsistent with welfare data, since even among black females, long-term utilization of welfare or long-term welfare dependency was the exception. Among black women who had received welfare at some time, only 30 percent were long-term recipients. Almost 60 percent of those black women who had received welfare did so in five or fewer years. Among all nonelderly black female heads of household or wives who were ever in a household that received welfare at some time during 1969 through 1978, only one-half were ever dependent on welfare income and only 15 percent were long-term dependent. For this reason, Coe concludes, "Even for the most disadvantaged of groups (black women), the welfare system does not appear to promote long-term dependency" (p. 45).

Liberal Views on Welfare Disincentives

Conservatives contend that welfare policies discourage work effort and encourage out-of-wedlock births and female-headed households. Liberals reject the view that welfare policies influence family structure. While they agree that welfare policies reduce work effort, liberals believe that this effect is quite small. This section details the liberal view.

Welfare Policies and Work Disincentives

Citing NIT studies, Murray (1984) contends that welfare policies reduce work incentives for women. He neglects to mention that the benefits given to participants in the Denver and Seattle NIT programs were among the most generous. Recipients were given guaranteed income transfers of more than $2,000 above welfare levels. Given the generous nature of these programs, liberals contend that declines in labor supplies were quite small. Danziger and Gottschalk (1985) note that when welfare guarantees increased by $2,180 per year, the labor supply of married women declined by only 2.2 hours per week, not the dramatic impact Murray perceives. Summarizing the liberal position, Ellwood and Summers (1986) conclude, "Restoring real

AFDC benefits to the levels of a decade ago . . . would do a great deal for people without much disincentive effect on work" (p. 97).

Welfare Policy and Out-of-Wedlock Births

Murray (1984) suggests that welfare policies were responsible for the rapid rise in the number of children born to unmarried women, but studies have not found this to be true. For instance, a 1978 survey of the literature by Maurice McDonald and Isabel Sawhill found no evidence of any significant connection between welfare and out-of-wedlock births. A more recent study by David Ellwood and Mary Jo Bane (1984), found that welfare had no impact on whether unmarried women, including teenagers, became pregnant or bore children. As further evidence, Greenstein (1985) notes that between 1972 and 1980, the number of children in black female-headed households increased by 20 percent, but the number of black children on welfare (AFDC) fell by 5 percent. He speculates, "If AFDC is to blame for illegitimacy, why did the black AFDC population decline at the same time that black female-headed households increased rapidly? How can welfare be encouraging more single black women to have children if many of these same women do not collect welfare when the children are born?" (p. 16).

Sara McLanahan (1985) has shown that the rise in out-of-wedlock births Murray (1984) portrays is quite sensitive to the organization of statistics. Murray uses an out-of-wedlock (illegitimacy) ratio—that is, the ratio of nonmarital births per hundred live births. This ratio began to increase during the late 1960s and grew even faster during the 1970s. The rising ratio does not necessarily indicate that there has been a change in the birthrate among nonmarried women, however. Suppose there were one hundred married and one hundred unmarried women, each given birth to eight children per year, or a 50 percent out-of-wedlock ratio. If the birthrate for married women declined to only four children per year, the ratio would rise to 67 percent, even though the behavior of unmarried women was unchanged. Similarly, if the marriage rate declined and there were fewer married women, there would be fewer births to married women. Again, the ratio would rise without a change in the behavior of unmarried women. McLanahan (1985) states, "[I]t is clear that the illegitimacy ratio jumped during the mid-sixties, not because of an increase in the rate of births to single women, but because of a dramatic decrease in marriage rates and a decline in the fertility of married couples" (p. 4).

McLanahan claims that the out-of-wedlock rate—the number of non-marital births per thousand unmarried women ages fifteen to forty-four—is a more appropriate measure. She found that the black out-of-wedlock rate increased between 1945 and 1965, declined dramatically between 1965 and

1974 when welfare guarantees were increasing, and began to rise again after 1975 when welfare guarantees were declining. The out-of-wedlock rate for unmarried white women also was inconsistent with changes in welfare guarantees.

Welfare Policies
and Marriage Decisions

Conservatives contend that if family structure had remained the same, poverty rates would have declined significantly from 1970 on. Mary Jo Bane (1986) argues that this contention is not necessarily correct. For Bane, wage income is a far more important determinant of poverty than changes in family composition: "It could be that the increased numbers in female-headed families . . . were people who were more likely to be poor, whatever type of family they lived in. Had they remained in husband–wife families, the poverty rate among that group would have been higher and the overall poverty rate perhaps not much different from what it turned out to be" (p. 216).

Danziger and Gottschalk (1985) point out that growth in female-headed never married households has not been dramatic. If the percentage of the population composed of women with children but never married had remained at its 1967 level, the 1980 official poverty rate would have dropped only slightly, from 13.0 percent to 12.4 percent. Rather, the rising divorce rate has been responsible for the large growth in female-headed households.

Even if welfare benefits are responsible for the rising divorce rate, Christopher Jencks (1985) contends that this might improve individual well-being. For Jencks, welfare frees many women from horrible marriages. Murray (1984) ignores the possibility that women married to low-wage-earning husbands are often trapped in an untenable situation. In his discussion, Murray implies that if these women had been forced to marry because of the absence of welfare, their lives would be better because their husbands would eventually attain some upward mobility in the work force and they would have a stable marriage. The possibility that the husband, feeling trapped in a dead-end minimum wage job, might take out his frustrations on his wife, mistreating her and the children, is not a future outcome Murray wishes to present.

Murray claims that the increased generosity of federal programs encouraged the growth in female-headed households. Many liberals believe that only in some short-run situations have benefits increased enough for them to have had a significant influence on the number of welfare recipients. Recent studies (Wilson and Neckerman 1986; Garfinkel and McLanahan 1987) suggest that rising divorce rates reflect the improved employment opportunities for women rather than the increase of welfare benefits.

Saul Hoffman and Greg Duncan (1986) also found that wage income is far more important to women than welfare payments. They analyzed the decisions of 767 divorced women between 1969 and 1982. For these women, an additional dollar of wage income was worth at least four additional dollars of AFDC income. Finally, between 1972 and 1980, the number of people on AFDC declined despite the dramatic increase in female headed households. As Ellwood and Summers (1986) note, "If AFDC were pulling families apart and encouraging the formation of single-parent families, it is hard to understand why the number of children on the program would remain constant throughout a period in our history when family structures changed the most" (p. 94).

Welfare Policies and
Black Family Structure

We have seen that the principal reason for the rise in female-headed households has been the rising divorce rate. Marriage rates have been unchanged within the white population, and this dominates aggregate statistics. But there has been a dramatic change in the marriage rate within the black population. Historically, 90 percent of black women were married by the age of forty-four. By 1975 the rate had dropped to 75 percent and by 1980 to 67 percent. Moreover, the remarriage rate for black women was substantially below the rate for white women. After six years, 60 percent of white women and only 40 percent of black women had remarried.

Hoffman and Duncan (1986) believe that the welfare system has had little influence on the remarriage decision of divorced black women. They estimate that lowering AFDC benefits by 25 percent would increase the remarriage rate of black women by only 10 percent. Many observers contend that the declining black marriage rate and the differentially lower black remarriage rate reflect the declining supply of marriageable black males. Darity and Myers (1986) summarized the evidence. They found that among blacks twenty to forty years old, the female–male population ratio was greater than 1.3. They believe that this reflects a widening gap in the proportion of males and females who make the transition from teenage to young adulthood. They estimate that in 1965 1 percent fewer males than females survived the transition, but this grew to 6 percent by 1970 and 9 percent by 1980.

Darity and Myers (1986) believe that even this understates the decline in the effective sex ratio, since there was a dramatic increase in the percentage of black males who were unavailable or undesirable. During this period, there was an increase in the rate of black male youth incarceration. The rate of incarceration of young black men on any given day rose from 2.0 percent in 1974 to 2.5 percent in 1979. For the white population, the incarceration rate was less than 0.5 percent.

Black men also are overrepresented in state and county mental hospitals. For males ages twenty to twenty-four, the black rate of institutionalization in mental hospitals is nearly nine times the white rate. Drug addiction also takes a much heavier toll in the black community. The black admittance rate to federally funded drug abuse treatment centers is more than four times the white rate.

Not only are an increasing number of black men unavailable for marriage due to institutionalization for criminal offenses, mental illness, or drug addiction, but an increasing number are financially unable to consider marriage. In 1980, 21 percent of all black men ages twenty to twenty-four had no earnings; this was more than double the white rate (and more than double the black rate ten years earlier).

Finally, an increasing number of eligible black men are career soldiers. Black representation in the armed forces rose from 15 percent in 1972 to 33 percent in 1980. Moreover, the reenlistment rate for black soldiers rose from 20.4 percent to 64.6 percent. Since the marriage rate for career soldiers is only one-fourth the marriage rate for all males, this also has lowered the black female marriage rate.

Black feminists (Omolade 1986) contend that the decline in black female marriage rates does not simply reflect the inability of black women to find eligible men; it also reflects their strong desire to escape from male control. They believe that black women are more willing to break with the traditional family structure because of the positive role extended families play within the black community.[3] Moreover, feminists reject the notion that single parenting by women is harmful to children. They note that in the traditional family, parenting is overwhelmingly done by women, with men often playing a destructive role.

Welfare Reform Proposals

Since 1986 there has been a concerted effort by many liberals and conservatives to initiate welfare reforms that do not reduce benefits but instead increase work incentives. This section summarizes the evolution of views that led to Congress's adoption of far-reaching welfare reform legislation in 1988. It also evaluates the Massachusetts Employment and Training (ET) program, which is thought by many to be a model of welfare reform legislation.

Evolution of
Federal Welfare Proposals

Ellwood and Summers (1986) summarize liberal criticisms of conservative claims as follows:

> Knowingly or unknowingly, we have been engaged in an experiment the past ten years. This experiment has been carried out at the expense of single mothers, and its results can be judged a failure. We have cut back AFDC benefits considerably. There has been no noticeable effect on family structure or work. . . . We have also conducted an experiment in allowing benefits to vary across states for years. Here, too, there is little evidence that these differences had any noticeable effect on work or family structure. We see no reason to continue with these experiments. . . . Without compelling evidence of damage caused by the programs, such stinginess seems mean-spirited and pointless (p. 97).

Despite Murray's (1985) response to such criticisms, it appears that his views are no longer accepted as a guideline for social policy, even by many conservatives. As a result, further cutbacks in government social programs have little support. Instead, efforts are now focused on reforming welfare to aid individuals in their transition from welfare to work. Lawrence Mead's (1985) proposals for welfare reforms have replaced Murray's proposals for welfare cutbacks as the most important issues debated by poverty specialists and government policymakers.

Mead has areas of broad agreement with Murray. He rejects discrimination as an explanation for the current economic and social problems experienced by the black community, he emphasizes the decline in work ethics among the poor, and he believes that the lack of employment is primarily due to internal inadequacies. Mead also agrees with Murray that the permissiveness of the welfare system "must get much of the blame" for the creation of an underclass that is increasingly welfare dependent (p. 23). He states, "Racism *per se* was harmful to blacks. The aim of Jim Crow, North and South, was to exclude and subordinate blacks. . . . [However,] permissive programs have replaced the racist regime with one that is, in its own way, equally destructive" (p. 67).

Mead is able to separate himself from Murray in one important way: He believes that the main problem with welfare "is its **permissiveness** not its size" (p. ix). Thus, Mead rejects proposals to cut welfare. He reviewed Work Incentive (WIN) programs and found that when work requirements were enforced, they were successful in shifting recipients to gainful employment. While he believes that the way welfare has been administered adds to the problem, he argues, "It is difficult to believe that an excess . . . of resources given to the poor explain their current problems. . . . While government programs in some sense reward dependency, it is 'rational' in only the most short-run sense for the poor to succumb to family and work problems or engage in crime" (p. 48).

Differences among Welfare Reform Advocates

With the shifting of conservative sentiment toward welfare reforms emphasizing work requirements rather than funding cutbacks, the views of many liberals and conservatives merged. As a result, welfare reform legislation passed the Senate and House of Representatives in 1988.

While these bills incorporate work requirements, even for women with small children, they differ from Mead's proposals in seemingly important ways. For example, Mead notes that the training desires of participants in the WIN programs he assessed were substantially above the skill requirements of the jobs they actually attained. Indeed, he found that the jobs obtained did not significantly differ from those that could have been obtained without additional training. However, he does not see this as a shortcoming.

In contrast, liberals believe that one of the major shortcomings of WIN programs was their lack of training. Gertrude Goldberg (1987) notes, "Only 12.5% or one-eighth of all activities were training, education, and work experience, with the other seven-eighths going to the less expensive and less intensive services: direct placement, individual job search, and group job search" (p. 6).

Similarly, liberals and Mead have different views on the role of day-care funding in welfare reform proposals. Both note that WIN programs provided minimal day-care funds. Mead (1985) does not believe this to be a "barrier, since most mothers, even those with preschool children, manage to arrange care informally if they seriously want to work" (p. 150). While day-care funding provided assistance to only 8 percent of WIN children under twelve, Mead contends that the informal arrangements WIN participants used were found to be satisfactory by most mothers.

Liberals provide a different assessment. They consider the lack of day-care funding deplorable. Supporting this contention, a report of New York City's mandatory workfare program (Statewide Youth Advocacy, Inc. 1987) found that "because of the inadequate service investments and the punitive approach of the program parents are being forced to leave their children in tenuous child-care situations or risk losing their families' only source of financial support" (p. 1).

The Massachusetts Employment and Training Program

Federal welfare reform legislation has similarities with Massachusetts's ET program. Initiated in 1983, ET is a voluntary program that emphasizes training rather than immediate work and provides substantial day-care and medical benefits to participants. In 1986 ET spent nearly half its total budget on day-care services. ET also provides extended medical care. Participants can continue on Medicaid for four months after obtaining employment. Since 30 percent of participants work in firms that offer no health benefits, Massachusetts is considering extending Medicaid benefits to one year for those who have no employment coverage.

Job training and education are an integral part of the program. Among the thirty-eight thousand participants in the first two years of the program, almost 30 percent received either basic or advanced education, while more than 14 percent entered government training programs and an additional 7 percent received extended on-the-job training in a subsidized employment situation. Teresa Amott and Jean Kluver (1986) note,

> Perhaps the best-known statistic about the ET program is the fact that in its first 30 months of operation over 23,000 ET graduates were placed in jobs. In fiscal year 1985, the AFDC caseload fell to its lowest level in 12 years, a decline of nearly nine percent during the three years of ET's operation. The Welfare Department claims savings in AFDC and Medicaid and additional tax revenues from working ET graduates totaling $107 million in fiscal year 1986, compared to program costs of approximately $30 million (p. 12).

Welfare reform critics suggest that the rosy picture Massachusetts's ET program projects is misleading. They believe that the employment generated by ET was lower, that wages were inadequate, and that initial participants were a biased sample of those most likely to be successful. Finally, critics contend that ET's performance cannot be duplicated nationally because Massachusetts's economy had above-average growth and ET's support benefits are far more generous than proposed federal legislation.

There is no disagreement as to the number of welfare recipients who gained employment after participating in ET programs. There is substantial disagreement, however, about the extent to which this was a result of the ET program, the extent to which this represented permanent employment, and the extent to which it represented a net employment expansion. First, in the absence of ET, we would expect a certain percentage of welfare recipients to gain employment. After all, more than 40 percent of all recipients leave welfare within one year. Second, the first three years of the ET program corresponded to the first years of a strong economic expansion, especially in Massachusetts. This expansion, rather than the ET program, could be responsible for the ability of ET participants to gain employment. Third, a substantial number of ET participants who obtained employment were back on welfare within one year, while others gained only part-time employment and continued to receive AFDC grants. Finally, there is some evidence (Goldberg 1987) that much of the employment gained by ET participants came at the expense of jobs for others. In this case, there would have been a reshuffling of welfare recipients—that is, jobs obtained by program participants would have been held by others, who then became eligible for AFDC or other benefits.

Critics also note that the initial ET participants were much more employable than the general welfare population. Amott and Kluver (1986) note,

> [Eighty-seven] percent of all first year participants in ET had some past work experience, compared to only 7.3 percent of AFDC recipients. Only 32 percent of AFDC recipients have worked in the last two years, compared to 70 percent of ET participants. Finally only half of AFDC recipients are high school graduates, compared to nearly three-fourths of ET participants (p. 22).

Whether or not employment gains are as robust as ET supporters contend, critics believe that the most serious problem with welfare reform programs is that they do not provide a living wage for workers. Amott and Kluver found that most ET training programs geared female participants for traditional women's work in clerical or service jobs. In 1985 the average hourly wage for full-time jobs gained by ET participants was $4.86 for white women and only $4.13 for black women. This indicates that it is unlikely that many welfare recipients would escape poverty even if they obtained full-time employment.

Amott and Kluver estimate that after adjusting for benefit reductions, the average ET participant who obtained full-time employment would have had $59 more per month than her pre-ET benefit package. However, they note, "Out of that $59, the ET graduate would have to pay transportation costs to and from the job and buy clothes to wear on the job" (p. 13). Thus, even for the successful ET participant, the benefits are meager. This finding is consistent with earlier studies. For example, Isabel Sawhill (1976) found that most of the women on welfare in the late 1960s had such a low earnings capacity that even if they worked full-time, more than half would still earn less than their welfare grant.

Critics also question the fairness of coercing welfare recipients into working full-time. Goldberg (1987) notes that "[t]he assumption that work is always preferable to welfare is rarely made in relation to the prime beneficiaries of AFDC, dependent children" (p. 14). McLanahan, Garfinkel, and

Watson (1987) point out that child-care costs for preschool children are quite expensive and may not be fully funded. Indeed, it is for this reason that the vast majority of all women with young children do not work full-time. (Only 23 percent and 37 percent of wives in married-couple households with children ages newborn to six and six to eighteen respectively work at least fifteen hundred hours per year). Thus, it would be not only inappropriate but also inequitable to shift AFDC mothers from welfare to full-time work.

Radical Assessment of Welfare Reform

Radicals believe that it is important to have a clear understand of why liberal politicians became active supporters of legislation that requires AFDC mothers to work. After all, since 1973 there has been no growth in the number of households receiving welfare. In addition, between 1967 and 1984, the percentage of household heads expecting to work remained constant at 70 percent. Among the poor, the percentage of household heads expecting to work increased.[4] Thus, politicians must have reasons other than the growth in number of welfare households or a declining work ethic for placing importance on welfare reform legislation. This section identifies some of these reasons and also details the reasons why radicals contend that increasing the minimum wage rate is necessary if welfare reform is to be beneficial.

Political and Economic Motives

Radicals contend that political and economic factors have motivated politicians to support welfare reform proposals. These motivations reflect responses to the growing federal deficit and to the changing size of the low-wage work force. During the 1980s, the federal budget deficit ballooned, increasing the vulnerability of U.S. financial markets to foreign capital flows. As a result, many politicians sought to reduce the federal deficit by reducing government spending. Because most politicians were unwilling to cut military expenditures significantly, large social spending reductions were required.

By 1985 social spending per recipient had been cut as much as possible, and further reductions could occur only if the number of recipients declined. Thus, the political motivation has not been welfare dependency but the growth of the federal deficit. Since politicians' concern continues to be social spending reductions, it is likely that many will seize upon liberal rhetoric to make workfare palatable. For these reasons, radicals expect that the touted funding for training and support services will not materialize and that programs will force AFDC mothers into the work force regardless of its impact on their well-being.

Radicals have always believed that the ebb and flow of welfare policies are related to changes in the low-wage labor market. Piven and Cloward (1971) document how welfare in the South rose during slack periods but declined during planting and harvest times when labor was needed. By 1985 demographic changes had reduced the number of young people entering the labor market, and there was also a reduction in the growth of undocumented foreign-born workers. As a result, a shortage of individuals willing to take low-wage, dead-end jobs appeared. Louis Uchitelle's (1987) article, which emphasizes that "jobs are going begging[, y]et a hard core of 'unemployables' now numbers in the millions," is but one example of the growing concern that there will be a severe shortage of low-wage workers. Gertrude Goldberg (1987) suggests that the desire to increase the supply of low-wage workers might have been one reason why the nation's governors overwhelmingly approved a plan to overhaul AFDC by requiring recipients with children over three to work or enroll in educational classes or job training. Again, this reinforces the fears radicals have that welfare reform will become "workhouses without walls" (Amott 1987, p. 6).[5]

*The Minimum Wage
and Welfare Reform*

Radicals believe that the central deficiency of welfare reform proposals is the inadequate wages available to AFDC mothers who enter the labor market. Welfare reform advocates expect educational and training programs to raise earnings levels well above government transfer payments. We have seen that this expectation was not fulfilled by the ET program. Radicals are not surprised, given the general wage patterns that currently exist. Danziger and Gottschalk (1986) document the growing percentage of households headed by individuals earning low wages. Table 7–4 indicates that this growth occurred for households headed by men as well as those headed by women.[6] Thus, welfare reform is being enacted in a period when all household heads are having increasing difficulty earning a living wage.

Table 7–4
Percentage of Households Headed by Low-Wage Earner, 1967–1984

Group	1967	1971	1979	1984
All households	19.4	19.1	19.7	26.1
Male	13.9	14.1	14.4	21.1
Female	53.4	47.8	42.2	44.9

Source: Danziger and Gottschalk 1986.

Statistics on hourly wages for all workers also indicate that it is unlikely that many AFDC mothers would obtain more than low-wage employment (Mellor and Haugen 1986). More than 60 percent of all female workers are paid hourly wages.[7] Among women paid an hourly wage, the median rate was $5.08 in 1984. For women over twenty-five years old and for those with a high school degree, the median wage rates were slightly higher— $5.51 and $5.41 respectively. Among all female hourly workers twenty-five years old or older, only 30 percent worked for at least $7 per hour. Thus, only if welfare reform programs raised skill levels of participants above those of the typical female hourly worker would significant numbers of AFDC mothers be able to support their families by entering the labor market.

Radicals note that increases in the minimum wage rate have not kept pace with the rate of inflation since 1968. At that time, the minimum wage had a purchasing power of almost $5 per hour in 1985 dollars. To regain the same purchasing power it had in 1981 (when the last adjustment was made), the minimum wage would have to have been increased to $4.45 per hour in January 1988.

Not only would a minimum wage increase to $5 per hour begin to make work a viable alternative to welfare, but it also would help many poor families who already rely on wage income. Smith and Vavrichek (1987) point out that in 1985, among all hourly workers in households with incomes below the poverty line, only 40 percent earned more than $4.35 per hour. Even among workers in households with incomes between 100 and 150 percent of the poverty line, only 58 percent earned more than $4.35 per hour. Thus, poor and near-poor households would benefit substantially from an increase in the minimum wage.[8]

Conclusions

This chapter has assessed contentions that generous welfare programs have been responsible for rising poverty rates and the growth of female heads of household and out-of-wedlock births. Data seem to indicate that welfare dependency is minor even among black female-headed households. Due to declining welfare guarantees and real wages in low-wage labor markets, it is surprising that poverty measures did not begin to increase until the 1980s.

Liberals claim that Murray (1984) drastically overstates the disincentives generated by social welfare programs. They note that Murray selected biased examples to judge the NIT studies, and even then it appears that welfare guarantees had only a modest impact on the labor market behavior of low-income households. Liberals also note that many studies have found that the wage conditions individuals face have a much stronger influence on the decision to enter or exit welfare than the size of the welfare guarantee. Indeed, in recent years many conservatives have come to believe that the generosity of welfare has little influence on the number of people who seek welfare.

We found that the growth in teenage out-of-wedlock births is misleading. This growth is a result of declining births among married women and the shrinking number of teenage marriages rather than an increase in the rate of births to unmarried women. Liberals reject the notion that welfare guarantees induce teenagers to have children out of wedlock. They have found that there is no relationship between the birthrate among unmarried teenagers and the size of welfare guarantees. Liberals also note that the out-of-wedlock rate declined during periods when welfare guarantees rose and increased during periods when guarantees declined.

In recent years, disagreements between liberal and conservative economists have narrowed. Both support work requirements, but they differ concerning the importance of training and day-care funding. Liberals are quite optimistic that only a modest amount of support would enable many women to escape welfare and become part of the paid labor force. This optimism is based on an upbeat evaluation of the Massachusetts ET program.

Radicals and some liberals are less optimistic that current federal welfare legislation will improve the situation of AFDC families, First, it was noted that for most married women with children, part-time work predominates and it would be discriminatory to require AFDC mothers to accept full-time work. Second, funding for support services—day-care and medical benefits—is critical, and federal legislation is likely to underfund them. Third, programs have tended to place women in jobs that pay low wages, which are often not enough to improve significantly their economic well-being. Thomas Glynn, deputy commissioner of the Massachusetts Public Welfare Department, said this concerning AFDC mothers who entered the Boston ET Choice program he runs: "These women want to work but at lower than than [$13,500 per year], recidivism is high" (Uchitelle 1987).

Radicals believe that the underlying motivation for current welfare reform legislation has little to do with a concern for the well-being of AFDC families. Radicals believe that it is a method to lower government social spending and to avoid labor shortages in low-wage service sector occupations. For these reasons, radicals believe that without a strong political movement to fight for adjustments in welfare legislation and for sizable increases in the minimum wage, AFDC families will be worse off as a result of the new legislation.

Notes

1. Each year the government estimates a poverty line threshold income—that is, the income just sufficient for a household to escape poverty. In 1984 this threshold

income for a family of four was $10,509. Radicals and many liberals believe that the government's low estimate of the Moderate-But-Adequate Income Budget is a more appropriate poverty measure. This budget is 50 percent more expensive than the government's poverty level budget.

2. This does not mean that they collected welfare for two years, as the figure would include individuals who lived in households that collected welfare only in December of one year and January of the following year.

3. Consistent with this assertion, Hoffman and Duncan (1986) found that black women place almost no value on male income when considering marriage. They conclude that an important reason for differentially lower marriage rates is that black women have a differentially lower preference for marriage than white women.

4. This was primarily the result of a dramatic decline in the percentage of elderly among the poor. Among poor households headed by women, however, the percentage not expecting to work remained constant between 1979 and 1984, and among all poor households, the percentage expecting to work full-time remained constant from 1971 to 1984 (Danziger and Gottschalk 1986).

5. Feminists contend that a major reason for the growing concern of legislatures is the fear that women are increasingly deciding to escape from patriarchy—the ability of men to control women in the traditional family. Strengthening the traditional family has certainly been one of the goals of the so-called Moral Majority. Feminists contend that the traditional family remains an important source of power for men and that welfare reform is a means of redirecting women back to patriarchy. For a discussion of feminist views, see chapter 9 of this book.

6. Danziger and Gottschalk (1986) define low-wage earners as household heads with weekly earnings below $204 per week. Such persons could not earn the poverty line annual income for a family of four if they worked full-time year-round. If $159 per week is used, results are unchanged. The percentage of household heads earning low wages then increases from 15.2 percent to 20.0 percent between 1967 and 1984.

7. The median wage of all female salaried workers is about 15 percent above that of all female hourly workers who work full-time.

8. Conservatives contend that these benefits would go only to those fortunate enough to maintain employment. Conservatives also claim that the minimum wage would reduce the total number of jobs available. For a discussion of these conservative claims and responses to them, see Cherry (1985) and chapter 6 of this book.

References

Amott, Teresa. 1987. "The Retreat from Welfare." *Dollars & Sense* 127:6–8.

Amott Teresa, and Jean Kluver. 1986. *ET: A Model for the Nation?* Philadelphia: American Friends Service Committee.

Bane, Mary Jo. 1986. "Household Composition and Poverty." In *Fighting Poverty: What Works and What Doesn't,* ed. Sheldon Danziger and Daniel Weinberg. Cambridge, MA; Harvard University Press, 209–31.

Bane, Mary Jo, and David T. Ellwood 1986. "Slipping In and Out of Poverty." *Journal of Human Resources* 21:1–24.

Blank, Rebecca, and Stanley Blinder. 1986. "Macroeconomics, Income Distribution, and Poverty." In *Fighting Poverty: What Works and What Doesn't,* ed. Sheldon Danziger and Daniel Weinberg. Cambridge, MA: Harvard University Press, 180–208.

Cherry, Robert. 1985. "Textbook Treatments of Minimum Wage Legislation." *Review of Black Political Economy* 13:25–38.

Coe, Richard. 1982. "Welfare Dependency: Fact or Myth?" *Challenge* 25:43–49.

Danziger, Sheldon, and Peter Gottschalk. 1985. "The Poverty of 'Losing Ground.' " *Challenge* 28:32–38.

———. 1986. "Work, Poverty, and the Working Poor: A Multifaceted Problem." *Monthly Labor Review,* September, 17–21.

Darity, William, Jr., and Samuel Myers, Jr. 1986. "The Marginalization of Black Males and the Rise of Female Headed Households." Paper presented at the Allied Social Science Association Meetings, New Orleans, 29 December .

Ellwood, David, and Mary Jo Bane 1984. "The Impact of AFDC on Family Structure and Living Arrangements." Report prepared for the U.S. Department of Health and Human Services, mimeo., Harvard University.

Ellwood, David, and Lawrence Summers. 1986. "Poverty in America: Is Welfare the Answer or the Problem?" In *Fighting Poverty: What Works and What Doesn't,* ed. Sheldon Danziger and Daniel Weinberg. Cambridge, MA: Harvard University Press, 78–105.

Garfinkel, Irwin, and Sara McLanahan. 1987. *Single-Mother Families and Public Policy: An American Dilemma?* Washington, DC: The Urban Institute.

Goldberg, Gertrude. 1987. "The Illusion of Welfare Reform and Some New Initiatives." Paper presented at the International Conference on Social Welfare, Rome, Italy, 19 September. I wish to thank Gertrude Goldberg for allowing me to quote from her unpublished work. Gertrude S. Goldberg, Center for Social Policy, Adelphi University School of Social Work.

Greenstein, Richard. 1985. "Losing Faith in 'Losing Ground.' " *The New Republic,* March 25, 12–17.

Hoffman, Saul, and Greg Duncan. 1986. "Race and Family Structure: Assessing the Role of Labor Markets, Marriage Markets, AFDC Benefits and Individual Preferences." Paper presented at the Allied Social Science Association Meetings, New Orleans, 29 December.

Jencks, Christopher. 1985. "How Poor Are the Poor?" *New York Review of Books,* February 12, 33–37.

Jones, Barbara. 1986. "Employment Opportunities for Black Female Heads of Households." Paper presented at the Allied Social Science Association Meetings, New Orleans, 28 December.

McDonald, Maurice 1985. "The Role of Multi-Benefits in Maintaining the Social Safety Net." *Journal of Human Resources* 20:421–33.

McDonald, Maurice, and Isabel Sawhill. 1978. "Welfare Policy and the Family." *Public Policy* 26:89–119.

McLanahan, Sara. 1985. "Charles Murray and the Family." In *Losing Ground: A Critique,* ed. Sara McLanahan et al., Madison, WI: Institute for Research on Poverty, University of Wisconsin–Madison, 1–7.

McLanahan, Sara, Irwin Garfinkel, and Dorothy Watson. 1987. "Family Structure, Poverty, and the Underclass." Discussion Paper #823-87, Institute for Research on Poverty, Madison, WI.

Mead, Lawrence. 1985. *Beyond Entitlement: The Social Obligations of Citizenship.* New York: The Free Press.

Miller, Earl, and Steven Haugen. 1986. "Hourly Paid Workers: Who They Are and What They Earn." *Monthly Labor Review,* February, 20–25.

Murray, Charles. 1984. *Losing Ground: American Social Policy, 1950–1980.* New York: Basic Books.

———. 1985. "Have the Poor Been 'Losing Ground?' " *Political Science Quarterly* 100:427–45.

Omolade, Barbara. 1986. *It's a Family Affair: The Real Lives of Black Single Mothers.* Latham, NY: Kitchen Table–Women of Color Press.

Piven, Frances, and Richard Cloward. 1971. *Regulating the Poor.* New York: Pantheon.

Sawhill, Isabel. 1976. "Discrimination and Poverty among Women Who Head Families." In *Women and the Workplace,* ed. Martha Blaxhall and Barbara Reagan. Chicago: University of Chicago Press, 201–11.

Smith, Ralph, and Bruce Vavrichek. 1987. "The Minimum Wage: Its Relation to Incomes and Poverty." *Monthly Labor Review,* January, 25–30.

Smith, James P., and Finis Welch. 1986. *Closing the Gap: Forty Years of Economic Progress for Blacks.* Santa Monica, CA: Rand Corporation.

Statewide Youth Advocacy, Inc. 1987. "New Report Details Pitfalls in NYC's Mandatory Workfare." Report of Statewide Youth Advocacy, Inc., Rochester, NY.

Uchitelle, Louis. 1987. "America's Army of Non-Workers." *New York Times,* 27 September, section 3 p. 1.

Wilson, William J., and Kathryn N. Neckerman. 1986. "Poverty and Family Structure: The Widening Gap between Evidence and Public Policy Issues." In *Fighting Poverty: What Works and What Doesn't,* ed. Sheldon Danziger and Daniel Weinberg. Cambridge, MA: Harvard University Press, 232–51.

8
Discrimination by Gender: Economic Theories and Policy Implications

T he average full-time year-round working woman earns less than 70 percent of her male counterpart. This figure has not changed dramatically during the post–World War II period. This chapter surveys various explanations for the persistence of lower female earnings. The first section details the data used to evaluate the economic position of women.

Conservatives believe that discrimination is minimal. They believe that women, having a different set of preferences than men, make choices that limit their market earnings. These decisions primarily influence the type of education they receive rather than the educational level. Thus, conservatives believe, the concentration of women in a few occupational categories is also a matter of choice rather than a product of discrimination. The second section of the chapter critically evaluates these conservative views. We will find that alternative data bases indicate that female labor market behavior is not very different from male labor market behavior and that these differences have declined dramatically in recent years. Thus, discrimination may be significant, and antidiscrimination policies may be warranted.

The third section of the chapter presents liberal explanations for the female–male earnings gap. Some liberals emphasize how women adapt to discrimination and the impact this has on the earnings of male workers and capitalists. Other liberals emphasize how women are crowded into low-wage occupations. The section concludes with a discussion of some liberal policy proposals.

The fourth section presents radical views of the earnings gap. Radicals contend that liberal explanations are inadequate because they minimize the profitability of discrimination and the inability of benefits from affirmative action to trickle down to women in female-dominated industries. Radicals also believe that reforms that undermine the traditional family, such as financial support for children, are unlikely to be enacted.

Economic Data

Overall Female–Male Differences

Table 8–1 presents two measures of the female–male earnings differential: the median yearly earnings of full-time year-round workers and the usual

Table 8–1
Female–Male Earnings Ratios, 1970–1986

Year	Yearly Earnings of Full-Time Year-Round Workers			Usual Weekly Wage of Full-Time Workers		
	Female	Male	Female–Male Ratio	Female	Male	Female–Male Ratio
1970	$ 5,323	$ 8,966	59.4	$ 94	$151	62.3
1972	5,903	10,202	57.9	106	168	63.1
1974	6,970	11,889	58.6	124	204	60.8
1976	8,099	13,455	60.2	145	234	62.0
1978	9,350	15,730	59.4	166	272	61.0
1980	11,197	18,612	60.2	200	317	63.1
1982	13,014	21,077	61.7	240	370	65.0
1984	14,780	23,218	63.7	262	393	66.5
1986	16,232	25,256	64.3	290	419	69.2

Sources: For 1970–1982: U.S. Department of Labor, Bureau of Labor Statistics, "The Female–Male Earnings Gap," Report #673 (September 1982). For 1984–1986 weekly data: U.S. Department of Labor, Bureau of Labor Statistics, *Employment and Earnings*. For 1984–1986 annual data: U.S. Department of Commerce, Bureau of the Census, *Current Population Reports*, P-60, nos. 150, 157.

weekly wage of full–time workers. Both ratios indicate that full-time working women receive 65 to 70 percent as much as full-time working men. If women had either a lower level or a lower quality of education than men, this would be one way to explain their lower incomes. However, women have only a slightly lower level of education than men. In 1980 median years of educational attainment were 12.6 and 12.4 for men and women respectively; a higher percentage of men than women attained at least a high school degree (67.3 percent of men versus 65.8 percent of women).[1]

Since the educational attainment of men and women is quite similar, we should not expect educational differences to have a significant influence on the earnings gap. In 1982 the female–male earnings ratios for full-time year-round workers with a high school degree, four-year college degree, and five or more years of college were 62.6 percent, 62.2 percent, and 66.3 percent respectively. Thus, even when men and women had a comparable education, the earnings gap did not change significantly.

There are some differences in the quality of men's and women's education. Until the 1980s, women generally entered fields with a lower earnings potential than fields entered by men. In 1975, 64.3 percent of female college graduates majored in either education, social sciences, letters, fine arts, or health professions. Men were more heavily concentrated in business and engineering, fields in which few women majored. These two fields accounted for 30 percent of male majors but only 5 percent of female majors (National Center for Educational Statistics 1977).

Another factor that could explain the earnings gap is the intensity of work effort among full-time workers. In 1982 the average workweek for males twenty-five to fifty-four years old was more than forty-three hours, while the average work week for comparably age women was thirty-eight hours. 36.1 percent of all full-time male workers and only 11.6 percent of all full-time female workers were employed more than forty hours per week. Full-time year-round working women also worked fewer weeks per year than their male counterparts. The mean number of weeks worked per year was 45.14 for men and only 43.85 for women who worked full-time year-round (U.S. Department of Commerce 1984, table 17).[2]

Earl Miller (1984) found that even after adjusting for these differences, the earnings gap was only slightly reduced. He estimated that if women had the same educational attainment and same average workweek as full-time male workers, their usual weekly wage would increase only from 65.0 percent to 69.5 percent of the usual weekly male wage.[3] Thus, these differences explain only 13 percent (4.5 divided by 35) of the earnings gap.

Exit/entry data and labor force participation rates from the 1970s appear to indicate that women had a more discontinuous work pattern than men. For example, in 1978, 1.8 percent of males and 11.0 percent of females ages twenty-five to fifty-nine who had worked in the previous twelve months were not currently in the labor force. Similarly, 16.0 percent of women, compared to only 3.7 percent of men, were new entrants in the labor force (Lloyd and Niemi 1979, table 2–7).

Discontinuous labor market behavior also can be assessed by looking at work experience and job tenure information. In 1975 the average male worker age forty-five to fifty-four had just over thirty years of work experience; for a similar age female, work experience was less than twenty years. Job tenure information for 1978 also demonstrates a stronger male labor market attachment. These men had on average 11.0 years of tenure at their current job; women had only 5.9 years of tenure (Lloyd and Niemi 1979, tables 3–6 and 3–7).

Since women had less work experience and job tenure than comparably aged men, it should not be surprising that the earnings gap grew with age. In 1983 women ages twenty to twenty-four who worked full-time year-round earned 84 percent as much as their male counterparts, while women ages thirty-five to forty-four earned only 60 percent as much as their male counterparts (O'Neill 1985, table 3). The earnings gap also grew with experience. For each additional year of experience, male earnings increased by a greater percentage than did female earnings.

The earnings gap also can be analyzed by looking at the occupational distribution of men and women. In 1981 women comprised 36.3 percent of the full-time work force, but they were overrepresented or underrepresented in many of the five-hundred three-digit occupations classified by the U.S. Department of Commerce. Holden and Hansen (1987) labeled all occupations in which the percent female deviated by more than 10 percent from the mean percentage of full-time jobs held by women as either female or male dominated. All occupations in which women comprised less than 26.3 percent were considered male dominated, occupations in which women comprised more than 46.3 percent were considered female dominated, and occupations in which women comprised between 26.3 and 46.3 percent were considered integrated. Table 8–2 indicates the distribution of female employment. As you can see, three out of every four working women were employed in female-dominated industries.[4]

Many studies have found that female-dominated occupations tend to be lower paying than male-dominated occupations. The hypothetical data presented in table 8–3 incorporate this observation. Table 8–3 illustrates that even if women earned more than men in each occupational category, because of their occupational distribution, the average wage for women would still be lower than the average wage for men. To the extent that women face discrimination, this infers that the wage differential results from their ina-

Table 8–2
Distribution of Female Employment by Sex-Labeled Occupations, 1971–1981

Occupation	Full-Time Jobs		Part-Time Jobs		All Jobs	
	1971	1981	1971	1981	1971	1981
Male-labeled	9.2	13.3	7.1	9.1	8.7	12.3
Female-labeled	79.7	73.9	83.1	81.0	80.4	75.4
Integrated	11.0	12.8	9.8	9.9	10.8	12.3

Source: Holden and Hansen 1987 (table 8).

Table 8–3
Impact of Occupational Distribution on Male and Female Earnings

Occupation	Mean Female Wages (thousands of dollars)	Mean Male Wages (thousands of dollars)	Occupational Distribution	
			Female Workers (percent)	Male Workers (percent)
Female-dominated	10	8	70	15
Male-dominated	20	18	10	60
Integrated	15	14	20	25
Total	12*	15.5†	100	100

*$10(0.7) + 20(0.1) + 15(0.2) = 12$
†$8(0.15) + 18(0.6) + 14(0.25) = 15.5$

bility to enter certain occupations rather than wage discrimination within individual occupations.

Many studies have estimated the extent to which differences in occupational distribution can explain the earnings gap. For each additional percent of female participation, Treiman and Hartmann (1981) estimate that the average annual earnings in an occupation would decrease by $42. Miller (1984) found that if the female labor force distribution was the same as the male distribution, the female–male earnings ratio would increase from 65.0 percent to 71.1 percent. In this case, we can say that differences in occupational distributions between men and women can explain 17.4 percent (6.1 divided by 35) of the earnings gap.

Black–White Differences

While the overall female–male earnings ratio was steady between 1950 and 1980, this was not the case for either the white or black female–male earnings ratio. In 1955 white female full-time year-round workers earned 65.3 percent as much as white male full-time year-round workers. By 1973 the figure had fallen to 55.9 percent. It then rose to 63.2 percent in 1986 (U.S. Department of Commerce 1987, table 52). For black women, the situation was dramatically different. In 1955 the female–male earnings ratio for blacks was 55.1 percent. It rose continuously to 74.1 percent by 1971, then after a lull, it again began to rise, reaching 80.1 percent in 1986.

The dramatic rise in the black female–male ratio was due to the rapid rise in black female earnings relative to other groups. Between 1955 and 1982, the female black–white earnings ratio rose from 51.4 percent to well over 90 percent for full-time year-round workers. When we look at occupational changes, the explanation of this rapid change in black female earnings becomes quite clear. Up until the 1950s, black women were heavily concentrated in domestic service and agricultural labor, two extremely low paying occupations. During the past three decades, black women have moved heavily into nondomestic service and blue-collar occupations. These new occupations are still low paying, but they pay better than the occupations in which black women were previously concentrated.

Black and white female occupational distributions are still somewhat different. Just as women compared to men are disproportionately concentrated in low-paying occupations, so are black women compared to white women. While more than 40 percent of black women working full-time year-round are located in nondomestic service and blue-collar occupations, less than 19 percent of white women work in these occupations. Within most of the broad occupational categories, black women earn more than white women.[5] Thus, the figures are similar to those in table 8–3 (substituting black women for women and white women for men). They indicate that if both groups had the same occupational distribution, black women would have a higher mean earnings than white women. In 1982 the mean earnings for white women working full-time year-round was $14,468. If white women had the same occupational distribution as black women, their mean earnings would have been only $13,217, slightly less than the black female mean earnings of $13,250 (U.S. Department of Commerce 1984, table 52).

Assessment of Conservative Views

Conservatives claim that women have a greater preference for child rearing and other household activities than men. Since conservatives emphasize how efficiency is usually associated with specialization, even if women have only a slightly greater preference for child-rearing activities than men, economic specialization would improve efficiency. Men should specialize in market activities and women in home activities. June O'Neill (1985) points out, "Thus traditional female jobs are not only compatible with the life-cycle investment profiles of women but also differ from men's jobs with respect to job amenities such as part-time work and flexible schedules" (p. S111).

Beginning with this perspective, conservatives go on to explain some of the data presented in the previous section. We found that women had much lower earnings than men with the same level of education. For conservatives such as Becker (1964), the answer is simple: Women seek further schooling in order to marry higher-earning males, not to increase their earning power.[6] This explains why women continue to seek further education despite its seemingly low labor market returns. In support of their contention, conservatives note the low (compared to men) labor force participation rates for women with college degrees: 50 percent in 1970 and 70 percent in 1980 (Miller 1984).

Conservatives also link discontinuous labor market behavior with the educational choices made by women. Expecting to leave the labor market for bearing and raising children, women choose occupations that have a low penalty for these absences. Since these occupations tend to have low earnings growth rates, men do not choose them, and thus segregation develops. In support of this hypothesis, Mincer and Polachek (1974) found that for an additional year of experience, yearly earnings increased 1.2 percent for married women, 2.6 percent for single women, and 3.4 percent for married men.

Limitations of the Conservative Model

Even if women have a weaker labor force attachment than men, conservative interpretations are subject to a number of criticisms. First, none of the conservative models explains more than 45 percent of the earnings gap. Conservatives usually contend that the residual—the unexplained 55 percent—is an overestimation of the portion of the wage gap due to discrimination. They contend that worker characteristics not included could account for an additional portion of the gap.[7]

In contrast, Barbara Bergmann (1986) points out that some of the measures that are excluded should increase the unexplained wage gap. For example, men are more likely than women to have alcohol problems, criminal records, or accident-studded driving records. If these productivity-related factors are included, less of the wage gap would be explained by supply-side differences. Thus, conservative models are still consistent with the view that much of the earnings gap results from discrimination.

Second, these models analyze differences among only full-time workers. A major feature of the labor market is the high proportion of women compared to men who work part-time. For the group aged twenty-five to fifty-nine, Holden and Hansen (1987) estimated that only 4.0 percent of the male labor force compared to 24.6 percent of the female labor force are employed part-time. If we compare all workers with positive incomes, the female–male earnings ratio drops to 45 percent. To the extent that discrimination causes many women to work part-time, studies that analyze only the full-time work force understate the earnings gap caused by discrimination.

Third, it is possible to find alternative explanations for the relationships conservative studies find. Does discrimination cause women to choose not to compete in certain fields and to shift to occupations in which discontinuous employment is acceptable? If so, the findings that women have more discontinuous work records would simply reflect female adaptation to discrimination.

According to Bergmann (1986), men receive more training and have longer tenure with their present employer as a result of discriminatory behavior. She contends that firms often withhold training from all female employees because they believe women quit jobs more often than men. Bergmann also believes that "[m]uch of women's lower seniority results from discrimination" (p. 81). She reasons that if women are unable to gain access to company training programs and promotions, they have little incentive to remain with the company. These interpretations justify aggressive affirmative action programs.

Many economists claim that higher turnover rates may have little to do with female motivations. Table 8–4 indicates a set of hypothetical data. Suppose male-dominated occupations tend to be good jobs all workers desire to keep while female-dominated occupations tend to be bad jobs all workers desire to quit. Although women have a lower turnover rate in each group of jobs, their average overall turnover rate is higher because they are concentrated more heavily than men in bad jobs. As a result, Blau and Jusenius

Table 8–4
Impact of Occupational Distribution on Female and Male Quit Rates

| | | | Occupational Distribution | |
| | | | Male Workers (percent) | Female Workers (percent) |
Occupation	Male Quit Rate*	Female Quit Rate*	Male Workers (percent)	Female Workers (percent)
Female-dominated	7.0	6.0	15	70
Male-dominated	4.5	4.0	60	10
Integrated	3.0	2.0	25	20
Total	4.5	5.0	100	100

*Quit rate is the percentage of workers expected to quit voluntarily within the next twelve months.

(1976)) claim, "To our knowledge no evidence exists to support the proposition that, *other things being equal,* women have higher rates of turnover and/or absenteeism [than men]" (p. 194n).[8]

Fourth, critics contend that discontinuous female labor market behavior does not explain occupational choices.[9] Conservatives believe that women with discontinuous labor market experience would choose occupations that have low penalties for exit and reentry. However, Paula England (1982) found that there was no difference between the occupational distribution of women with more continuous and women with less continuous labor market experience.[10]

Conservative economists Smith and Ward (1984) emphasize how more continuous employment will eventually be reflected in higher average years of experience of working women. They project that a forty-year-old working woman will have 2.8 more years of work experience in the year 1990 and 5.2 more years of work experience in the year 2000 than a forty-year-old working woman in 1980 (Smith and Ward 1984, table 32). They contend that the substantial increase in the female–male earnings ratio from 60 percent in 1980 to 64 percent in 1983 reflected the growth in average work experience of working women during the early 1980s.

Critics contend that work experience has little to do with the low wages female workers receive. Data seem to indicate that there is no difference between the earnings of women with continuous and those with discontinuous work experience. The U.S. Census Bureau (U.S. Department of Commerce 1987) separated female workers between the ages of twenty-one and sixty-four into two groups—those who had at least one work interruption of six months or more since their twenty-first birthday and those with no work interruptions. Women with work interruptions had the same earnings as those with no interruptions. The Census Bureau study contends that structural factors and discrimination rather than discontinuous employment explain the earnings gap.

The Census Bureau study notes that the evidence Smith and Ward (1984) cite is misleading, as much of the female "gain" reflected declining median male wages. During the early 1980s, a deep recession and overvalued dollar caused declining demand in many high-wage manufacturing industries. The impact these changes had on male wages rather than growing female work experience may very well explain the closing of the gender earnings gap.

Finally, child-rearing responsibilities may reflect patriarchy rather than personal choice. In this case, women should not be penalized for the extra burden they have.[11] Government-funded day-care centers can ease their child-rearing burden and reduce their labor market disadvantage.

Discrimination within Occupations

Critics point to the persistence of wide intraoccupational wage differentials as evidence that additional work experience will not substantially reduce the earnings gap between men and women. Miller (1984) estimated that in each of the eleven one-digit occupations, 40 percent of male workers earned more than all except the top 10 percent of female workers. Studies by Osterman (1978), Hartmann (1987), and Bielby and Baron (1986) demonstrate that within firms women are crowded into the bottom categories of each job cluster while men are crowded into the upper end.

Osterman (1978) studied 759 salaried employees, employed in eleven job clusters, in a publishing company. He found that most of the earnings differential came from unequal treatment of women and men within the clusters and not from their different allocation across clusters. To the degree discrimination occurred, it was the inability of women to be promoted within job clusters. Hartmann (1987) studied the employment pattern of a major insurance company that employed more than five thousand full-time workers. She found that women had extreme difficulty attaining the highest grade levels within occupations. After adjusting for performance and tenure, Hartmann found that women had a significantly lower probability of being promoted than men.

Numerous studies have found that within occupations men and women are not randomly distributed among firms. Blau (1977) found that women were more likely than men to be employed by low-paying firms. Within occupations such as accounting clerk, women were more likely to be employed by firms in lower-profit industries, in nonunionized firms, and in smaller firms within industries. She found that more of the earnings gap between women and men in the same occupations can be explained by pay differences among firms than by pay differences within firms.

Many observers note that mixed occupations are extremely segregated at the firm level and even more so within firms. William Bielby and James Baron (1986) assessed the employment data of 290 firms that employed more than 50,000 individuals, 40,000 males and 11,000 females.[12] When they analyzed all job classifications with at least two employees, they estimated that the index of segregation was more than 96 percent. Virtually all job classifications, even among those within integrated occupations, were gender segregated. They caution,

> Although aggregate statistics on occupational composition show a very modest trend toward gender integration, this may partly reflect increased sex-based differentiation of *jobs* as men and women have become more similar occupationally. . . . Therefore, a more balanced sex mix in a given occupational category need not reflect increased equity of job opportunities in specific work settings (p. 788).

Bielby and Baron analyzed the employment distribution within integrated occupations. They found that within these occupations, jobs assigned to female workers tended to reflect statistical discriminations—that is, they had characteristics associated with female stereotypes. Bielby and Baron found little evidence, however, that these assignments reflected objective differences in the skills or motivations of women.

These studies indicate that within occupations, there are wage differentials independent of work experience and job tenure information. They persist even for women with extensive work experience within occupations, and stereotypic job assignment continues even when women leave female-dominated occupations. Thus, conservative theories postulating that women earn less than men because they lack work experience and job tenure or because they remain in traditional female occupations are inadequate.

Liberal Explanations of the Earnings Gap

If we reject conservative contentions that discrimination is minimal, we are still left to explain the source and the process by which women end up in lower-paying jobs. Is discrimination inadvertent or consciously undertaken? Is discrimination psychologically or financially motivated? Do owners and male workers benefit from labor market discrimination against women?

Myrdal's Cumulative Process

In chapter 3, we noted that Myrdal's (1944) theories of discrimination have been used to explain the situation of women in the labor market. As long as there is a sufficient number of qualified male candidates, the firm has no incentive to screen female applicants extensively. While the firm is not motivated by discrimination, it nonetheless ends up rejecting qualified female applicants. Facing this situation, women adapt, shifting their occupational goals. However rational, their actions reinforce the stereotype that female applicants have little long-term attachment to the labor market.

If follows immediately that this form of discrimination can be reduced through affirmative action programs. By requiring firms to interview a minimum percentage of their applicants from disadvantaged groups, affirmative action forces them to expend a significant amount of resources on the screening of female applicants. The expenditure of resources would result in the identification of employable women. Since the firm's decision would be motivated by profitability rather than discrimination, once qualified women were identified, they would be hired.

Bergmann's Crowding Hypothesis

Barbara Bergmann (1971) claims that however inadvertently the exclusion of women from better-paying occupations begins, male workers realize that it enables them to obtain better jobs. Since employers often have little incentive to seek qualified female workers, they accommodate their hiring process to the demands of male workers. As a result, women are crowded into secondary occupations. This reduces the wage rate secondary employers must pay and the working conditions they must provide. These firms organize production in a discontinuous fashion, not because women prefer it that way, but because of the limited choice available to women. Since firms hiring secondary workers benefit financially, they also favor the discriminatory hiring practices used by firms offering better jobs.[13]

Bergmann's crowding hypothesis suggests that discrimination will be more resilient than Myrdal's cumulative process envisioned. Discrimination is more consciously motivated because male workers and secondary employers have a financial stake in its perpetuation. Also, women do not adapt and develop discontinuous labor market behavior; they are exploited by secondary firms that have a captive labor force. Both theories emphasize, however, that the main source of discrimination is the inability of women to enter high-paying occupations.

These theories also suggest that women in secondary labor markets would benefit from policies that improved female access to primary jobs. If more women obtained primary jobs, the conditions and wages for women in secondary markets also would improve. For this reason, Bergmann (1986) states, "[If] affirmative action were proceeding rapidly, a pay equity campaign might be redundant" (p. 191). Both theories also minimize the financial gains major corporations receive as a result of discrimination against women.

Radical Views

Radicals believe that liberals understate the forces opposed to antidiscrimination regulations. Radicals contend that besides secondary firms and primary workers, major corporations benefit from discriminatory hiring practices. Intraoccupational wage differentials indicate that major corporations are able to create secondary tracks within primary labor markets in which women (and blacks) will be underpaid. Major corporations also gain when they either hire secondary workers or purchase inputs from suppliers who hire them. Radicals contend that these cost savings to major corporations more than offset the slightly higher wages they must pay male workers in the high-wage tracks.

Even if antidiscrimination regulations were enacted, radicals believe that they would not benefit many women. As a result of the strong forces opposed to these regulations, a trickle-down process could take a great deal of time and affect only a modest proportion of female-dominated professions. Many professions would not be affected at all, and women in these occupations would continue to receive low earnings.

Most importantly, radicals question the assumptions upon which this trickle-down process relies. Radicals believe that the dominant reason for low wages is the existence of a reserve army of the unemployed. Piore (1979), in particular, has argued that even if some workers gained access to primary jobs, wages in secondary markets would not be forced up. He believes that firms would find other sources of cheap (captive) labor that were not previously needed.

Teresa Amott (1988) cites welfare reform proposals offered during the late 1980s. Once affirmative action began to reduce the number of women forced to accept service-sector jobs, government officials sought reforms that would coerce welfare recipients to enter the labor market. This parallels previous welfare policies used to reduce labor supply shortages described by Piven and Cloward (1971).

Radicals and some other economists note that many female-dominated occupations would not experience wage increases even if severe labor shortages appeared. In response to nursing shortages, for example, hospitals have attempted to increase their recruitment of foreign nurses. In addition, Killingsworth (1985) contends that the labor market for nurses has been cartelized—that is, hospitals and other large employers of nurses have agreed not to compete with each other by offering higher wages to attract nurses. This indicates that to the extent welfare reforms are instituted, foreign recruitment of nurses is successful, and the cartelization of female-dominated labor markets persists, benefits from affirmative action programs will not trickle down to women and other workers remaining in low-wage occupations.

These doubts concerning the trickle-down approach have led to an increased emphasis by activists on policies that directly affect earnings in female-dominated occupations.[14] One such policy, known as comparable worth or pay equity, attempts to determine relative salaries of different occupations within the same firm or agency independent of market wages. Comparable worth proposals assume that objective measures would allow investigators to compare the productive worth of different occupations. Each occupation would be evaluated and allocated a number of points. Occupations that scored the same number of points would be considered equivalent and receive the same salaries.

Comparable worth studies have sometimes been conducted by firms seeking an integrated pay system. The most publicized example was the job evaluation studies conducted by Westinghouse in the late 1930s. At that time, production jobs were almost completely segregated by sex and were known as either female or male jobs. At one Westinghouse plant, after making a point evaluation of each position, female jobs were assigned to five grades, 1 through 5; male jobs with the same job evaluation scores were assigned to parallel labor grades, 1 through 5; and five additional labor grades were specified for male jobs with higher scores. The wage rates for male and female labor grades did not reflect evaluation scores. The hourly wage rates were established so that all female grades earned less than the lowest male labor grade, despite the fact that parallel male and female grades represented jobs of comparable worth according to the company's own criteria.

After the Civil Rights Act of 1964, Westinghouse eliminated the separate series for male and female jobs. If Westinghouse had followed its own evaluations, it should have combined male and female classifications for grades 1 through 5. This would have eliminated the higher male earnings in each of these classifications. However, male grades 1 through 10 were simply relabeled 6 through 15, and earnings differentials between men and women were preserved.

Comparable worth studies also have been conducted in response to lawsuits alleging discrimination. In 1974 a study of state government jobs was conducted in the state of Washington. Claims had been made that the state, by using traditional wage rates found in private industry, were simply reproducing the discrimination existing there. The study assigned job evaluation scores of fifty-nine female-dominated and sixty-two male-dominated occupational categories. The study found that, holding job worth constant, earnings in female occupations averaged 20 percent less than earnings in male occupations.

Jeanneret (1980), using a somewhat different procedure, conducted job evaluation studies for a number of utility companies. Using questionnaires to evaluate the basic human behaviors in jobs, he placed various utility jobs in several pay grades. Jeanneret then compared the average actual pay of men and women in each of these grades. He found a salary difference of $108 a month in favor of men. In a similar study for a savings and loan company, Jeanneret found similar salary differences. In each of these cases, the salaries of women were subsequently adjusted.

Many economists criticize comparable worth proposals. First, critics believe that wage differentials are appropriate even when two jobs require the same skill levels. If society placed more value on rock than classical guitarists, then even though skill levels were the same, the market wages of the former would be greater than those of the latter for each song produced. Only if differential wages existed could consumers signal guitar players that they preferred rock to classical songs. Thus, comparable worth would undermine consumer sovereignty.

Critics also contend that wage differentials reflect the amenities embedded in different jobs: Some jobs have safe or preferred working conditions, while others have unsafe or undesirable working conditions. In a competitive market, firms would offer a wage premium for those jobs with undesirable working conditions to attract workers. These workers would value the additional income more than preferable working conditions. To the extent female workers prefer certain job amenities, including flexible hours or occupations compatible with feminine qualities, firms would be willing to accommodate them only if wages could be reduced. In both these situations, wage differentials would reflect the desires of workers. Comparable worth policies, by requiring wage equality, would undermine worker sovereignty.

Critics point out that, besides restricting consumer or worker sovereignty, comparable worth proposals can reduce efficiency. For example, in most state-supported universities, faculty salaries and rank are based on comparable worth; it is assumed that in all academic fields there should be the same criteria for determining salary and rank. Thus, philosophy and accounting professors must meet the same criteria (publication, education, teaching experience, and so on) to attain the same salary and rank. Basing salary and rank on comparable worth has created some problems for universities, since the supply and demand situation differs among academic disciplines. For disciplines such as philosophy, where there are few non-academic options, a particular salary structure is likely to generate an excess labor supply. For disciplines with extensive high-salary nonacademic options, however, there is likely to be an excess labor demand. With salary structures based on comparable worth, some universities have too many philosophers and too few accounting instructors.[15]

Comparable worth advocates agree that certain arbitrary judgments not reflecting consumer or worker values would be made and that certain inefficiencies due to labor market imbalances would be generated. Advocates also agree that there might be some adverse employment effects if comparable worth policies were implemented.[16] Julianne Malveaux (1985) expects some workers who were formerly employed in the public sector to have their jobs subcontracted to private employers. These workers, who are disproportionately black and female, are employed primarily in food and cleaning service occupations. Since subcontractors compete on the basis of the lowest bid, it is likely that wages and working conditions of workers would decline when their jobs moved from the public to the private sector.

Malveaux lists other limitations of comparable worth policies. She notes they are limited to employed workers and would have little impact on unemployed female workers, who are disproportionately black. She anticipates that these policies would not affect women forced to participate in workfare programs or in the underground economy. Malveaux also believes that female-dominated occupations considered unskilled or semiskilled would not benefit, as only unionization could raise the wages for these workers. Finally, Malveaux believes that advocates must address the question of who will fund comparable worth policies. It is clear that the dominant approach is to raise wages in female-dominated occupations without lowering wages in the comparable male-dominated occupations, resulting in higher costs. Malveaux fears that the government might raise taxes or reduce the level of services to fund these programs, which might have an adverse effect, especially on black communities.

Comparable worth advocates, including Malveaux, believe these limitations can be minimized and are small when compared to the benefits of implementation. Advocates contend that modest labor demand declines are offset by substantial wage increases. When comparable worth was widely implemented in Australia, the female–male earnings ratio rose from 60 percent to 75 percent, the equivalent of a 25 percent wage increase for all female workers (Malveaux 1985).

Advocates note that since many comparable worth adjustments are within firms, issues of consumer sovereignty are generally irrelevant. Advocates also believe that issues of worker sovereignty are overstated. Most studies have shown that wage premiums for undesirable working conditions are minor. Radicals believe this reflects the inability of workers to dictate their working conditions, while conservatives believe it reflects the low value many workers place on their health. In either case, if wage premiums are small, comparable worth pay schedules will not create significant wage distortions.

Advocates also question relying on female preferences to defend the need for wage differentials. Even if women had a different set of preferences, wage differentials might be unnecessary. As long as female preferences for some occupations were balanced with male preferences for others, both female- and male-dominated occupations would be equally desirable. Only if men simply preferred money while women had preferences for certain occupational characteristics would gender-based wage differentials be appropriate.

Finally, advocates question the association of wage differentials with economic efficiency. They note that U.S. and Japanese firms in the same industry, using the same technology, have widely differing wage scales. In this case, it would appear that wage differentials cannot be based on productivity criteria alone.

Conclusions

We have found that conservative assertions concerning the limited amount of labor market discrimination against women is consistent only with a questionable selection of relevant data. If alternative data were used, female labor market behavior would be much closer to that of males, and the differences would appear to have declined dramatically in the past few decades. Even if the remaining differences in behavior are relevant, many argue that they result from female adaptation to discrimination. If this is the case, only through antidiscrimination policies can we expect female behavior to change.

We also found that it is likely that inadvertent discrimination might explain only a small portion of the discrimination women experience. Economic benefits received by male workers and secondary employers might play a much greater role. Given studies that indicate that discrimination within occupations is substantial, increased female access to higher-paying professions will only modestly reduce gender discrimination. In this case, a set of antidiscrimination policies that is much more activist than affirmative action guidelines is warranted.

Since it is unlikely that benefits will trickle down to women in low-wage occupations, equal pay for equal work proposals will have a limited impact on the earnings gap. For these reasons, comparable worth has become a dominant policy proposal. Studies consistently indicate that when occupations within firms are evaluated, those in which female workers are crowded tend to have lower wages than male-dominated occupations of comparable worth. While comparable worth policies have some limitations and create some inefficiencies and inequities, advocates believe that the benefits far outweigh the costs.

Notes

1. The percentage of men and women with four years of college was 9.7 percent and 7.3 percent respectively, while the percentage with at least five years of college was 10.3 percent and 5.3 percent respectively (U.S. Department of Commerce 1984, table 37).

2. This explains why the earnings gap is larger when measured by yearly earnings than when measured by usual weekly wage.

3. Using a slightly different data base, June O'Neill (1985) estimates that the male–female ratio of median usual weekly earnings of full-time workers would increase from 65 percent to 71 percent if adjustments for hours or work were made.

4. Using a 20-percent deviation, Rytina and Bianchi (1984) estimated that between 1971 and 1981, the percentage of female workers employed in female-dominated occupations declined from 74.6 percent to 63.3 percent. Holden and Hansen (1987) also computed an index of segregation—that is, the proportion of women in the labor force that would have to switch occupations in order to be distributed in the same way male workers are distributed. They estimated that the index of segregation declined from 69.0 percent in 1971 to 61.8 percent in 1981.

5. Although black women have higher earnings, they do not have higher hourly wage rates than white women. Their higher earnings reflect more hours worked per week and more weeks worked per year. See Blau 1984 (pp. 75–76).

6. Becker (1985) suggests that working women have reduced productivity, since "women with household responsibilities would have less energy available for the market than men would" (p. S35).

7. Randall Filer (1985) contends that men tend to hold jobs with more difficult or more dangerous working conditions than jobs held by women. These jobs must, therefore, pay higher wages to compensate workers. Filer claims that these differences in working conditions help explain the female–male earnings gap.

8. For additional studies that come to the same conclusion, see Viscusi (1980) and Blau and Kahn (1978).

9. Liberals also believe that aggregate data overstates the differences in experience between working women and men. Corcoran (1978) found that by restricting comparisons to workers—those employed more than five hundred hours a year—the experience differential between men ages forty-five to fifty-four and comparably aged women is reduced from ten to six years. Smith and Ward (1984) report similar results.

10. For additional criticisms of the conservative contention, see Beller (1982); Corcoran and Ponza (1983); Zellner (1975); and Angle and Wissman (1983).

11. Numerous studies (see, for example, Robinson 1977; Quinn and Staines 1979) have documented that when women enter the labor market, their spouses increase only marginally their time spent on family responsibilities.

12. Manufacturing establishments were overrepresented, and major industries not represented include construction trades, trucking, department stores, insurance carriers, and miscellaneous business services. Using standard measures of occupational segregation, Bielby and Baron (1986) note that "it seems unlikely that our sample is biased toward establishments and industries that are more segregated than average" (p. 775n).

13. Solomon Polachek (1979) claims that the crowding hypothesis is inconsistent with productivity data. Many economists (see, for example, Goldberger 1984; Green and Ferber 1984) contend that the statistical procedure used by Polachek—reverse regressions—might be seriously flawed.

14. Chapter 7 noted the low earnings of women with less than a college degree.

It was suggested there that raising the minimum wage to $5 an hour might be one way to help women in low-paying occupations.

15. Some universities have been able to solve this problem by circumventing comparable worth and hiring accountants at much higher salaries and rank than their academic record would warrant. In some fields, such as law and medicine, universities have set up separate salary schedules to attract faculty.

16. Killingsworth (1985) cites the Australian experience, in which estimates indicate that the growth rate of female employment was one-third lower than it would have been in the absence of comparable worth programs.

References

Amott, Teresa. 1988. "Welfare Reform: A Workhouse without Walls." In *The Imperiled Economy: Through the Safety Net,* ed. Robert Cherry, et al. New York: Union for Radical Political Economies.

Angle, John, and David Wissman. 1983. "Work Experience, Age, and Gender Discrimination." *Social Science Quarterly* 65:66–83.

Becker, Gary S. 1964. *Human Capital.* New York: Columbia University Press.

Beller, Andrea H. 1982. "Occupational Segregation by Sex: Determinants and Changes." *Journal of Human Resources* 17:371–82.

Bergmann, Barbara. 1971. "The Effects on White Incomes of Discrimination in Employment." *Journal of Political Economy* 79:294–313.

———. 1986. *The Economic Emergence of Women.* New York: Basic Books.

Bielby, William, and James Baron. 1986. "Men and Women at Work: Sex Segregation and Statistical Discrimination." *American Journal of Sociology* 91:759–99.

Blau, Francine D. 1977. *Equal Pay in the Office.* Lexington, MA: D.C. Heath.

———. 1984. "Discrimination Against Women: Theory and Evidence." In *Labor Economics: Modern Views,* ed. William Darity, Jr. Boston: Kluwer-Nijhoff, 53–90.

Blau, Francine D., and Carol Jusenius. 1976. "Economists' Approaches to Sex Segregation in the Labor Market: An Appraisal." In *Women and the Workplace,* ed. Martha Blaxall and Barbara B. Reagan. Chicago: University of Chicago Press, 181–200.

Blau, Francine D., and Laurence Kahn. 1978. "Race and Sex Differences in the Probability and Consequences of Voluntary Turnover." Mimeo.

Corcoran, Mary. 1978. "Work Experience, Work Interruption, and Wages." In *Five Thousand American Families: Patterns of Economic Progress,* ed. Greg Duncan and James Morgan. Ann Arbor, MI: Institute for Social Research, 3–46.

Corcoran, Mary, and Michael Ponza. 1983. "A Longitudinal Analysis of White Women's Wages." *Journal of Human Resources* 18:497–520.

England, Paula. 1982. "The Failure of Human Capital Theory to Explain Occupational Sex Segregation." *Journal of Human Resources* 17:358–70.

Filer, Randall. 1985. "Male–Female Wage Differences: The Importance of Compensating Differentials." *Industrial and Labor Relations Review* 38:426–37.

Goldberger, Arthur. 1984. "Reverse Regression and Salary Discrimination." *Journal of Human Resources* 19:293–318.

Green, Carole, and Marianne Ferber. 1984. "Employer Discrimination: An Empirical Test of Forward versus Reverse Regressions." *Journal of Human Resources* 19:557–69.

Hartmann, Heidi I. 1987. "Internal Labor Markets and Gender: A Case Study of Promotions." In *Gender in the Workplace*, ed. Clair Brown and Joseph Pechman. Washington, DC: The Brookings Institute, 59–91.

Holden, Karen C., and W. Lee Hansen. 1987. "Part-Time Work, Full-Time Work, and Occupational Segregation." In *Gender in the Workplace*, ed. Clair Brown and Joseph Pechman. Washington, DC: The Brookings Institute, 217–37.

Jeanneret, R. 1980. "Equitable Job Evaluation and Classification with a Positive Analysis Questionnaire." *Compensation Review* 3:32–42.

Killingsworth, Mark. 1985. "The Economics of Comparable Worth: Analytical, Empirical, and Policy Questions." In *Comparable Worth: New Directions for Research*, ed. Heidi Hartmann. Washington, DC: National Academy Press, 85–115.

Lloyd, Cynthia B., and Beth T. Niemi. 1979. *The Economics of Sex Differentials*. New York: Columbia University Press.

Malveaux, Julianne. 1985. "Comparable Worth and Its Impact on Black Women." *Review of Black Political Economy* 14:47–62.

Miller, Earl. 1984. "Differences in Weekly Earnings of Men and Women." *Monthly Labor Review* 107:32–37.

Mincer, Jacob, and Solomon Polachek. 1974. "Family Investments in Human Capital: Earnings of Women." *Journal of Political Economy* 82:S76–S108.

Myrdal, Gunnar. 1944. *An American Dilemma: The Negro Problem and Modern Democracy*. New York: Harper and Row.

National Center for Educational Statistics. 1977. *Earned Degrees Conferred, 1974–75*. Washington, DC: U.S. Government Printing Office.

O'Neill, June. 1985. "The Trend in the Male–Female Wage Gap in the United States." *Journal of Labor Economics* 3:S91–S116.

Osterman, Paul. 1978. "Sex, Marriage, Children, and Statistical Discrimination." Discussion Paper #16, Department of Economics, Boston University.

———. 1979. *Birds of Passage*. New York: Cambridge University Press.

Piven, Frances, and Richard Cloward. 1971. *Regulating the Poor*. New York: Pantheon.

Polachek, Solomon. 1979. "Occupational Segregation among Women: Theory, Evidence, and Prognosis." In *Women in the Labor Market*, ed. Cynthis Lloyd, Emily Andrews, and Curtis Gilroy. New York: Columbia University Press, 137–57.

Quinn, Robert, and Graham Staines. 1979. *The 1977 Quality of Employment Survey*. Ann Arbor, MI: Survey Research Center.

Robinson, J. 1977. *How Americans Use Time: A Social Psychological Analysis*. New York: Praeger.

Rytina, Nancy F., and S. Bianchi. 1984. "Occupational Reclassification and Distribution by Gender." *Monthly Labor Review* 107:38–44.

Smith, James, and Michael Ward. 1984. *Women's Wages and Work in the Twentieth Century*. Santa Monica, CA: Rand Corporation.

Treiman, Donald J., and Heidi I. Hartmann. 1981. *Women, Work and Wages: Equal Pay for Jobs of Equal Value*. Washington, DC: National Academy Press.

U.S. Department of Commerce, Bureau of the Census. 1984. *Current Population Reports*, P60, no. 142.

———. 1987. *Current Population Reports*, P70, no. 10.

U.S. Department of Labor, Bureau of Labor Statistics. 1982. *The Female–Male Earnings Gap: A Review of Employment and Earnings Issues*, Report #673.

Viscusi, W. Kip. 1980. "Sex Differences in Worker Quitting." *Review of Economics and Statistics* 35:388–98.

Zellner, Harriet. 1975. "The Determinants of Occupational Segregation." In *Sex, Discrimination and the Division of Labor*, ed. Cynthia Lloyd. New York: Columbia University Press, 125–45.

9
Feminism and the Family

C hapter 8 detailed competing assessments of gender discrimination in labor markets, in some cases suggesting that female and male labor market decisions differ as a result of contrasting household responsibilities. This chapter describes various feminist assessments of the impact of family structure on labor market outcomes. The first section enumerates the reasons why most feminists claim that it is inadequate to analyze the labor market without a systematic analysis of the family.

Any systematic analysis of female household responsibilities must assess the origins and role of the nuclear family. This form of family organization emerged as the dominant household structure during the capitalist era. Both mainstream and Marxist theorists believe that there are reasons for this linkage. The second section of the chapter describes the mainstream views of Talcott Parsons, who contends that the nuclear family replaced other household forms because it best served the needs of individuals living in a capitalist economy. These views are contrasted with those of Marx and other more recent writers working in the Marxist tradition.

Patriarchy can be defined as a set of social relations enabling men to benefit materially and ideologically from women's work (Sokoloff 1980, 154; Hartmann 1981, 14). Feminists reject both theories presented in the second section because neither correctly describes the patriarchal aspects of the nuclear family. Whereas mainstream theories postulate that the nuclear family emerged because it served both men and women, feminists contend that the family does not serve women because of its patriarchal nature. Some feminists accept the Marxist view that capitalism significantly influences the family structure, but they believe that Marxists inadequately understand the ways capitalism benefits from patriarchy and underestimate the benefits of patriarchy to men. The third section of the chapter details the views of those critics who have been identified as left feminists.[1]

Traditional Marxists contend that left feminists overstate the ways in which capitalists benefit from the patriarchal nuclear family and equivocate on the method by which patriarchal relations are enforced. Moreover, traditional Marxists suggest that conflicts between bourgeois and working-class women are more consistent with a class analysis than left feminists believe. These and other criticisms of left feminist views are presented in the concluding section.

Labor Market Discrimination and the Family

All feminists agree that discrimination is the cause of unequal relationships and believe that organizational efforts are required to bring about greater equality. Historically, feminist thought also has identified a distinction between the public and private spheres. The public sphere includes work and organizations in the larger society, while the private sphere is dominated by family and personal relations. Depending on how feminists have viewed these two spheres, different perspectives have emerged.

Alice Kessler-Harris (1987) has identified two directions feminists have taken. One group, which she labels humanist, has fought for equality in the workplace as the primary means by which equality can be achieved. The humanist position emphasizes eliminating all discriminatory barriers to female occupational mobility and the preeminence this plays in the overall liberation of women.[2] These feminists believe that changes in the labor market conditions women face will force changes in the family. Thus, labor market benefits for women will result in a trickling down of benefits to them within the family. From this perspective, the public sphere can be analyzed relatively independently of the private sphere. This viewpoint is reflected in the liberal and radical perspectives presented in chapter 8.

The more dominant feminist perspective does not favor an emphasis on policies that eliminate occupational restrictions. While this group certainly wants women to have the chance to compete on equal terms for all available jobs, it believes that feminist strategies should acknowledge the differences between men's and women's situations. This group contends that legislation should be enacted to help female workers who have special needs owing to their continued responsibility for child care and household services. These feminists believe that women should remain a special interest group fighting for women's special needs and that changes in the private sphere may be necessary before changes in the public sphere occur. This second group does not believe that the public and private spheres are separate and rejects reliance on a trickle-down theory to change social relations within the family. These women believe that a systematic analysis of the family is necessary before one can undertake an adequate analysis of the labor market discrimination women face. These are the feminist views most relevant to the issues discussed in this chapter.

There are many reasons why this group of feminists believes that an analysis emphasizing labor market aspects is inadequate.

1. Nonincome Dimensions. If we look only at labor market outcomes, we will be measuring only economic effects. This narrow focus ignores the harassment female workers face. Recall that in chapter 2 conservatives claimed that market forces would discipline individuals to separate their personal attitudes from their market behavior. Sexual harassment occurs, however, because men may not separate the sexist behavior that occurs in the private sphere from their actions in the public sphere. Thus, we must analyze the private sphere if we are to understand behavior in the public sphere.

Feminists point out that sexual harassment often includes physical abuse, with its most extreme form being rape. Rape has been consciously used in a wide range of societies to discipline women and to symbolize the conquering of an enemy. In the United States, men often receive minimal punishment for sexual excesses and the female victim is often treated as the criminal.[3]

Moreover, feminists point out that the benefits of gender discrimination are not necessarily reflected in changes in family income. For example, there might be evidence that the lack of male–female unity lowers family income—that is, lower wives' wages are not offset by higher husbands' wages. This would appear to indicate that husbands should fight against gender discrimination in the labor market, but many feminists contend that men benefit from patriarchal relations within the family. They suggest that even if gender discrimination lowers family income somewhat, men more than benefit from it through the strengthening of their patriarchal control. Only by systematically analyzing the family can we assess the degree to which men benefit from patriarchal relations and determine whether the household benefits men receive, rather than the impact of discrimination on family income, dominate male behavior.

2. Inadequate Analysis of Marriage. In previous chapters, female marriage decisions were thought to be determined by changes in female preferences for private sphere production or changes in female benefits from market labor. Most feminists would conclude that these are inadequate analyses because they do not question the allocation of private sphere production to wives. In addition, focusing on female behavior may be misguided. According to many observers (Galbraith 1973), patriarchy enables men to obtain domestic services at much more favorable prices through marriage than if purchased in the marketplace. Once women expect more egalitarian relations, the benefits of marriage for men decline. Thus, Barbara Ehrenreich (1983) contends that it is men rather than women who are fleeing marriage. Only a systematic analysis of the family would enable us to judge why marriage rates have declined.

3. The Occupational Choices of Women. Women's activities in the public sphere often mirror their activities in the private sphere. These activities include child care and adult care, servicing, and nurturing through early education and social work. Equality could occur if women no longer perceived their roles in the labor market to be the same as their household roles. In this case, role models and affirmative action might help bring about labor market equality.

Many feminists reject the view that equality will be advanced when women no longer disproportionately seek nursing and elementary school employment and instead seek to be options traders. They contend that this analysis ignores the positive aspects of the nurturing and caring roles women perform. Women are the providers of nonalienating humanistic values and services, and, they believe, equality will occur when men change by adopting these values and sets of behavior. Until then, women should continue to maintain their distinctive values and force society to acknowledge their role.

From this perspective, comparable worth strategies take on increased importance. Comparable worth suggests that we should be more supportive of jobs that are currently distinctly female. Moreover, comparable worth is consistent with the view that women enter these fields for positive reasons and not because they have been acculturated to accept these positions.

4. The Work of Women. Any analysis that ignores the family underestimates the value of the women's work efforts. This devaluation is reflected in many television sitcoms, which posit a hardworking husband and a housewife with extensive idle time. At best the wife is seen providing emotional support, often through nurturing of children. Meaningful productive labor is almost always nonexistent. This view devalues women because it ignores the domestic services they provide, including child rearing, cleaning, cooking, washing, transporting, and so on. Just as importantly, it ignores the often extensive home production that provides revenues to the family—for example, making clothes, taking in boarders, or making products for corporations (piecework).

Women have often been perceived as individuals earning income to spend on frivolous personal consumption. Many feminists contend that the wife's income is used primarily to offset fluctuations in her husband's earnings—that is, she works not to obtain discretionary income but to balance family income. The wife's supplemental earnings often makes a crucial difference in the family's standard of living or ability to respond to unexpected financial needs. Only by seeing women's situation in its entirety—in both the private and public spheres—can an accurate assessment of the value of women's work be undertaken.

5. Inadequate Understanding of Labor Market Behavior. Feminists note that many jobs are structured by patriarchal notions of the family. For many professional and managerial positions, employers expect spouses to accommodate the responsibilities placed on employees. If the firm requires overtime, unexpected rescheduling of work hours, or other adjustments, spouses are expected to adjust their schedules. As long as many jobs are structured in this way, job applicants who do not have a spouse willing to accommodate to the firm's prerogatives are at a disadvantage. Patriarchy posits that women be the accommodating spouse. Thus, even if firms are genuinely antidiscriminatory, without a change in job requirements, women will continue to be at a disadvantage.[4]

According to choice theory, women weigh income benefits from market employment against the costs to the family from lost household services. This would appear to indicate that firms can increase the labor supply of married women only by increasing the wages offered to them. In this case, mothers are not a reserve army capable of keeping down wages in secondary labor markets. Critics note that the constraints on mothers also have an attitudinal component. For example, the way society views the value of home child rearing versus day care may affect the costs mothers perceive if they were to enter the labor market. Capitalists would then be able to draw women into the labor market by influencing public attitudes rather than raising wages.

Many feminists contend that this revision is inadequate because it still assumes that women control their labor supply decisions. Although many women desire paid employment, they are not working because men control their access to jobs. Women are often restricted by the patriarchal attitudes of their husbands. Thus, capitalists may be more concerned with manipulating the attitudes of husbands than wives when they desire changes in female labor supply decisions. More importantly, capitalists determine hiring practices. By subsidizing day-care expenses or facilitating part-time employment, firms would quickly find many women willing to work.

Feminists point to the way women were drawn into the work force during World War II. As a result of the war effort, female labor was needed in industry. Articles and stories championed the value of day care and the benefits of market work for women. Firms also provided day care and a willingness to hire women in nontraditional occupations. With their patriarchs at war, women were less constrained and there was a dramatic increase in female labor force participation. With the ending of the war and the return of men, articles changed. Now it was found that absent mothers were responsible for juvenile delinquency and that certain jobs detracted from femininity. Feminists (Milkman 1976; Beechey 1978) detail how firms eliminated day-care facilities and again refused to hire women for certain jobs. Men began to reinforce their desire for women to be full-time mothers and housekeepers. Not surprisingly, many women left the work force, resigning themselves to becoming "happy homemakers."

Capitalism and
the Nuclear Family

The emergence of the nuclear family as the dominant form of social organization is a relatively recent phenomenon. As late as the sixteenth century, most cultures were dominated by kinship relationships. Over the next few centuries, household structures evolved until the nuclear family predominated. For this reason, many social scientists have conjectured that there is an important relationship between the emergence of capitalism and the nuclear family.

Parsonian Views

Typified by the work of Talcott Parsons (1954) and Parsons and R.F. Bales (1956), many social scientists believe that the benefits from kinship relationships declined with capitalism.[5] Louis Wirth (1956) claimed that a capitalist society required individuals to develop specialized fragmented relationships. In particular, business relations would be separate from social relations. Thus, Wirth believed that individuals from cultures that emphasized kinship relationships would be unsuccessful in capitalist environments.

Parsons (1954) considered other aspects of the extended family ill-suited for success in capitalist societies. In an extended family, benefits are spread among all so that individual risk taking is unprofitable. Even if risk takers were successful, the benefits to them would be limited. Extended families also restrict the mobility of individuals. Thus, the nuclear family was better suited for the risk-taking behavior and spatial mobility necessary for success.

Parsons thought that the nuclear family minimized interpersonal conflicts. In capitalist societies, individual behavior generates unequal incomes. This generates conflicts and disagreements in extended families with many (male) wage earners. In contrast, the nuclear family avoids conflict by assigning complementary roles to spouses. Men specialize in market production, while women specialize in home activities.

Underlying much of Parsons's analysis is the belief that the industrialization process separated work from the home, fostering the need for husbands and wives to develop specialized functions for which the extended family was ill-suited. Critics question this viewpoint. Elizabeth Pleck (1976) points out that the separation of work and home occurred only for the bourgeois family; for other families, home production declined gradually and maintained its importance until World War II.

Census data indicating low labor force participation rates for married women during the pre–World War II period overstate the separation of home and production. Matthaei (1980) estimates that for every five women in the official labor force in 1900, another four were not included: Three took in boarders, and one did laundry or dressmaking at home.[6] For most working-class wives, home production remained a fundamental part of their work effort. For these reasons, the bourgeois family described by Parsons may have had little relationship to the working-class family during this period.

Finally and most importantly, the Parsonian view assumes that capitalism has no interest in the social organization chosen by workers. This implies that the nuclear family was chosen because it served the interests of workers. In contrast, traditional Marxists believe that the nuclear family could be sustained only if it served the interests of capitalists, while feminists contend that the benefits all men derive explain its persistence. For these reasons, traditional Marxists and feminists reject Parsonian explanations.

Traditional Marxist Views

While not systematically incorporating insights into their major works, Karl Marx (1967) and Frederick Engels (1972) did make substantive comments concerning patriarchy. They imagined the prehistoric period to be one of equality between men and women. In agreement with Marx and Engels, Joan Kelley-Gadol (1976) writes,

> [I]n societies where production for exchange is slight and where private property and class inequality are not developed . . . sexual inequalities are less evident. Women's roles are as varied as men's, although there are sex-role differences; authority and power are shared by women and men rather than vested in a hierarchy of males; women are highly evaluated by the culture; and women and men have comparable sex rights. (p. 818)

This period of equality ends with the domestication of animals, which becomes the first important form of private property. Reflecting this transformation, Kelley-Gadol continues: "[Women] steadily lose control over property, products, and themselves as surplus increases, private property develops, and the communal household becomes a private economic unit. . . . [I]t becomes evident that sexual inequalities are bound to the control of property" (p. 819).

Though generally agreeing with this thesis, contemporary Marxists have begun to correct some of its shortcomings. While Gough (1975) believes that a distinct change occurred with the development of family property around 4000 B.C., she rejects the notion of prior equality. She finds inequality in hunting societies and hypothesizes that this was the result of men having a monopoly of heavy weapons. Gough concludes,

> From the start, women have been subordinate to men in certain key areas of status, mobility, and public leadership. But before the agricultural revolution . . . the inequality was based chiefly on the unalterable fact of long

child care combined with the exigencies of primitive technology. . . . But [inequality] was largely a matter of survival rather than of man-made cultural impositions. Hence the impressions we receive of dignity, freedom, and mutual respect between men and women in primitive hunting and horticultural societies. (p. 74)

In its initial stages, capitalism assigned industrial production to men and household production to women. Marx and Engels thought that the exclusion of women from social production subordinated women to men. In the bourgeois household, this separation was complete, reducing women to the private property of men. Within the proletarian family, however, Marx thought patriarchal relationships were not as strong. Working-class men had little property, and working-class women had some independence owing to their continued presence in the labor market.

As capitalism developed, Marx thought that the dominant tendency would be to incorporate working-class women into the production process. According to Engels (1972) this would cause "the last remnants of male domination in the proletarian home [to lose] all foundation" (p. 508). Indeed, Marx (1967) believed that capitalism was destroying working-class families by drawing women and children indiscriminately into the production process, but he claimed,

> However terrible and disgusting the dissolution, under the capitalist system of the old family ties may appear, nevertheless, modern industry, by assigning as it does an important part in the process of production, outside the domestic sphere, to women, to young persons, and to children of both sexes, creates a new economic foundation for a higher form of family and of relations between the sexes (p. 489–90).[7]

Some traditional Marxists believe that even under capitalism there will be a gradual transformation of relationships within the family. This optimism is generally combined with a view that men are limited by the emotional restrictions that patriarchy burdens them with. Julie Matthaei (1980) writes, "[M]ore and more men are interpreting women's development as an opportunity to free themselves from subordination to the requirements of advancement at work" (p. 370).

Michele Barrett (1980) also believes that men are increasingly realizing that the rigid definition of masculinity is oppressive to them. She finds "a growing expression of dissatisfaction with the degree to which this definition has deprived men of significant access to their children" (p. 217). Thus, some Marxists see the possibility of men supporting changing relationships and conclude that "marriage is being transformed from a complementary relationship, based on masculinity and femininity, to a symmetric one, based on a new kind of personhood" (Matthaei 1980, 325).[8]

When discussing the subsistence wage paid to male workers, Marx (1967) claims that the wage must be high enough to purchase the goods necessary to maintain and reproduce the working class. In this case, domestic work has no impact on capitalists' profits. But if it has no influence on profits, capitalists have no stake in the perpetuation of the patriarchal nuclear family.

Contemporary Marxists have modified this view by linking domestic work with the creation of surplus value (profits). Mariarosa Dalla Costa (1972) argues that the subsistence wage paid to married men does not fully compensate them for the full value of the necessary services women's domestic labor provides.[9] Sokoloff (1980) points out that capitalist exploitation of the family is most apparent when the husband's wages decline. Women and children reduce their consumption in order to maintain the wage earner and take over certain functions, such as care for the sick and elderly, in response to government cutbacks.

Left Feminist Views

While these modifications correct for the devaluation of domestic labor found in many earlier Marxist analyses, they are still inadequate from the standpoint of most feminists. First, all Marxist analyses assume that patriarchy persists only as long as it is in the interest of capitalists. Most feminists believe that patriarchy is an independent system that, while influenced by capitalism, is not controlled by capitalist needs. Feminists agree that it is men rather than capitalists who are the principal beneficiaries of patriarchy and that these benefits are both material and ideological.

Second, feminists reject the belief of Marx and Engels that capitalism weakens rather than strengthens patriarchy in working-class households. These feminists contend that the development of capitalism strengthened patriarchy. Moreover, feminists believe that the evolution of capitalism will not undermine patriarchy, since capitalists also benefit from its continuation.

These critics claim that a true merging of feminism and Marxism can occur only if patriarchy is considered a system maintained by men, who are the main beneficiaries, and if capitalism is thought to have intensified patriarchy in addition to benefiting from it. This is the perspective that unites those women who I identify as left feminists.[10]

Left feminists contend that patriarchy is not dependent on capitalist profitability and that it thrived long before private property arose. Gayle Rubin (1975) notes that the abuses women must endure in a range of societies have nothing to do with material wealth. Zillah Eisenstein (1979) concludes that patriarchy arose when men chose particular ideological and political interpretations of biological differences.[11] Well before commercial relationships developed, most societies became patrilocal, with the power and privilege gravitating to males.

In these societies, Chevillard and Leconte (1986) emphasize, almost all the productive work was performed by women. Men were idle, occupying most of their time with leisure activities. Louise Michel's (1981) observation of Kanakan men illustrates this point. While in a penal colony in New Caledonia during the 1870s, she wrote,

> I saw warriors loading their women as if they were mules . . . but if the gorges and mountains closed up and hid them from view, or if the path were deserted, then the warrior, moved by pity, would unload some of the burden from his human mule and carry it himself. . . . But if a shadow appeared on the horizon—even if only a cow or a horse—quickly the load went back on the woman's back (p. 140).

Gayle Rubin (1975), citing the work of Levi-Strauss, emphasizes that patriarchy allowed men to develop kinship systems in which women could be traded to facilitate alliances, extend male bonding, and engage in reciprocity. Thus for Rubin, the "traffic in women" is crucial to the cultures upon which virtually all societies are sustained. While aware that these cultural patterns did have some material basis,[12] she concludes, "The economic oppression of women is derivative and secondary" (p. 177).

In contrast to Marx and Engels, left feminists contend that capitalism increases the oppression of working-class women. This thesis is presented by Dorothy Smith (1987) in her description of the North American farm family. She characterizes the initial homestead household as one of relative equality of the sexes. This all changed once capitalist forces became more developed, forcing farmers to emphasize cash crops sold in highly competitive markets. Owing to their small scale and undercapitalization, these farmers were always on the brink of bankruptcy. In this context, Smith writes,

> [W]omen's labor is substituted for hired labor in working the land and in the production of subsistence for the family. . . . Increased inputs of her labor [compensate for] the lack of money at every possible point in the enterprise. Her time and energy, indeed her life, are treated as inexhaustible. She must, in addition, bear children because their labor is also essential. Women were virtually *imported* into Canada in this period to serve these functions (p. 29).[13]

Sarah Deutsch (1987) also found that capitalist development intensifies the oppression of women. Until the 1880s, Chicano society was based on subsistence farming supplemented by a modest amount of external trade. While there was sexual division of labor, both men and women were engaged in social production: Men raised grain and livestock, while women raised produce and cash items such as chilies and eggs. While men made adobes and built basic structures, women did all the plastering and built adobe ovens and fireplaces. Within the community, women had property rights and authority equal to men.

All this changed when these families were forced to migrate to permanent jobs in Colorado. This migration destroyed the independent production of Chicano women, as well as their community network and status. Deutsch concludes,

> Increasingly at the center of village life, Hispanic women found the move north anything but liberating. Both men and women settling permanently in the Anglo north suffered from narrow opportunities, but . . . women found that their activities declined in significance relative to men's. . . . In a sense, this development was an Americanization of gender roles. It echoed the experiences of U.S. women during nineteenth century industrialization as well as those of immigrant groups at the turn of the century. Areas of female authority, such as food production, nonwage work, and kin and community affairs—for Chicanas became as they were in Anglo society, increasingly peripheral to the main concerns of subsistence in a centralized, male-dominated and cash economy (p. 737).[14]

Not only do left feminists believe that capitalism intensifes inequalities, but unlike Marx and Engels, most believe that "a strong and healthy partnership exists between patriarchy and capitalism" (Hartmann 1981, 19). Hartmann contends that the material base of patriarchy is not primarily capitalist benefits but men's control over women's labor power. She enumerates these benefits to men: excluding women from the best jobs, receiving personal service work from women, not having to do housework or rear children, and having access to women's bodies for sex.

For a strong bond to exist, capitalists must choose to maintain the patriarchal nuclear family. Left feminists offer a number of ways capitalists are served by the nuclear family. First, it is argued that the nuclear family reduces labor militancy (Barrett 1980). Having a family to support, husbands are pressured into remaining docile politically. Also, capitalist ideology encourages the working class to see the development of a stable nuclear family as a measure of success. As a result, many workers focus on the impact of class conflict on their nuclear family rather than on workers as a group. Thus, class solidarity and working-class militancy are weakened.[15]

Second, left feminists contend that the family offsets the alienating nature of market labor, which also reduces the conflict between workers and the production process. Barrett (1980) suggests that the anger men may feel from failure in the business world is deflected by their compensation from "ruling in the family" (p. 192). Indeed, feminists have often argued that the construct of femininity—women making themselves sexually appealing to their husbands—has been endorsed primarily because it provides a relief to husbands from the alienation and conflicts experienced in the labor process.

Third, many left feminists emphasize that the family serves capitalism by increasing consumer spending. For some Marxists, the possibility of underconsumption—that is, not enough demand to purchase capitalist production—has become the major difficulty capitalists face. Adopting this position, Baxandall, Ewen, and Gordon (1976) contend that the nuclear family has enabled capitalism to create a fine-tuned consumer who is capable of reducing problems of underconsumption.

Left feminists do not believe that women have been liberated by modern household appliances. According to Rothschild (1983), "Household technology has aided a capitalist-patriarchal political order to reinforce the gender divisions of labor and to lock women more firmly into their traditional roles in the home" (p. 79). She believes that home technology has not reduced domestic labor but has shifted it to shopping and transportation activities, which reflect an increased emphasis on consumer spending. Barrett (1980) identifies two links between increased consumer spending and the nuclear family: A nuclear family requires each household to own its own consumer goods, while the time required to purchase and utilize many items effectively "may depend upon the fulltime housewife" (p. 221).[16]

Fourth, left feminists believe that patriarchal attitudes enable capitalists to exploit those women who enter the labor force. By generating the impression that women do not support families, capitalists justify paying low wages to all women workers. No wonder Louise Michel (1981) considers working women's wages to be "a snare because they are so meager that they are illusory" (p. 141). She says that many women do not work because they would "rather die of hunger, living in a cave, than do a job which gives them back less than enough to live on and which enriches the entrepreneur at the same time" (p. 141).

Fifth, many left feminists (see, for example, Bentson 1969; Mitchell 1971; Beechey 1978) consider married women especially useful to capitalists as a reserve army. Beechey contends that firms anticipating variable production can more easily rationalize layoffs if they hire married women on a temporary basis.[17] She also believes that the docility of married women reduces their ability to unionize, which in turn makes it easier for firms to lay them off during periods of slack demand. In addition, when married women are laid off, they often resume full-time domestic responsibilities until jobs begin to expand. As a result, government unemployment statistics (and transfer payments) do not increase as quickly as when other workers experience unemployment.

Jane Humphries (1976) identifies a final way in which patriarchal attitudes are useful to capitalists. During the Great Depression, the U.S. bourgeoisie was partially able to divert working-class anger by convincing some that married women were responsible for unemployment. Humphries cites articles in magazines and statements by national leaders claiming that married women were working for pin money while depriving male bread-winners of jobs.

Not surprisingly, during the 1930s many workers demanded that married women be fired rather than fighting for more jobs for all workers. Legislation was passed requiring the government, when undertaking layoffs, to fire married women with working husbands first. Huckle (1982) documents the enforcement of this legislation on schoolteachers. Humphries (1976) notes that these policies not only weakened a united effort to combat the lack of jobs but resulted in women accepting an increasing burden of the Depression.

Critical Evaluation of Left Feminist Views

The previous section depicted the left feminist viewpoint. This position has much in common with the neo-Marxist views presented in chapter 4. Both viewpoints criticize traditional Marxist theories for exaggerating the influence of capitalists. For both neo-Marxists and left feminists, white male workers play the decisive role. Just as Baron (1975) emphasizes how white workers benefit from racism by having a group below them, left feminists emphasize how patriarchy enables working-class men to have power over women. Just as Bonacich (1976) suggests that white workers use racism to monopolize the higher-paying jobs, left feminists contend that men use patriarchy to obtain these jobs.

Both the neo-Marxist and the left feminist viewpoints minimize differences within oppressed groups, reducing the relevance of a Marxist class analysis. In contrast, traditional Marxists believe that left feminists analyze incorrectly the impact of patriarchy on capitalists, the ability of men to enforce patriarchy, and the conflict between bourgeois and working-class women.[18]

Benefits to Capitalists

Left feminists have identified a number of ways in which capitalists appear to benefit from the nuclear family. At closer inspection, some of these claims are questionable. For example, neither Barrett (1980) nor Milkman (1976) believes that married women function as a reserve army. Milkman points out that women are primarily in sex-segregated occupations. Thus, only in female-dominated occupations do firms have the ability to lay off married workers first. Barrett stresses how patriarchal attitudes undermine the ability of capitalists to use married women as a threat to working males. Thus, even when occupational segregation does not preclude the use of married women, cultural constraints limit capitalists.

In chapter 8, we found that the supply of female workers influences the wages paid to all workers in secondary labor markets. By restricting the labor force participation of married women, patriarchy may cause wages in secondary labor markets to rise. We also found that women in male-dominated primary labor markets receive inferior wages and working conditions. Thus, to the extent patriarchy restricts female entrants into these occupations, wages in primary labor markets also are raised. Finally, patriarchal attitudes strengthen the struggle by male workers for a family wage, further increasing labor costs.

Many left feminists respond that even if some individual capitalists did suffer short-term losses as a result of patriarchy, the nuclear family would be maintained because it serves the long-term interests of the capitalist class as a whole. In chapter 4, two important examples of this willingness of capitalists to accept system-reinforcing reforms were cited. Some neo-Marxists cite the willingness of the largest companies to accommodate unionism. Presenting a similar line of argument, Baran and Sweezy (1965) claim that the elite Kennedy administration was quite willing to reduce labor market discrimination against black workers, as short-run production cost increases would be more than offset by the strengthening of U.S. corporate long-term interests in Third World countries. Similarly, left feminists contend that whatever short-term costs some firms absorb, the family wage increases the long-term stability of capitalism. They contend that as a result of patriarchy, both male and female workers are less militant, less class conscious, and hence less antagonistic toward the capitalist system.

Reforms become even less costly if we accept the Baran and Sweezy thesis that deficient demand (underconsumption) rather than rising costs is the major contradiction capitalists face. In this case, reforms that put more funds in the hands of the working class can restore profits. From this perspective, capitalists favor paying only male workers more so that the ideological benefits from patriarchy can be maintained.

Traditional Marxists have always criticized the monopoly capitalist thesis that underconsumption rather than rising labor costs is the main threat to profit rates.[19] Martin Feldstein and Lawrence Summers (1977) estimate that between 1965 and 1973, the rate of profit declined from 13.7 percent to 6.3 percent. In response, capitalists did not seek ways to increase spending but instead sought to lower labor costs by undermining unions and intensifying racism.[20] In addition, traditional Marxists contend that the falling rate of profit forced capitalists to seek out a cheaper source of labor—married women. To facilitate their entry into the labor market, capitalists chose expansion of part-time labor rather than provision of day-care facilities. Moreover, once large numbers of women entered the labor force, capitalists were able to limit wage increases to men. This occurred not because capitalists threatened men with being replaced by lower-paid female workers but because firms were no longer bound by family wage requirements. This facilitated lowering wages and generating new male jobs with lower pay scales, which resulted in a growing number of male heads of household who no longer earned even a living wage.[21]

Ann Ferguson and Nancy Folbre (1981) indicate additional reasons why capitalism has grown increasingly antagonistic toward the patriarchal family. When raising a large number of children, women remained outside the labor force for most of their adult lives. With eight pregnancies common during the nineteenth century, women often had to spend close to twenty years outside the labor force. Given life expectancies, this meant that there was little to be gained by encouraging female entry into the labor force when their child-rearing days were over. This has changed dramatically, however, now that many women have only two children and life expectancies have increased. In this case, the primary function of the full-time housewife has shifted to serving her husband rather than the interests of capitalism. As a result, patriarchy has lost its value to capitalists, as the benefits of child-rearing activities no longer offset the higher costs resulting from reduced female labor supplies.[22]

The Enforcement of Patriarchy

Traditional Marxists suggest that left feminists have not clearly specified how working-class men enforce patriarchy. Since working-class men have little property, left feminists infer that control over the paycheck has enabled them to enforce patriarchy. With the increasing ability of women to obtain market employment, welfare transfers, and divorces, it has become less likely that the husband's paycheck will enforce patriarchy.[23] In response, some left feminists (see, for example, Brown 1981) now identify the state as the primary enforcer of patriarchy.

Traditional Marxists find a number of problems with Brown's formulation of public patriarchy. First, Marxists contend that the state is run by capitalists, while public patriarchy implies that it is run by men. Second, it appears that the government has legislated many rulings that free women from patriarchy. Summarizing the impact of U.S. courts on women through 1945, Eileen Boris and Peter Bardaglio (1987) write, "If at first the courts reinforced the status quo . . . they gradually began to promote the rights of individual family members at the expense of the patriarchal father" (p. 132). Since World War II, changes in divorce laws, abortion laws, maternity leave policies, welfare regulations, and pending child-support legislation have tended to increase the freedom of women and their access to financial support.

Patricia Huckle (1982) envisions the possibility that women will be able to collect disability income while on maternity leave. Looking favorably upon the resources provided by the federal welfare state, Frances Fox Piven (1987) concludes that "the state is turning out to be the main recourse of women" (p. 514). Thus, even many feminists believe that the state has weakened rather than enforced patriarchy.

Radical feminists offer a differ explanation. For them, men, not the state, are still the primary enforcers of patriarchy. Radical feminists believe that men obtain services from women in the home, in nonmarriage personal relations, and in the workplace as a result of physical intimidation—the threat of rape.[24] Some radical feminists suggest that with the declining ability of men to use their financial power to coerce women, violence has become more important. Consistent with this thesis, Jacqueline Hall (1983) notes that there was a 49 percent increase in the incident of rape between 1969 and 1974. The continuing high level of physical abuse in the home and sexual harassment at work also is consistent with this hypothesis (MacKinnon 1979).

That women sometimes perceive marriage as a refuge from physical assault is exemplified by the history of black women in the post–Civil War South. As Barbara Omolade (1983) notes, during slavery the concept of the white man's unconstrained rights to a black woman's body was buttressed by two notions: It avoided the horrors of prostitution and increased the slave population.[25]

With emancipation, the upsurge of rape and other sexual atrocities endured by black women strengthened their commitment to the nuclear family. Hall (1983) writes,

> After the Civil War, the informal sexual arrangements of slavery shaded into the use of rape as a political weapon, and the special vulnerability of black women helped shape the ex-slaves' struggle for the prerequisites of freedom. Strong family bonds had survived the adversities of slavery; after freedom, the black family served as a bulwark against a racist society (p. 332).

Traditional Marxists suggest that the reasons for this increased violence against women are complex. Ehrenreich (1981) suggests that the upsurge in male violence reflects the media's attempt to pervert the feminist message into the threatening image of the sexually and economically liberated woman. Hall (1983) contends that it has more do with the fear and rage working-class men develop when confronted with growing economic uncertainty and weakening community institutions. Thus, increased male violence against women may not be the result of their desire to maintain benefits from patriarchal relations but a manipulation of their anxieties and hostilities. Traditional Marxists hope that these antagonisms can be redirected toward their source—the capitalist economy—which is generating increasingly lower standards of living and further fragmentation of people's lives.

Disunity among Women

Feminists believe that working-class women have more in common with upper-income (professional) women than they do with working-class men. In contrast, traditional Marxists perceive a much more complex situation. Jane Humphries (1977) found that many working-class women considered the struggle for the family wage in their interest. Once husbands earned a reasonable living, it often allowed wives to remain at home, where the supplemental income from home production would be sufficient for the family to attain an acceptable material standard of living. While feminists emphasize images of women being relegated to "alienating janitorial services" or seeking "ecstatic love" (Gordon 1976, 360), for most of the pre-World War II period, women remained at home for child-rearing purposes. Rather than being alienated, women found their nurturing function meaningful and rewarding. In contrast, working-class men had not only alienating, but often oppressive, jobs with little family interaction possible.

Feminists cite studies indicating that men appropriate the largest share of discretionary income to buttress claims of patriarchy (see Oren 1973). George Stigler's (1946) study of household expenditures on domestic servants conflicts with this view. As income rose, Stigler found, households dramatically increased their expenditures on domestic servants; this was especially true for working-class households.[26] Thus, in conflict with feminist claims, domestic help to ease the wife's burden was a priority expenditure in working-class households.

Time studies summarized by Bergmann (1986) indicate that between 1967 and 1976, husbands increased their time spent on domestic work only from eleven to twelve hours per week.[27] Feminists often cite this as evidence of the continuation of patriarchy despite the entrance of women into the work force. More relevant would be a comparison of the total hours spent by both men and women on work and domestic chores.

Bergmann tabulated survey data for households in which husbands averaged more than thirty hours per week of paid employment. Table 9–1 indicates that for households in which women were not full-time workers, men spent substantially more time at work than women. Even among households in which wives had substantial paid employment, husbands totaled more work hours. These findings are consistent with Humphries's (1977) position that for many women, the family wage was in their interest.

Table 9–1
Paid and Unpaid Labor Effort by Husbands and Wives in a Sample of American Married Couples, 1975–1976
(hours per week)

Wife's Paid Employment	Paid Employment*		Housework†		Other Family Work‡		All Work	
	Husband	Wife	Husband	Wife	Husband	Wife	Husband	Wife
Less than 5 (n = 128)	51.0	0.1	4.0	31.6	8.2	17.6	63.2	49.3
5–30 (n = 59)	51.1	18.9	4.7	23.8	8.3	13.0	64.1	55.6
More than 30 (n = 103)	50.5	38.0	4.9	15.6	7.8	8.6	63.2	62.2
Total (n = 290)	50.9	17.4	4.4	24.3	8.0	13.5	63.4	55.1

Sources: *American Use of Time, 1975–76* (Ann Arbor, MI: Survey Research Center) as tabulated by Bergmann 1986 (p. 263).
*Including commuting time.
†Including meal preparation and cleanup, indoor and outdoor cleaning, laundry, and everyday shopping.
‡Including other shopping, child care, baby-sitting, travel with children, medical care, gardening, pet care, household repairs, other services, and associated travel.

Feminists respond that these studies understate women's work. Whereas men have free leisure time, women must continue to provide men with the emotional support they expect and guarantee the interaction children desire. As a result, women are always on call, making quantitative measures inadequate and biased.

Since World War II, there has been a dramatic decline in availability of domestic servants. In 1900 there were ninety-five domestic servants per one thousand women. This declined to fifty-five in 1930 and thirty-three in 1960. Thus, unlike previous generations, post–World War II middle-class women were less able to use servants to ease family domestic labor conflicts.[28] While the servant crisis may have increased marital conflicts, it has implications for the relationships among women. By purchasing household services, wealthier women can escape oppressive marriages. Cheap service help also enables them to have expanded employment possibilities. Just as many careers require men to have an accommodating wife, many women now require paid service help to pursue careers. As a result, there is a conflict between wealthier and poorer women, as the wage demands of poorer women are a threat to the quality of life of upper-income women.

Bonnie Dill (1983) and Evelyn Glenn (1985) highlight this conflict as it relates to black women. Dill rejects suggestions that sisterhood is all-inclusive. She claims that the lack of a common experience has led the feminist movement to support racist positions. Glenn points out that in the early industrial period, "[t]he labor of black and immigrant servants made possible the women belle ideal for white middle class women. Even where white immigrant domestics were employed, the dirtiest and most arduous tasks, laundering and heavy cleaning—were often assigned to black servants" (p. 104).

Glenn then proceeds to apply a split labor market analysis to the relationship of black and white working-class women. She writes,

> Within female-typed reproductive work, there is further stratification by race. Racial ethnic women perform the more menial, less desirable tasks. They prepare and serve food, clean rooms and change bed pans, while white women, employed as semi-professionals and white collar workers, perform the more skilled and administrative tasks. The stratification is visible in hospitals, where whites predominate among registered nurses, while the majority of health aides and housekeeping staff are black and latinas. . . . [In general,] white women professionals enjoy more desirable working conditions because racial ethnic women perform the less desirable service tasks. . . . [As a result,] white women have gained an advantage from the exploitation of racial ethnic women (p. 104).

Thus, Glenn suggests, even working-class white women have benefited from the oppression of black women. This underlies claims that there should be a separate black feminist movement.

Conclusions

This chapter began by enumerating the reasons why most feminists believe it is inadequate to analyze the labor market without a systematic analysis of the family. Without such an analysis, issues of sexual harassment, home production, marriage decisions, and female labor market behavior will be ignored or distorted.

Next, liberal and Marxist assessments of the rise of the nuclear family during the capitalist era were detailed. Liberals believe that the nuclear family enhances risk taking and spatial mobility, allowing greater economic gains for individuals. Also, the nuclear family reduces intrahousehold conflicts and fosters more specialized social relationships. Marxists believe that capitalism leads to increased patriarchal oppression of bourgeois women, but they also believe that capitalism will undermine patriarchy in working-class households.

We found that left feminists reject important aspects of the traditional Marxist analysis. First, left feminists believe that capitalism intensifies the oppression of working-class women. Second, they reject the Marxist notion that capitalists are indifferent to patriarchy. For left feminists, there is a strong alliance between elite and working-class men in defense of patriarchy. Left feminists enumerate the ways in which capitalists benefit from patriarchy:

1. It reduces the militancy of working-class men.
2. It diverts the exploitation and alienation working-class men experience.
3. It stimulates consumerism, which offsets underconsumption problems.
4. It enables capitalists to exploit working-class women.
5. It lowers the economic and political costs of economic downturns.

Traditional Marxists believe that left feminists overstate the benefits of patriarchy to working-class men, mistake the ways capitalists are affected by patriarchy, do not specify clearly enough the method of enforcement of patriarchy, and minimize the conflicts between working-class and bourgeois women. In particular, traditional Marxists believe that when capitalists were confronted with a falling rate of profit in the 1970s, they chose to undermine patriarchy by bringing married women into the labor force and using the courts and government to facilitate this process. Traditional Marxists also point out that once domestic workers are incorporated into the analysis, it is difficult to maintain an all-inclusive feminist perspective.

Traditional Marxists find the same weaknesses in the left feminist theories as they find in other neo-Marxist theories. Whereas neo-Marxist theories postulate that capitalists will often accommodate reforms that raise labor costs, traditional Marxists believe that reducing labor costs dominates capitalist decisions. Thus, traditional Marxists reject notions that capitalists support patriarchy because it enhances long-term political stability or solves problems of underconsumption. As long as patriarchy raises labor costs to individual firms, traditional Marxists believe, capitalists will undermine it. Whereas these neo-Marxist theories imply further fragmentation of movements against capitalism, even justifying a split between working-class black and working-class white women, the traditional Marxist view again emphasizes the benefits of the unity of all working-class elements.

Notes

1. This chapter does not present radical feminist views in a systematic manner. For a summary of this viewpoint, see Shulamith Firestone (1970) and Hester Eisenstein (1983). For criticisms of the radical feminist viewpoint, see Michele Barrett (1980, 195–98) and Zillah Eisenstein (1979, 18–22).

2. For examples of this type of feminism, see Bergmann (1983).

3. Berger (1977) and Johnson (1980) found that up to 90 percent of rapes go unreported, 50 percent of assailants who are reported are never caught, and 70 percent of all prosecutions end up with acquittals.

4. See Kingson (1988) for details of how the continued belief that women should have primary responsibility for child rearing has resulted in women being relegated to a lower track within the most prestigious law firms.

5. See Edwards and Lloyd-Jones (1973) for a discussion of how the early development of commerce began to change the basis of kinship relationships.

6. For detailed data on the incidence of home boarding among Irish and Puerto Rican immigrant households, see Groneman (1977) and Sanchez-Korrol (1979) respectively.

7. Linda Lim (1983) takes this position when assessing the impact of multinational corporations on patriarchy in Third World countries. She finds that the multinational manufacturing enterprises set up in Third World countries primarily employ women who are liberated from family patriarchy. She writes, "[T]he availability of jobs in multinational and local export factories allows women to leave the confines of the home, delay marriage and childbearing, increase their incomes and consumption levels, improve mobility, and expand personal independence" (p. 83).

8. This reflects the delayed-androgyny thesis (Hunt and Hunt 1987).

9. It would be inappropriate to associate this necessary domestic labor only with wives. In many households, this labor also is provided by sisters, aunts, mothers, daughters, and so on.

10. Distinctions between the traditional Marxist, Marxist feminist, and socialist feminist viewpoints are somewhat arbitrary. For example, Sokoloff (1980) considers those who modified Marx as "early" Marxist feminists and those who support the three criticisms noted as "later" Marxist feminists. Also, Hartmann's (1981) conception of Marxist feminism and Zillah Eisenstein's (1979) conception of socialist feminism are quite similar. More recently, Marxist feminists have broadened their differences with socialist feminists, while narrowing their differences with traditional Marxists. Rather than detailing these shifting positions, I have chosen to use the term

left feminist and present the views held by socialist feminists and most Marxist feminists.

11. Other feminists, including Juliet Mitchell (1974) add that patriarchy has a psychological basis rooted in the Oedipus complex.

12. Polygamy was favored because it allowed a man to increase his wealth by having more workers. Female children were favored because they had value, since fathers received bridewealth when selling them into marriage.

13. This description emphasizes how competitive pressures within capitalism intensify discriminatory practices. Recall from chapter 4 that the cottage industry, under intense pressure from the technologically advanced factory system, increasingly resorted to the use of superexploited child and female labor.

14. Strobel (1982) suggests that capitalist penetration of African agricultural markets reduced female access to the land, while commercialization of cloth production undercut previous female domestic production.

15. It can be argued that this ideology has encouraged an indifference on the part of more fortunate workers to the plight of victims of recent disruptions in the economy. Among these victims are the homeless, the poor, family farmers, and displaced industrial workers. This indifference has made it easier for the federal government to avoid aiding these groups.

16. Feminists also point to the multibillion-dollar cosmetics and weight-loss industries, which thrive as a result of patriarchal attitudes emphasizing the beauty requirements to which women must aspire.

17. Recall in chapter 8 that conservatives, including Feldstein (1973), believe that married women desire these layoffs and impose their preferences on employers.

18. Marxist feminists do not agree with some of the points presented in the previous section. As a result, this section uses the views of individual Marxist feminists to criticize specific aspects of the left feminist viewpoint.

19. Marx (1967) thought that automation might momentarily neutralize the impact of rising labor costs on profits. However, automation, by raising the organic composition of capital—that is, the capital–output ratio—tends to lower the profit rate as well. For a discussion of various Marxist theories of the falling profit rate, see Cherry, et al. (1987).

20. For details of these attacks, see Cherry et al. (1988), especially the chapters by David Gordon and Sam Rosenberg.

21. Recall that table 7–4 indicated that between 1979 and 1984, the percentage of male household heads earning less than $204 a week rose from 14.4 percent to 21.1 percent.

22. Left feminists respond that capitalism generates a hierarchy and inequality. As a result, the elite fear that creating equalitarian relationships within the family might undermine the legitimacy of inequalities within the workplace.

23. See Sorensen and McLanahan (1987) for measures of the decline in the income dependency of married women from 1940 to 1980.

24. Johnson (1980) estimates that, at a minimum, 20 to 30 percent of girls now twelve years old will suffer a violent attack sometime in their lives.

25. Jacqueline Jones (1982) documents the brutal treatment of black women as workers. Black women predominated in field labor, while at least some black men

were allowed to learn skilled jobs. She notes, "[I]n the 1850s at least 90 percent of all female slaves over sixteen years of age labored more than 261 days per year, eleven to thirteen hours each day" (p. 243).

26. Stigler (1946) estimates that the income elasticity of demand for domestic servants was +2 for upper-middle-class households and +4 for lower-middle-class households.

27. During this period, domestic work fell from fifty-seven to forty-eight hours per week for nonworking wives and from thirty-four to twenty-three hours per week for full-time working wives.

28. Reflecting the situation in Third World countries, Beneria and Sen (1982) write, "Domestic service reduces gender tensions among the upper classes, at the expense of the double oppression of the female domestic servants" (p. 170).

References

Baran, Paul, and Paul Sweezy. 1965. *Monopoly Capital.* New York: Monthly Review Press.

Baron, Harold. 1975. "Racial Domination in Advanced Capitalism: A Theory of Nationalism and Divisions in the Labor Market." In *Labor Market Segmentation,* ed. Richard Edwards, Michael Reich, and David Gordon. Lexington, MA: D.C. Heath, 173–216.

Barrett, Michele. 1980. *Women's Oppression Today: Problems in Marxist Feminist Analysis.* London: Verso.

Baxandall, Rosalyn, Elizabeth Ewen, and Linda Gordon. 1976. "The Working Class Has Two Sexes." *Monthly Review* 28:1–9.

Beechey, Veronica. 1978. "Women and Production: A Critical Analysis of Some Sociological Theories of Women's Work." In *Feminism and Materialism: Women and Modes of Production,* ed. Annette Kuhn and AnnMarie Wolpe. London: Routledge and Kegan Paul, 155–97.

Beneria, Lourdes, and Gita Sen. 1982. "Class and Gender Inequalities and Women's Role in Economic Development." *Feminist Studies* 8:157–75.

Bentson Margaret. 1969. "The Political Economy of Women's Liberation." *Monthly Review* 21:13–27.

Berger, Vivian. 1977. "Man's Trial, Women's Tribulation: Rape Cases in the Courtroom." *Columbia Law Review* 1:3–12.

Bergmann, Barbara. 1983. "Feminism and Economics." *Academe* 14:22–25.

———. 1986. *The Economic Emergence of Women.* New York: Basic Books.

Bonacich, Edna. 1976. "Advanced Capitalism and Black/White Relations in the United States: A Split Labor Market Interpretation." *American Sociological Review* 41:34–51.

Boris, Eileen, and Peter Bardaglio. 1987. "Gender, Race, and Class: The Impact of the State on the Family and the Economy, 1790–1945." In *Families and Work,* ed. Naomi Gerstel and Harriet Engel Gross. Philadelphia: Temple University Press, 132–51.

Brown, Carol. 1981. "Mothers, Fathers, and Children: From Private to Public Patriarchy." In *Women and Revolution,* ed. Lydia Sargent. Boston: South End Press, 239–68.

Cherry, Robert, et al. 1987. *The Imperiled Economy: Macroeconomics from a Left Perspective.* New York: Union for Radical Political Economics.

———. 1988. *The Imperiled Economy: Through the Safety Net.* New York: Union for Radical Political Economies.

Chevillard, Nicole, and Sebastien Leconte. 1986. "The Dawn Lineage Societies: The Origins of Women's Oppression." In *Women's Work, Men's Property: The Origins of Gender and Class,* ed. Stephanie Coontz and Peta Henderson. London: Verso, 76–107.

Dalla Costa, Mariarosa. 1972. "Women and the Subversion of Community." In *The Power of Women and the Subversion of the Community,* ed. Mariarosa Dalla Costa and Selma James. Bristol, England: Falling Wall Press, 1–58.

Deutsch, Sarah. 1987. "Women and Intercultural Relations: The Case of Hispanic New Mexico and Colorado." *Signs* 12:719–39.

Dill, Bonnie. 1983. "Race, Class, and Gender: Prospects for an All-Inclusive Sisterhood." *Feminist Studies* 9:131–50.

Edwards, MM., and R. Lloyd-Jones. 1973. "N.J. Smelser and the Cotton Factory Family: A Reassessment." In *Textile History and Economic History: Essays in Honour of Miss Julia de Lacy Mann,* ed. N.B. Harte and K.G. Ponting. Manchester, England: University of Manchester Press, 304–19.

Ehrenreich, Barbara. 1981. "The Women's Movement: Feminists and Antifeminists." *Radical America* 15:93–101.

———. 1983. *Hearts of Men.* New York: Doubleday.

Eisenstein, Hester. 1983. *Contemporary Feminist Thought.* Boston: G.K. Hall and Company.

Eisenstein, Zillah. 1979. "Developing a Theory of Capitalist Patriarchy and Socialist Feminism." In *Capitalist Patriarchy and the Case for Socialist Feminism.* ed. Zillah Eisenstein. New York: Monthly Review Press, 5–40.

Engels, Frederick. 1972. "The Origins of the Family, Private Property, and the State." In *Selected Works,* ed. Karl Marx and Frederick Engels. London: Lawrence and Wishart, 455–593.

Feldstein, Martin. 1973. "The Economics of the New Unemployment." *The Public Interest* 33:1–21.

Feldstein, Martin, and Lawrence Summers. 1977. "Is There a Falling Rate of Profit?" *Brookings Papers* 1:211–27.

Ferguson, Ann, and Nancy Folbre. 1981. "The Unhappy Marriage of Patriarchy and Capitalism." In *Women and Revolution,* ed. Lydia Sargent. Boston: South End Press, 313–38.

Firestone, Shulamith. 1970. *The Dialectic of Sex: The Case for Feminist Revolution.* New York: William Morrow.

Galbraith, John Kenneth. 1973. *Economics and the Public Purpose.* Boston: Houghton Mifflin.

Glenn, Evelyn Nakano. 1985. "Racial Ethnic Women's Labor: The Intersection of Race, Gender, and Class Oppression." *Review of Radical Political Economics* 17:86–108.

Gordon, Linda. 1976. *Woman's Body, Woman's Right*. New York: Grossman Publishers.

Gough, Kathleen. 1975. "The Origins of the Family." In *Toward an Anthropology of Women*, ed. Rayna R. Reiter. New York: Monthly Review Press, 51–76.

Groneman, Carol. 1977. " 'She Earns as a Child; She Pays as a Man': Women Workers in a Mid-Nineteenth Century New York City Community." In *Class, Sex, and the Woman Worker*, ed. Milton Cantor and Bruce Laurie. Westport, CT: Greenwood Press, 83–100.

Hall, Jacqueline. 1983. " 'The Mind That Burns in Each Body': Women, Rape, and Racial Violence." In *Power of Desire: The Politics of Sexuality*, ed. Ann Snitow, et al. New York: Monthly Review Press, 328–49.

Hartmann, Heidi. 1981. "The Unhappy Marriage of Marxism and Feminism: Toward a More Progressive Union." In *Women and Revolution*, ed. Lydia Sargent. Boston: South End Press, 1–42.

Huckle, Patricia. 1982. "The Womb Factor: Pregnancy Policies and Employment of Women." In *Women, Power and Policy*, ed. Ellen Bonaparth. New York: Pergamon Press, 144–61.

Humphries, Jane. 1976. "Women: Scapegoats and Safety Valves in the Great Depression." *Review of Radical Political Economics* 8:98–121.

———. 1977. "Class Struggle and the Persistence of the Working Class Family." *Cambridge Journal of Economics* 1:241–58.

Hunt, Janet, and Larry Hunt. 1987. "Male Resistance to Role Symmetry in Dual-Earner Households: Three Alternative Explanations." In *Families and Work*, ed. Naomi Gerstel and Harriet Engel Gross. Philadelphia: Temple University Press, 192–203.

Johnson, Allan Griswold. 1980. "On the Prevalence of Rape in the United States." *Signs* 6:136–46.

Jones, Jacqueline. 1982. " 'My Mother Was Much of a Woman': Black Women, Work, and the Family Under Slavery." *Feminist Studies* 8:233–69.

Kelley-Gadol, Joan. 1976. "The Social Relation of the Sexes: Methodological Implications of Women's History." *Signs* 1:809–24.

Kessler-Harris, Alice. 1987. "The Debate Over Equality for Women in the Workplace." In *Families and Work*, ed. Naomi Gerstel and Harriet Engel Gross. Philadelphia: Temple University Press, 520–39.

Kingson, Jennifer. 1988. "Women in the Law Say Path Is Limited by 'Mommy Track.' " *New York Times*, 8 August #A1.

Lim, Linda. 1983. "Capitalism, Imperialism, and Patriarchy: The Dilemma of Third-World Women Workers in Multinational Factories." In *Women, Men, and the International Division of Labor*, ed. June Nash and Maria Fernandez-Kelly. Albany: State University of New York Press, 70–91.

MacKinnon, Catharine. 1979. *Sexual Harassment of Working Women*. New Haven, CT: Yale University Press.

Marx, Karl. 1967. *Capital*. Vol. 1. New York: International Publishers.

Matthaei, Julie. 1980. *An Economic History of Women in America*. New York: Schocken Books.

Michel, Louise. 1981. *The Red Virgin: Memoirs of Louise Michel*. Edited and translated by Bullitt Lowry and Elizabeth Ellington Gunter. University, AL: University of Alabama Press.

Milkman, Ruth. 1976. "Women's Work and Economic Crisis." *Review of Radical Political Economics* 8:69–97.

———. 1986. "Women's Work and the Economic Crisis: Some Lessons from the Great Depression." *Review of Radical Political Economics* 8:73–97.

Mitchell, Juliet. 1971. *Woman's Estate.* New York: Vintage Books.

———. 1974. *Psychoanalysis and Feminism.* New York: Pantheon Books.

Omolade, Barbara. 1983. "Hearts of Darkness." In *Power of Desire,* ed. Ann Snitow, et al. New York: Monthly Review Press, 350–66.

Oren, Laura. 1973. "The Welfare of Women in Laboring Families: England, 1860–1950." *Feminist Studies* 1:107–21.

Parsons, Talcott. 1954. *Essays in Social Theory.* New York: The Free Press.

Parsons, Talcott, and R.F. Bales. 1956. *Family: Socialization and Interaction Process.* London: Routledge and Kegan Paul.

Piven, Frances Fox. 1987. "Women and the State: Ideology, Power and the Welfare State." In *Families and Work,* ed. Naomi Gerstel and Harriet Engel Gross. Philadelphia: Temple University Press, 512–19.

Pleck, Elizabeth. 1976. "Two Worlds in One: Work and Family." *Journal of Social History* 10:178–95.

Rothschild, Joan. 1983. "Technology, Housework, and Women's Liberation: A Theoretical Analysis." In *Machina Ex Dea: Feminist Perspectives on Technology.* ed. Joan Rothschild. New York: Pergamon Press, 79–93.

Rubin, Gayle. 1975. "The Traffic in Women: Notes on the Political Economy of Sex." In *Toward an Anthropology of Women,* ed. Rayna R. Reiter. New York: Monthly Review Press, 157–210.

Sanchez-Korrol, Virginia. 1979. "On the Other Side of the Ocean: The Work Experience of Early Puerto Rican Migrant Women." *Caribbean Review* 8:22–28.

Smith, Dorothy. 1987. "Women's Inequality and the Family." In *Families and Work,* ed. Naomi Gerstel and Harriet Engel Gross. Philadelphia: Temple University Press, 23–54.

Sokoloff, Natalie. 1980. *Between Money and Love.* New York: Praeger.

Sorensen, Annemette, and Sara McLanahan. 1987. "Married Women's Economic Dependency, 1940–1980." *American Journal of Sociology* 93:659–87.

Stigler, George. 1946. "Domestic Servants in the United States, 1900–1940." Occasional Paper #24, National Bureau of Economic Research.

Strobel, Margaret. 1982. "African Women: Review Essay." *Signs* 8:109–31.

Wirth, Louis. 1956. *City Life and Social Policy.* Chicago: University of Chicago Press.

10
The Economic Success
of American Jewry

At the end of the nineteenth century, massive immigration to the United States from eastern and southern Europe began. Of all the ethnic groups that came, Jews seem to have been the most successful. Children of Jewish immigrants appear to have entered universities in large numbers, and others developed highly successful businesses. During the twentieth century, many Jews rose to national prominence by becoming entertainers, motion picture executives, Nobel Prize–winning scientists, and presidential advisors.

Today, economic data indicate that American Jews have higher median earnings than any other ethnic minority group in the United States. This comparative success appears to hold even after adjusting for age, education, and other factors. Since it is also widely accepted that Jews have historically been victims of persecution, their economic success has had an important impact on the debate among various viewpoints. In particular, conservatives believe that the economic success of Jews demonstrates that discrimination is not a significant impediment and that cultural attributes are much more important.

This chapter evaluates the conservative explanation for the differential success of Jewish immigrants. The first section presents the conservative view that the unique cultural values of Jews enabled them to overcome whatever discrimination they faced. The next section assesses the level of discrimination Jews experienced compared to other immigrant groups. We will find that most historical accounts indicate that the level of discrimination Jews experienced was much lower than that faced by other immigrant groups. This alone could explain the more rapid upward mobility of Jews.

The third section assesses the degree to which Jewish cultural traits are significantly different from those of other immigrant groups. We will find that conservative claims are inconsistent with the Jewish experience in Europe and even the experience of the first few generations of Jewish immigrants to the United States. This section presents some alternative explanations for the success of Jewish immigrants.

The final section contrasts small business activity in the Jewish and black communities. We will find that the disproportionately large number of Jewish owners has provided an important stepping-stone for Jews. In contrast, the share of small businesses owned by blacks is exceedingly small and does not aid black upward mobility. This section summarizes the theories developed to explain the low ownership rate among blacks.

Conservative Explanations of Jewish Success

By numerous measures, the income of Jews is substantially higher than the income of other ethnic groups. Census data provide no specific estimate for the income of Jewish households but only estimate incomes by country of national origin. However, Erich Rosenthal (1975) found that there was a strong correlation between incomes of households listed as having a Russian origin and incomes, estimated from other sources, of Jews. Using this approach, Jews appear to have a median income 30 percent higher than the national average. Using the National Jewish Population Survey, Thomas Sowell (1981) estimates that Jewish family income is 73 percent above the national average.

Not surprisingly, educational attainment data also show high Jewish achievement. In 1971 Massarik and Cherkin (1973) found that 36 percent of the adult Jewish population had graduated from college, as compared with 11 percent of non-Jews. Among those aged twenty-five to thirty-nine, 59 percent of Jews had graduated from college, as compared with 17 percent of non-Jews. Phillips (1986) estimates that in Los Angeles in 1980, Jewish adults were twice as likely as non-Jewish adults to be college graduates. These figures are more striking when only elite universities are considered. For example, David Riesman (1973) estimates that in 1973 Jews represented more than one-quarter of the student body and more than one-third of the faculty at Harvard.

Barry Chiswick (1983) found that education explains only part of the Jewish economic success. After correcting for educational and other factors, he estimates that second-generation Jewish men have 16 percent higher earnings than the national average. Moreover, he found that these Jewish men have a higher rate of return from education than the national average and a steeper experience–earnings profile than the national average. Chiswick believes that cultural traits explain these higher returns.

All conservatives contend that cultural differences are responsible for the rapid Jewish upward mobility. While most note that Jewish immigrants were more urbanized than other turn-of-the-century immigrants, conservatives generally focus on values thought to run deep in the Jewish community. Nathan Glazer (1955) believes that religious values emphasize "the traits that businessmen and intellectuals require" (pp. 31–32). Moreover, Glazer (1958) contends, "The strong emphasis on learning and study can be traced that far back, too. The habits of foresight, care, and moderation probably arose early during the two thousand years that Jews have lived primarily as strangers among other peoples" (p. 143).

Thomas Sowell (1981) also believes that Jews have a love of learning that transcends financial considerations. He says, "Russian-Jewish tenement [dwellers read] . . . Tolstoy, Dumas, and Dickens, not frothy best-sellers. . . . [Jewish] pushcart peddlers, butchers, grocers, and other occupations where book learning was of no economic value . . . went to all sorts of public lectures on topics far from relevant to their daily lives" (p. 86).

Sowell discounts the independent role of urbanization. First, he associates the Jewish cultural superiority with factors such as cleanliness, rejection of crime, and aversion to alcoholism, which should not distinguish individuals emigrating from urban environments from those emigrating from rural areas (Sowell 1981). Second, in his explanation for the lack of success of southern Italian immigrants, Sowell (1975) contends that long after they became urbanized, they still maintained anti-intellectual characteristics.

In general, Sowell considers family stability necessary for the transmission to children of the important values of work, thrift, and education. This is why Sowell believes that those cultures lacking a stable family, such as Irish immigrants and blacks, have attained success only in areas requiring emotion (not hard work or education), oratory, sports, or music (Sowell 1975).

According to Sowell (1981), the Jews' willingness to work long hours in sweatshops enabled unskilled illiterate Jewish immigrants to gain skills and an economic foothold. As for education, Sowell notes that the rate of graduation from either high school or college of children of Jewish immigrants was not very high. However, he believes that education "helped not only the few who went on to higher education but also those for whom eight years of schooling was a ticket to white-collar jobs at the time" (p. 84).

While Sowell believes that a stable family is necessary for the transmission of important values, he does not believe it is sufficient. Sowell contends that although the Italian community has very stable families, the persistence of rural values affects the businesses they own. According to Sowell (1975), Italian Americans enter "small businesses under the immediate direction of the owner and often in close touch with the local community, rather than businesses requiring a broader vision and a wide range of abstract skills" (p. 132).

In contrast, Sowell assumes that deeply held cultural values are responsible for the long tradition of broad business acumen within the Jewish community. In a telling discussion of the persistence of cultural inheritance, Sowell (1984) states, "[T]he reality of group patterns that transcends any given society cannot be denied. Jewish peddlers followed in the wake of the Roman legions and sold goods in the conquered territories. How surprising is it to find Jewish peddlers on the American frontier or on the sidewalks of

New York two thousand years later—or in many other places in between"
(pp. 28–29).

Anti-Semitism in
the United States

From most accounts, it appears that anti-Semitism was most intense during
the period 1877 to 1927, from the time Joseph Seligman was refused admittance to the Grand Hotel in Saratoga, New York, until Henry Ford publicly apologized for anti-Semitic articles in his *Dearborn Press*. Prior to this
period, there were examples of anti-Semitism, beginning with the reluctance
of Peter Stuyvesant to allow the first group of Jews to enter New York in
1654. Anti-Semitism also was part of the Know Nothing party's anti-
immigration campaign in the 1850s and General Grant's policies during the
Civil War. However, anti-Semitism became widespread only during the latter
part of the nineteenth century.

Oscar Handlin (1951) and Richard Hofstadter (1955) identify anti-
Semitism with the short-lived agrarian Populist movement of the 1890s.
They contend that the Populists associated traditional Jewish stereotypes
with the evils faced by the yeomanry. Increasingly forced into debt peonage,
the yeomanry demanded elimination of the gold standard. However, President Cleveland pursued a scheme with the Rothschild banking empire to
protect the gold standard. This led many Populists to attack Jews for what
they perceived as Jewish control of world finance. Also, the yeomanry often
divided society into those who engaged in productive labor and those who
did not. Typically, Jews in rural areas were identified with nonproductive
labor—that is, they were commercial and financial middlemen who gained
income from the work of others.

Other historians claim that early twentieth century anti-Semitism was
associated with xenophobic fears fueled by mass immigration. Later Jewish
immigrants tended to be poorer, less skilled, and less urbanized than the
Jews who had emigrated from Germany during the 1850s. They were considered a dangerous criminal element. In 1908 New York City's police commissioner Theodore Bingham suggested that half of all criminals were Jews.
The 1910 report of the Dillingham commission claimed that large numbers
of Jews scattered throughout the United States seduced and kept girls in
prostitution and that many were petty thieves, pickpockets, and gamblers.
The report stated, "Jews comprise the largest proportion of alien prisoners
under sentence for offenses against chastity" (Dobkowski 1979, 66).

During this era, Jews were not pictured simply as petty criminals. The
stereotypic Jewish businessman was one who manipulated laws and engaged
in white-collar crimes, especially insurance fraud. Dobkowski (1979, 59–

68) gives numerous examples of how these stereotypes became part of the popular culture. In describing a Jewish businessman, *Puck,* a popular New York City humor magazine, noted that "despite hard times, he has had two failures and three fires." It claimed, "There is only one thing [their] race hates more than pork—asbestos." (p. 64) So pervasive were these images that the Anti-Defamation League (ADL) in 1913 noted, "Whenever a theatre producer wishes to depict a betrayer of the public trust, a white slaver or other criminal, the actor is directed to present himself as a Jew." (p. 60) Indeed, for more than fifty years, *Roget's Thesaurus* included the word *Jew* as a synonym for usurer, cheat, extortioner, and schemer (McWilliams 1948, 90).

Some historians, including John Higham, believe that anti-Semitism was more significant among the elite than among either the rural yeomanry or middle-class xenophobic nativists. Higham (1966) notes that the patrician class, typified by Henry and Brooks Adams, realized that the industrialization process was transforming the United States into a materialistic, pragmatic society that had less concern for tradition and culture than previously. This transformation, which meant the end of patrician hegemony over political and economic affairs, was thought to be the result of Jewish influence.

According to Higham, the patrician class believed that Jewish commercial values undermined basic American traditions. While most became defeatist, some, including Henry Cabot Lodge and John J. Chapman, attempted to reduce Jewish influence. In 1896 Lodge proposed legislation requiring immigrants to be literate in the language of their country of origin rather than in another language. Since most Polish and Russian Jews were literate in Yiddish but not in Polish or Russian, this would have made them ineligible for immigration. Lodge's legislative proposal was defeated, and Jewish immigration continued. Chapman was an active urban reformer who did not have anti-Semitic values until the time of World War I. Dobkowski (1979) contends that his inability to reform urban society led him to agree with Henry Adams that the reason for urban decay was growing Jewish influence.

Dobkowski documents how progressive muckrakers, including George Kibbe Turner, Jacob Riis, and Emily Balch, echoed many of the charges against Jews made by the patrician class. Lamenting the decay of cities, Turner considered Jewish immigrants to be at the "core of this festering human cancer" (Dobkowski 1979, 65). Riis believed that the lack of social values among Jewish immigrants was overwhelming urban society. He thought that recent Jewish immigrants believed that "[M]oney is God. Life itself is of little value compared with even the leanest bank account" (p. 99–100). Even Balch, a leading defender of social welfare reforms, accepted negative Jewish stereotypes.

Liberal sociologist E.A. Ross (1972) believed that Jewish immigrants were cunning in their ability to use their wit to undermine business ethics and to commercialize professions and journalism. He claimed that attempts to exclude Jews from professional associations and social clubs had nothing to do with discrimination; instead they reflected a strong desire not to associate with individuals from an immoral culture. Tom Watson, a former Populist and later KKK leader, used Ross's writings to justify his organization's anti-Semitism.

These examples of anti-Semitic views sometimes provides the basis for contentions that Jews faced discrimination similar to that of other groups.[1] Thomas Sowell (1981) implies this when he states, "Anti-Semitism in the United States assumed growing and unprecedented proportions in the last quarter of the nineteenth century with the mass arrival of eastern European Jews. . . . [H]elp wanted ads began to specify 'Christian,' as they had once specified 'Protestant' to exclude the Irish" (p. 82).

This is an incorrect assessment. During the last quarter of the nineteenth century, the United States adopted a reservation program for American Indians, an exclusionary policy for Orientals, Jim Crow laws for blacks, and an anti-immigration movement to harass Italian and Polish newcomers. In contrast, before World War I, Jewish immigrants faced few anti-Semitic barriers to their advancement. For example, in 1910 it was estimated that only 0.3 percent of employment advertisements specified Christians and no colleges had adopted restrictive entrance policies (McWilliams 1948).

Only after World War I and the Bolshevik Revolution when xenophobic fears peaked did anti-Semitic restrictions become significant. Zosa Szakowski (1974) documents the vigorous attack on Jews during the anti-immigrant Palmer raids in 1919. In 1920, 10 percent of employment ads specified Christians, rising to 13.3 percent by 1926. Steinberg (1981) summarizes the restrictive entrance policies many prestigious universities, including Columbia and Harvard, adopted at that time to reduce Jewish enrollment.

At about this time, Henry Ford began publishing anti-Semitic tracts in his *Dearborn Press*. Like Ross, Ford was a Progressive. He supported Wilson, social legislation, antilynching laws, and urban reforms. Unlike Ross, Ford had nothing but praise for the ordinary Jewish businessman, and he could count Jews among his personal friends. However, Ford thought that industrialists were at the mercy of financial institutions controlled by international Jewry (Ribuffo 1978).[2]

Adopting a similar perspective, Robert La Follette introduced a petition to Congress in 1923 assigning responsibility for World War I to Jewish international bankers. This petition also asserted that Wilson, Lloyd George, Clemenceau, and Orlando—the officials in charge of negotiating the peace treaty at Versailles—were surrounded by Jewish advisors (Dobkowski 1979).

World's Work and other liberal publications also complained that Jews were not 100 percent American. They not only identified Jews with draft dodgers and war profiteers, but also complained that Jews, though taking advantage of the opportunities given by democracy, had not taken "the one essential act of a democratic society. . . . They are not willing to lose their identity" (Dobkowski 1979, 148). By the end of the decade, however, after immigration restriction laws had been passed and the anticommunist hysteria had subsided, anti-Semitism again subsided to a minimum level (see, for example, Stember 1966).

The Inadequacy of Internal Theories

Stephen Steinberg (1981) and others have pointed out that conservative claims that cultural values are the primary reason for Jewish success have, to a large extent, substituted cultural determinism for the genetic determinism of the social Darwinists.[3] In both case, ethnic differences are transmitted from one generation to the next without change. Unlike Myrdal (1944) and even the Progressives, the modern cultural determinist believes that institutions and policies will have little impact on the deeply held cultural values that result in the success of some groups (Jews) and the permanent lagging behind of others (Italians and blacks). For this reason, Steinberg has characterized those who advocate the cultural determinist view as the new social Darwinists. Thus, critics caution that we should not accept conservative claims without hard evidence, as they provide a very powerful rationale for a return to indifference to the plight of less fortunate ethnic groups.

Much of the conservative view is based on anecdotal evidence and stereotypic imagery rather than on detailed statistical testing. For example, Sowell (1981) accepts without evidence that Jewish families place more importance on education than do other cultures, yet he never explains why they entered the United States with, in his words, more "illiteracy than other immigrants" (p. 93).

We are told that a thirst for education explains Jewish success but find that higher educational attainment belongs to the second generation after initial economic success occurred. Sowell is then left to claim that this desire for education is reflected in the relatively large percentage of first-generation Jews who completed eight years of schooling. However, turn-of-the-century evidence seems to indicate that even the attainment of an eighth-grade education was not an objective fulfilled by the majority of first-generation Jewish immigrants. For example, in New York City, Selma Berrol (1976) found that in 1908 there were 25,534 Jewish students in the first grade but only 11,527 in the seventh and 2,549 in the ninth. This indicates that even for the group of Jewish children who had entered the school system, more than half dropped out by the end of the sixth grade. Moreover, Steinberg

(1981) notes that preliminary research by Herbert Gutman indicates that within the Jewish community, only children from more prosperous households remained in school. He observes that virtually all Jewish children living in the poorest sections of the ghetto dropped out of the school system.

Sowell (1981) contends that "even when Jews lived in slums, they were slums with a difference" (p. 94). One of these differences, according to Sowell, was the lower rate of juvenile delinquency and, by inference, the lower rate of criminal behavior. Steinberg (1981) points out, however, that after Bingham's assertion that half the criminals in New York City were Jewish, a Yiddish paper began to monitor the arrests in night court. It found that "only" 28 percent of prostitutes were Jewish. A 1907 study found that Jews made up 16 percent of those convicted of felonies and a much higher percentage of those arrested for lesser crimes. Within the Jewish community, many considered crime a serious problem resulting from the breakdown of the Jewish family. Subsidized by contributions from the German Jewish community, organizations were set up to supply information to the police on illicit activities in the Jewish ghettos.

That contemporary Jewish accounts should consider the breakdown of the family to be a cause of Jewish criminal behavior brings into question the core of the conservative theory, the stable Jewish family. Data indicate that at the turn of the century, Jewish husbands' desertion of their wives was widespread. The *Jewish Daily Forward* routinely ran a "Gallery of Missing Husbands" to assist women in locating their errant husbands, and Jewish charities received thousands of applications for relief from deserted women (Steinberg 1981).

It is certainly possible that Jewish immigrants, compared to others, had lower desertion rates, lower crime rates, and higher rates of completion of eight years of education. But critics contend that it is at most a matter of degree. Jewish family instability, criminal behavior, and limited education seem to have been widespread and in accordance with what one would expect given their situation as immigrants. To what extent they had unique cultural values that enabled them to resist these pressures to a greater degree than other immigrants is highly speculative. These meager differences may very well reflect different external factors and, in any case, are not large enough to warrant a cultural determinist viewpoint. Let us now identify some of these external differences.

Demographic Differences

During the nineteenth century, significant numbers of eastern European Jews lived in rural communities called shtetls. Sociologist Louis Wirth (1928), writing about the ghettos formed by the eastern European Jewish immigrants during the early twentieth century, emphasizes this rural character when comparing them to the earlier German Jewish immigrants.

Wirth believed that immigrants (and black migrants) to cities from rural cultures had extreme difficulty adjusting. Whereas in rural cultures personal relationships are dominated by family ties, in urban society they must be functional. Whereas in rural cultures superstition and fatalism, often embedded in fundamentalist religion, dominate, in urban society rationality is valued. Thus, Wirth believed that many of those from rural cultures would be unable to adapt to the demands of urban society because they would develop pathological disorders and their institutional arrangements—family ties and religion—would be unstable. Since the eastern European Jewish immigrant had some of these rural characteristics when compared to the German Jewish immigrant, Wirth thought this explained significant differences within the Jewish community.

Wirth did not use this urban–rural dichotomy to evaluate the differences between eastern European Jewish immigrants and non-Jewish immigrants from Poland and southern Italy. In this comparison, the eastern European Jewish immigrant was much more urbanized. Moreover, while Jewish immigrants from shtetls had some of the characteristics of rural societies, they were primarily merchants, traders, and small producers. They purchased agricultural produce from peasants in exchange for products the Jewish merchant or trader had bought in large urban areas. Since Jews in rural areas helped connect rural and urban economies, their culture and life patterns had much in common with urban society. Thus, even rural Jews came with cultural values that were more adaptable to American city life than were those of immigrants from Italian or Polish agrarian societies.

Economic conditions faced by eastern European Jews at the end of the nineteenth century made their urban character even more pronounced. In Poland and Russia, increased anti-Semitic incidents, including progroms, made life in the rural shtetl too vulnerable, forcing many Jews to migrate to larger urban areas. Also, legal restrictions imposed on commerce reduced the ability of Jews to act as middlemen, undermining the economic viability of the shtetl. By the beginning of the twentieth century, Polish and Russian Jews were highly urbanized, even if many were less than one generation removed from shtetl life. According to an 1897 census, of the five million Jews in Russia, as many as three-quarters lived in urban areas (Steinberg 1981). Thus, it is possible that the adjustment to urban cultural requirements of functionalism and rationality was easier for eastern European Jews than for other immigrant groups from rural cultures.

Occupational Differences

According to the cultural determinist viewpoint, Jews came with assets quite similar to those of their Italian and Polish counterparts. Nathan Glazer (1955) notes, "Jewish immigrants were scarcely distinguishable from the huge mass of depressed immigrants, illiterate and impoverished" (p. 15). Echoing the same view, Marshall Sklare (1971) believes that Jewish immigrants "arrived without capital or marketable skills" (p. 60). Indeed, Thomas Sowell (1981) claims that Jews "were more destitute and illiterate than other immigrant groups" (p. 80).

We have already seen that Jewish immigrants may have faced less discrimination and their urbanized culture may have enabled them to adapt more easily to American city life. Jews also were more skilled in industrial occupations than other immigrant groups. Steinberg (1981) indicates that 67 percent of Jewish immigrants entering the United States between 1899 and 1910 were classified as skilled workers, compared to less than 10 percent of Italian and Polish immigrants.

Not only were Jewish immigrants more skilled generally, but they were especially adept at skills required by the garment industry. This is not surprising, since the Russian census of 1897 estimated that one-sixth of the entire Jewish work force was employed in the garment industry. As Steinberg (1981) states, "It would be difficult to exaggerate the significance of this single industry for the economic adjustment of Jewish immigrants" (p. 99).

During the 1880s, with the perfection of the sewing machine by Isaac Singer, it became possible to mass-produce clothing. Over the next forty years, garment production grew at almost three times the national average for all industries. Much of the financial success of the German Jewish immigrants derived from their early and sizable entry into garment production. By 1885 of the 241 garment factories in New York City, 234 were owned by Jews.

Jewish immigrants had just the skills the growing garment industry required and, thanks to Jewish ownership, were able to find employment quickly despite their inability to speak English or to work on the Sabbath. Moreover, the low capital requirements of garment production, which enabled the German Jews to enter successfully at the end of the nineteenth century, also allowed relatively easy access to ownership for eastern European Jews a generation later.

The trading background of many eastern European Jews provided the basic business and networking skills necessary for small business ownership. Jacob Lestchinsky (1946) found that Jews in New York City were far more likely to be owners than workers. He notes that in New York City in 1933, among Jews within the wholesale/retail trades and manufacturing, 29 percent and 8 percent respectively were owners, whereas among non-Jews only 12 percent and 1 percent respectively were owners. Thus, it is incorrect to assume that eastern European Jews were simply harder working and more industrious than other immigrants. Italian and Polish immigrants had neither the skills and employment in the garment trades nor the business and networking background of eastern European immigrants.

Educational Differences

Conservatives claim that religious values are responsible for the emphasis Jews place on education. Critics indicate that this linkage is highly questionable. First, there are substantial differences in the educational attainment between Ashkenazic and Sephardic Jews, even though they follow virtually the same religious rituals and traditions.

Second, critics contend that the intellectual environment of eastern European Ashkenazic Jewish immigrants was not necessarily conducive to secular education. When detailed, the distinct intellectual image that the cultural determinists use to characterize the eastern European immigrant is that of *kheyder* study in shtetls. Kheyders were operated by ultraorthodox and Hasidic rabbis. They emphasized ritualistic memorization and obedience to fundamentalist beliefs, many of which conflicted with scientific developments.

In their classic book on Jewish life in the shtetl, Mark Zborowski and Elizabeth Herzog (1962) claim, "Not every Jew in the shtetl is a scholar [but] . . . there are few Jews from eastern Europe who have not attended the kheyder for a short time" (p. 102). Whether this image of scholastic-oriented shtetl children is correct or not, Miriam Slater (1969) demonstrated that the style and content of kheyder scholarship was fundamentally at odds with the requirements of modern education. If anything, it would have operated as a deterrent to educational achievement in the United States.

Steinberg (1981) suggests that modest differences in the educational attainment of immigrant groups might result from the urbanization of Jewish immigrants rather than from any distinctive characteristics of their culture. According to the U.S. Immigration Report of 1911, the rate of illiteracy for eastern European Jews was 26 percent. This was much higher than the illiteracy rates of more urbanized immigrant groups and lower than the rates of less urbanized immigrant groups. For example, the illiteracy rate of (urbanized) northern Italian immigrants was only 12 percent, while the illiteracy rate of (rural) southern Italian immigrants was 54 percent.

Data indicate that American Jews eventually sought careers that require extensive education to a greater degree than others. For example, Sherry Gorelick (1979) found that among Russian Jews graduating from City College (New York City) between 1895 and 1935, more went into teaching than into any other profession. Critics suggest that this choice of career reflected the occupational opportunities available to Jews rather than any cultural predispositions. During the first few decades of the twentieth century, there was a dramatic increase in the number of public school teaching positions available to Jews. Later, after World War II, college teaching positions became available in large numbers. Thus, when children of Jewish immigrants wished to build on the often very modest initial financial success of their parents, teaching provided a natural avenue for upward mobility.

Anti-Semitism also shaped Jewish career opportunities. While Gentile college graduates could expect to find employment as managers with large corporations or white-collar employment in banking, Jews could not. The corporate sector, manufacturing as well as banking, maintained anti-Semitic hiring policies throughout the pre–World War II period. In this environment, it is predictable that Jews would seek employment in teaching or in fields such as law, medicine, and accounting, where they could be independently employed.

Infrastructure Support Differences

Not only did the already established German Jewish community provided easy entry of skilled Jewish immigrants into the garment industry, but it provided other advantages as well. Although German Jews generally looked down on the eastern European Jewish immigrants, they accepted the responsibility of providing aid and support for these new arrivals. Thus, the German Jewish community funded an extensive range of social agencies that helped Jewish immigrants to adjust to American urban life. While other immigrant communities also developed self-help organizations, none had financial resources of comparable size.

The German Jewish community also had sufficient economic and political influence to respond to anti-Semitic actions. For example, when President Lowell of Harvard suggested that Jewish quotas be adopted, Jewish politicians in the Boston area and Jewish Harvard graduates sparked large protests. Similarly, as a result of pressure from influential German Jews, Police Commissioner Bingham was forced to retract his claims concerning Jewish criminality. Thus, the existence of a wealthy and influential German Jewish community afforded eastern European Jews not only access to employment, but also a social support infrastructure and protection from discriminatory behavior to a degree not available to other immigrant groups.

Black and Jewish
Small-Business Ownership

Since the end of World War II, Jewish success has often been contrasted with the persistence of poverty among blacks. When *Brown v. the Board of Education* (1954) signaled that policies must be enacted to uplift the black population, Jewish success became a political instrument. As Sherry Gorelick (1980) notes, "Scholarly support for the rewards of a Jewish passion for education was particularly useful for liberal, social policy makers of the late 1950s and 1960s. Conventional wisdom perceived education as the panacea for social problems" (p. 40). Thus, instead of policies that responded directly to racist employment practices, liberals, emphasizing the Jewish experience, claimed that funding for education would be sufficient.

Given the conventional wisdom that children of uneducated Jewish immigrants were able, through hard work, to succeed once barriers were lifted, there were high expectations of black success. When supportive educational policies did not result in dramatic increases in black college graduates, many decided that internal inadequacies were responsible.

As we have seen, critics contend that the conventional wisdom is mistaken. The high educational attainment of American Jewry was a result of the particular occupational distribution of Jewish immigrants. Jewish college students were the children of skilled workers and small-business owners. For some Jews, small-business ownership made them wealthy. For most Jews, however, the modest income from ownership simply generated a more stable financial and social infrastructure. This stable environment was conducive to the educational advancement of their children. Once Jews had access to higher education, the proportion of the labor force who were owners declined. Brenner and Kiefer (1981) note that by 1973 only 14 percent of the Jewish labor force consisted of self-employed owners, a decline from 20 percent in 1933. Thus, for Jews family businesses provided a stepping-stone to higher education.

Jews continue to be self-employed to a greater extent than other groups. For example, Barry Chiswick (1983) found that 1970 national data show that Jews were more than twice as likely to be self-employed as non-Jews. In contrast, blacks are quite underrepresented. E. Franklin Frazier (1962) summarizes the state of black-owned firms during the pre–World War II period as follows: "[B]lack business was insignificant from the standpoint of the American economy and provided an exceedingly small amount of employment and income for Negro workers" (p. 129).

More recent evidence continues to find that black-owned firms are very small and provide little employment for the black community. Summarizing the 1977 business census, Don Markwalder (1981) reaches the same conclusions as Frazier. Markwalder notes that only 113 firms had at least one hundred employees, while only 716 had annual sales of more than $1 million. At the other extreme, more than 90 percent of black firms had no paid employees, and 78 percent had annual sales of less than $25,000. Moreover, he found that the situation was deteriorating when compared to the previous 1972 data. Over the five-year period, annual sales of black-owned firms, adjusted for inflation, declined by 22 percent, and the average number of employees declined from 6.0 to 4.1 among firms with paid employees.

According to the 1982 census of small businesses (U.S. Small Business

Administration 1986), while 13 percent of the overall labor force was self-employed, only 6 percent of the black labor force was self-employed. If we exclude self-employed workers, the figures for the general and black populations are 11 percent and 3 percent respectively. Moreover, blacks owned much smaller businesses than whites. Among white-owned firms, 70.5 percent were sole proprietorships, while 29.5 percent were either partnerships or corporations. Among black-owned firms, 95.2 percent were sole proprietorships.

Black-owned firms also are exceedingly small. In 1982, almost 90 percent had no paid employees. Indeed, only 2 percent of all black businesses had at least five paid employees. Of the 339,000 black-owned firms, only 1,100 employed at least twenty workers and only 360 employed at least fifty workers. Most strikingly, the number of black-owned firms with at least one paid employee actually declined between 1977 and 1982.

The smallness of black-owned businesses also is reflected in sales receipt information. In 1982, 46 percent of all black firms had annual sales receipts of less than $5,000, and only 20 percent had annual sales receipts of more than $20,000. Thus, unless there was dramatic underreporting, black business and entrepreneurial activities were not only small in number but often reflected disguised unemployment and erratic part-time behavior rather than providing a foundation for upward mobility.

In explaining the minimal black ownership, Frazier (1962) was predisposed to accept some aspects of the cultural determinist viewpoint: "[T]he fundamental causes of the failure of Negroes to carry on successful business enterprises . . . [reflects the] fundamental sociological fact that the Negro lacks a business tradition or the experience of people who, over generations, have engaged in buying and selling" (p. 139). This thesis is somewhat supported by Strang's (1971) survey of one hundred black firms. Strang believes that the black business failure reported in this survey reflects a lack of managerial ability and business education. A more recent study by Scott, Furino, and Rodriquez (1981) disputes these claims. They found that after adjusting for age of owner, size of business, and business location, there was no difference between the mean rates of return of black-owned and white-owned firms. Thus, structural factors rather than ability differences were responsible for black–white performance differences.

Other observers also have found that external factors have had an important impact on black business performance. In a government commissioned report, David Swinton and John Handy (1983) try to explain the "strikingly low participation rates of blacks as owners" (p. i). They divide explanations into supply-side and demand-side theories. Supply-side theories emphasize the lack of external financing available to black owners, while demand-side theories emphasize factors that restrict the demand for products supplied by black-owned businesses.

According to the demand-side view, discrimination limits the ability of black-owned firms to service a white clientele. As a result, black-owned firms are limited to servicing the black population. Brimmer and Terrel (1971) suggest that the low income within the black community is the primary reason why there are few black firms and those that exist are very small. Moreover, Wallach (1967) points out that because black owners are restricted to a black-only clientele, they are unable to attain a scale of operation that would enable them to compete successfully against white firms in the same line of trade. Since black customers are free to shop at these lower-cost white-owned stores, black firms are often rejected by black consumers. Finally, some researchers (Brimmer 1969; Markwalder 1972) have suggested that black-owned firms are disproportionately affected by economic downturns. During downturns, not only does the income of blacks decline more rapidly than that of whites, but they also lose the little discretionary income they possess. In this case, blacks reduce their purchases from ghetto restaurants, beauty parlors, and other stores to a greater extent than do customers of other businesses.

Many researchers also have noted the limited capital resources available to black business owners. Studies show that even after controlling for earnings, blacks have far fewer assets than whites. Having fewer assets, blacks have much less collateral against which they can borrow. Moreover, since black owners locate in depressed economic areas, their access to bank credit is severely restricted. Summarizing the literature, Swinton and Handy (1983) contend that black banks may play an important role in overcoming the credit restrictions black firms face when seeking loans from white-owned financial institutions.

Conclusions

This chapter began by presenting the conservative view that unique cultural traits explain the relative economic success of Jewish immigrants. Conservatives believe that Jewish values pertaining to education, family stability, and delayed gratification derive from their religious and cultural heritage rather than from their urbanism. Conservatives believe that some cultural differences will not change quickly and that these differences are responsible for the relative success of Jewish immigrants.

Critics have found this cultural determinist view wanting. First, it appears that Jewish immigrants faced less discrimination than other groups. Critics of the conservative view note that differences between eastern European Jews and other turn-of-the-century immigrant groups, with respect to education, family stability, and criminal behavior, may be quite modest—so modest, in fact, that they would be insufficient to support a cultural determinist viewpoint. Moreover, critics note that arguments attempting to trace Jewish educational values to religious traditions are at odds with important facts.

We also saw that urbanization may explain the higher literacy and greater adaptability of Jewish immigrants to American urban life. We found that Jewish immigrants were much more skilled than other turn-of-the-century immigrants, making their transition into American industrial life easier. Moreover, since many Jewish immigrants possessed skills required by the burgeoning garment industry, they were able to prosper as workers and small-business owners more quickly than other immigrants. The presence of an already established German Jewish community also provided access to employment, a social infrastructure, and protection from discriminatory behavior to a degree unmatched by other immigrant communities. Thus, external factors are quite sufficient to explain the differential success rate among immigrants.

Finally, we found that whereas small-business ownership provided a stepping-stone to intergenerational upward mobility for Jews, this has not been the case for blacks. The differences in small-business ownership between Jews and blacks does not appear to reflect cultural differences. Instead, the lack of access to financial markets and to a white clientele has limited blacks to business areas that are too small and unstable to provide the financial and social stability necessary for advancement.

Notes

1. Booker T. Washington (1907), noting that "no race has suffered as much," suggested that blacks would succeed only when they "imitate the Jew" (p. 182).

2. That Ford should identify finance capital with international Jewry is odd, given the overwhelmingly Protestant character of American banking (for instance, the Morgan, Mellon, and Rockefeller families). Lee Levinger (1972) claims that Ford was won over to anti-Semitism by two factors: First, he blamed Jews for the failure of Wilson's peace efforts, and second, he was convinced by White Russian émigrés of the authenticity of the Protocols of the Elders of Zion.

3. This section closely follows the line of argument and sources found in Steinberg 1981.

References

Berrol, Selma C. 1976. "Education and Economic Mobility: The Jewish Experience in New York City, 1880–1920." *American Jewish Quarterly Review* 65:257–71.

Brenner, Reuven, and Nicholas Kiefer. 1981. "The Economics of the Diaspora: Discrimination and Occupational Structure." *Economic Development and Cultural Change* 29:517–33.

Brimmer, Andrew. 1969. "The Negro in the National Economy." In *Race and Poverty*, ed. John Kain. Garden City, NY: Prentice-Hall.

Brimmer, Andrew, and Henry Terrel. 1971. "The Economic Potential of Black Capitalism." *Public Policy* 19:379–405.

Chiswick, Barry. 1983. "The Earnings and Human Capital of American Jews." *Journal of Human Resources* 18:313–35.

Dobkowski, Michael N. 1979. *The Tarnished Dream*. Westport, CT: Greenwood Press.

Frazier, E. Franklin. 1962. *The Black Bourgeoisie*. New York: Collier.

Glazer, Nathan. 1955. "Social Characteristics of American Jews, 1954–1964." *American Jewish Yearbook* 56:1–25.

———. 1958. "The American Jew and the Attainment of Middle-Class Rank." In *The Jews*, ed. Martin Sklare. 138–46. Glencoe, IL: Free Press.

Gorelick, Sherry. 1979. *Social Control, Social Mobility, and the Eastern European Jews*. New Brunswick, NJ: Rutgers University Press.

———. 1980. "Jewish Success and the Great American Celebration." *Contemporary Jewry* 4:40–55.

Handlin, Oscar. 1951. "American View of Jews at the Opening of the Twentieth Century." *Publication of the American Jewish Historical Society* 40:324–45.

Higham, John. 1966. "American Anti-Semitism Historically Reconsidered." In *Jews in the Minds of America*, ed. Charles Stember. New York: Basic Books, 237–58.

Hofstadter, Richard. 1955. *The Age of Reform*. New York: Alfred A. Knopf.

Lestchinsky, Jacob. 1946. "The Economic Development of Jews in the United States." *The Jew: Past and Present* 1:391–406.

Levinger, Lee. 1972. *Anti-Semitism in the United States*. Westport, CT: Greenwood Press.

Markwalder, Don. 1972. "The Potential for Black Business." *Review of Black Political Economy* 3:87–93.

———. 1981. "Potential for Black Business." *Review of Black Political Economy* 11:301–12.

Massarik, Fred, and Alvin Cherkin. 1973. "United States National Jewish Population Study: A Preliminary Report." *American Jewish Yearbook* 74:270–93.

McWilliams, Carey. 1948. *Mask of Privilege*. Boston: Little, Brown.

Myrdal, Gunnar. 1944. *An American Dilemma: The Negro Problem and Modern Democracy*. New York: Harper and Row.

Phillips, Bruce A. 1986. "Los Angeles Jewry: A Demographic Portrait." *American Jewish Yearbook* 86:126–95.

Ribuffo, Leo. 1978. "Henry Ford and the International Jew." *American Jewish Quarterly Review* 69:437–78.

Riesman, David. 1973. "Education at Harvard." *Change*, September, 24–37.

Rosenthal, Eric. 1975. "The Equivalence of United States Census Data for Persons of Russian Stock or Descent with American Jews: An Evaluation." *Demography* 12:275–90.

Ross, Edward A. 1972. "The Old World and the New." In *Kike,* ed. Michael Selzer. New York: World Publishing, 63–76.

Scott, William D., Antonio Furino, and Eugene Rodriquez. 1981. *Key Business Ratios for Minority-Owned Businesses.* San Antonio: Center for Studies in Business, Economics and Human Resources.

Sklare, Marshall. 1971. *American's Jews.* New York: Random House.

Slater, Miriam. 1969. "My Son the Doctor: Aspects of Mobility Among American Jews." *American Sociological Review* 34:359–73.

Sowell, Thomas. 1975. *Race and Economics.* New York: McKay.

———. 1981. *Ethnic America.* New York: Basic Books.

———. 1984. *Civil Rights: Rhetoric or Reality?* New York: Morrow.

Steinberg, Stephen. 1981. *The Ethnic Myth.* New York: Antheneum.

Stember, Charles. 1966. *Jews in the Mind of America.* New York: Basic Books.

Strang, William. 1971. "Minority Economic Development: The Problem of Business Failures." *Law and Contemporary Problems* 36:17–23.

Swinton, David, and John Hardy. 1983. *The Determinants of the Growth of Black-Owned Businesses: A Preliminary Analysis.* Washington, DC: U.S. Department of Commerce.

Szakowski, Zosa. 1974. *Jews, Wars, and Communism: The Impact of the 1919 Red Scare on American Jewish Life.* New York: KTAV.

U.S. Small Business Administration. 1986. *The State of Small Business: A Report of the President.* Washington, DC: U.S. Government Printing Office.

Wallach, Henry. 1967. "The Negro Economy." *Newsweek,* September, 70.

Washington, Booker T. 1907. *The Future of the American Negro.* Boston: Small, Maynard.

Wirth, Louis. 1928. *The Ghetto.* Chicago: University of Chicago Press.

Zborowski, Mark, and Elizabeth Herzog. 1962. *Life Is with People.* New York: Schocken Books.

11
Middleman Minority Theories and Black–Jewish Relations

I n recent years there has been growing antagonism between leaders of the black and Jewish communities. In 1984 this was highlighted by statements made by Muslim leader Louis Farrakhan. In 1988 Steve Cokely, an aide to Chicago mayor Eugene Sawyers, was forced to resign after a series of public speeches in which he claimed that Jews control the media and controlled former mayor Harold Washington and that the AIDS epidemic is spread by Jewish doctors who inject AIDS into blacks (Kennedy 1988).

Survey data also seem to indicate that anti-Jewish attitudes among black Americans have increased substantially. Reporting on surveys conducted in 1964, Gary Marx (1967) states, "Negroes consistently emerge as less anti-semitic [than whites]. . . . Negroes see Jews in a more favorable light than they see non-Jewish whites" (pp. 147, 163). Similarly, Celia Heller and Alphonso Pinkney (1965) found that 42 percent of adult blacks polled found Jews helpful, while only 9 percent found Jews harmful to black Americans. Summarizing a more recent survey, Charles Silberman (1985) states, "When the last comprehensive survey was taken in 1981, proportionately twice as many blacks as whites displayed significant prejudice against Jews. . . . Th[e] concentration of anti-semitism among the best educated and most affluent members of the black community [was striking]" (p. 339).

Major Jewish organizations have identified these emerging black anti-Jewish attitudes as the major danger faced by American Jewry. Writing for the American Jewish Committee (AJC), Arnold Forster and Benjamin Epstein (1974) claim that the "new" anti-Semitism among blacks reflects left-wing rhetoric—that is, that blacks are exploited by Jewish ghetto merchants and slumlords and are controlled by Jewish teachers and social workers. Forster and Epstein note that anti-Semitism was a staple of previous black nationalists, including Marcus Garvey and Malcolm X, but the recent upsurge is more intense and more dangerous.[1] The first section of this chapter shows that major Jewish organizations might be seriously underestimating the significance of elite anti-Semitism.

Many radicals contend that black antagonism reflects the economic roles played by Jewish middlemen. Other radicals believe that black animosity toward Jews is misguided and that Jews and blacks have common interests and should maintain unity. From this perspective, anti-Semitism splits the working class, harming both Jews and blacks. The remainder of the chapter evaluates these competing views.

Leftist theorist Edna Bonacich (1973) has attempted to explain Jewish attainment of middleman positions and why this generates anti-Jewish sentiment. Her sojourner theory suggests that other workers (blacks) develop antagonistic relationships with Jews as a result of Jewish economic activities. The second section of this chapter presents Bonacich's sojourner theory and shows its similarities to her broader split labor market models discussed in earlier chapters (Bonacich 1972, 1975, 1976).

The third section demonstrates that Bonacich is incorrect when she associates Jewish immigrants with a sojourner outlook, with attainment of middleman positions, and with clannish behavior. We will find that before World War II, Jewish immigrants were predominantly working-class and were active in multiethnic movements.

The fourth section updates the analysis. Today the Jewish working class has been replaced by a Jewish professional class, many members of which service the black community as teachers, government administrators, and social workers. It is the role of this group that is critical to evaluating the relationship of blacks and Jews.

Elite Anti-Semitism

As noted in chapter 10, influential historians claim that after immigration restrictions were imposed, anti-Semitism in the United States declined dramatically. Since the 1950s, the AJC and Anti-Defamation League (ADL) of B'nai Brith have minimized the seriousness of anti-Semitic attitudes among the general public and the inability of Jews to advance within the corporate and financial communities. Selectively summarizing evidence, Charles Silberman (1985) claims that "anti-semitism is rapidly becoming a thing of the past" (p. 94).

These contentions are not consistent with most studies. As late as 1978, an ADL study conducted by Ira Gissen found only five Jews among the top three hundred executives in the six leading oil companies. Gissen (1978) concludes that this resulted from "recruitment avoidance, promotion levels beyond which Jews cannot go, non-assignment to certain job areas, and stereotyped employment (i.e. in such departments as legal, accounting, and research)" (p. 3).

ADL studies of hiring in the automobile (Anti-Defamation League 1963) and insurance (Anti-Defamation League 1968) industries found similar exclusionary policies. These studies demonstrate that Jews have little influence over the policies of major corporations. In contrast to these findings, Martire and Clark (1982) found that 37 percent of Americans polled believed that

"Jews have too much power in the business world" and 23 percent thought that "Jews have too much power in the United States" (p. 17). In 1964 these views were held by 33 percent and 13 percent respectively of those polled. Thus, in conflict with the evidence, a growing section of the U.S. public believes Jews are too powerful.

Although Martire and Clark found that 43 percent of the non-Jewish public believed international banking is pretty much controlled by Jews, nothing is further from the truth. An AJC study (American Jewish Committee 1973) did not find a single Jew among the 176 senior executives of the fifteen largest U.S. commercial banks, eight of which are located in New York City. Even at middle-level management, there were only 14 Jews out of 1,757 executives.

Major corporations and financial institutions hire executive trainees primarily through interviewing at college campuses. Not surprisingly, these firms do very little interviewing at schools with a high Jewish enrollment. Slavin and Pradt (1983) surveyed the 1972–73 recruiting patterns of major firms at 128 colleges. In twenty-one of these colleges, Jewish enrollment was more than 30 percent. These "Jewish" colleges were among the most prestigious. They included Wesleyan, Yale, Johns Hopkins, Washington University, Columbia, and the University of Pennsylvania.

Slavin and Pradt (1982, 50) found that these "Jewish" colleges "were off-limits for corporate and bank recruiters." While corporations in the Fortune 500 made a total of more than forty visits a year to the typical school with a Jewish enrollment of less than 20 percent, they averaged twenty-three and eight visits to schools with Jewish enrollments of 30 to 39 percent and over 40 percent respectively. When the recruitment patterns of individual corporations are analyzed, the biases are even more striking. Of the eighty-five corporations that visited at least twenty colleges, only eight visited more than two "Jewish" colleges, thirty-two visited one, and twenty-four visited none.

Richard Zweigenhaft analyzed the makeup of the board of directors of the largest corporations and interviewed a sample of recent Harvard MBA graduates. In *Jews in the Protestant Establishment,* Zweigenhaft and G. William Domhoff (1982) found that Jews were still underrepresented at the very largest corporations and that the few who attained directorships did so in atypical ways. They found that "few Jews have been able to start at the bottom and prove themselves in the usual way. Climbing the corporate ladder still remains problematical for Jews" (p. 46).

In addition, Zweigenhaft (1984) surveyed seventy-five Harvard MBA graduates. In order to dismiss corporate anti-Semitism, Silberman (1985, 94–95) quotes only those respondents who said anti-Semitism "is not relevant anymore" and those who believed corporations had become real meritocracies in which "people who deliver make it." Silberman fails to mention that more than half of Zweigenhaft's respondents graduated in 1980, so most had little direct knowledge of corporate promotion procedures.

Zweigenhaft (1984) found that while few respondents had experienced anti-Semitism, most felt that it would have a significant influence at the highest promotion levels. They believed that Jews continue to face the risk of reaching a plateau above which they cannot advance. Many respondents believed that corporations require social and political conformity, particularly as you climb the corporate ladder. As a result, they were reluctant to show their Jewishness. Finally, Zweigenhaft quotes Simon Rifkin, a longtime Jewish leader and corporate director, who still contends, "Jews have traditionally been successful bankers and yet if you look at most of the commercial banks you will not find a Jewish name at all. . . . The same is true of insurance companies. I would say the same is true of the bigger corporations" (p. 11).

Silberman (1985) and others overstate the progress Jews have made because they ignore objective factors that limit the ability of Jews to move into positions of power within the corporate structure. In chapter 2, we found that conservatives believe that individuals separate their social and economic behavior—that is, people maintain their discriminatory beliefs in social settings but not in their business activities. It is often difficult to make this separation at higher corporate levels, however. In commercial banking and corporations, senior officers are expected to attract corporate clients through social contacts. If prestigious social clubs continue to exclude Jews, Jewish executives are at a disadvantage. They are unable to develop the personal contacts necessary to attract major corporate accounts.[2]

Discrimination against Jews by prestigious social clubs has lessened somewhat in recent years. In 1969 the AJC found that approximately 80 percent of the social clubs surveyed nationally had no Jewish members, whereas a decade earlier there had been a 90 percent exclusion rate (Carlson 1969). A more recent AJC survey (American Jewish Committee 1980) found that discrimination by suburban country clubs was still widespread. Using 1976 data from the forty most prestigious social clubs nationally and the seven most prestigious clubs in New York City, Zweigenhaft (1982) found that few Jews were members; whereas 73 of the 219 non-Jewish leaders belonged to these clubs, only 13 of the 219 identified Jewish leaders were members.

Some corporations might adopt anti-Semitic executive hiring practices in response to the wishes of their customers. Major oil companies and other firms engage in business with many countries, most notably Saudi Arabia, which are openly hostile to Jews. It stands to reason that these companies would be reluctant to hire Jewish executives. This was especially true when the Arab countries maintained an official list of U.S. corporations from which they would not make purchases. Companies were subject to an Arab boycott if they did business with Israel or purchased supplies from firms that did business with Israel.

In their book summarizing the Arab boycott, Walter Nelson and Terence Prittie (1977) contend that voluntary compliance was widespread. They found that many firms hoping for Arab business "often 'launder' themselves of Jewish connections, associations and employees without ever having been asked to do so by the Arabs" (p. 77). According to Nelson and Prittie, Pepsi Cola (p. 55), Bechtel Construction (p. 94), American Express (p. 56), and Chase (p. 114) were among the major corporations that refused to enter into business relations with the Israeli government because doing so would harm their corporate operations in countries hostile to Israel. Thus, Jewish executives are a liability for many major corporations.

Mainstream Jewish organizations would have us believe that right-wing anti-Semitism is merely a nuisance, since it lacks political power. But there are many examples that contradict this assertion. A striking example was the case of General George S. Brown, chairman of the Joint Chiefs of Staff, who stated, "Jewish influence is so strong, you wouldn't believe it, now. They own, you know, the banks in the country, the newspapers. Just look at where the Jewish money is" (Finney 1974).

Many claim that anti-Semitism flourished during the Reagan administration. When Congress refused to approve the sale of AWACS to Saudi Arabia in 1981, AJC director Milton Ellerin (1982) claimed that President Reagan resorted to anti-Semitism. Nathan Perlmutter (1982) reports that only the threat of public pressure forced the Reagan administration to stop the appointment of Warren Richardson, chief lobbyist for the anti-Semitic Liberty Lobby, to a high-level position within the government. Under Reagan, the major conduit for covert aid to the mercenaries attempting to overthrow the Nicaraguan government was retired general George Singlaub, chairman of the World Anti-Communist League. This organization has a long history of anti-Semitism that was documented by Scott and John Anderson (1986).

Similarly, the CIA-funded Radio Liberty, which broadcasts into the Soviet Union, has enlisted Soviet émigrés who weave anti-Semitism into their airings. Lars-Erik Nelson (1985/86) documents how Radio Liberty has allowed right-wing émigrés to set the tone for many important broadcasts. Nelson notes that many of these émigrés were linked to the People-Labor Alliance (NTS), an organization accused of collaborating with the Nazis in the early stages of World War II. A report by the General Accounting Office in June 1985 corroborated Nelson's charges. It cited a broadcast dealing with Aleksandr Solzhenitsyn's book, *August 1914,* as "anti-semitic and the most offensive program aired by the Russian service in ten years" (Nelson 1985/86, 191).

In this section, we have seen that U.S. corporations continue to exclude

Jews and to accommodate the anti-Semitic attitudes of their customers. We also found that right-wing anti-Semites are not merely nuisances, but individuals with important political ties.

Bonacich's Middleman Minority Theory

During the 1970s, Edna Bonacich (1973) proposed a sojourner theory to explain why certain groups have been associated with particular economic positions in societies and why this has engendered hostility toward them. According to Bonacich, the economic objectives of sojourners explain their attainment of middleman positions. As a result of this sojourner outlook, these immigrant groups have little reason to develop lasting relationships with members of the surrounding society but have strong incentives to maintain ethnic ties. Although Bonacich is well aware that Jewish immigrants were not sojourners,[3] she claims that they had a sojourner outlook because of their deeply held religious attachment to Palestine.

Bonacich claims that group solidarity generates preferential economic treatment. Credit is available on more favorable terms, job seekers are more likely to be hired, and retailers are more likely to be given favorable prices from manufacturers if both are from the same sojourner group. Since workers in the sojourner community have more loyalty to their employers, they are hostile to union organizing. Since sojourners have only financial interests in the host country, Bonacich found that they are rightly accused of maintaining "dual loyalty" and draining away resources (p. 591). This unites both native workers and capitalists in their opposition to sojourners.

Bonacich does not believe discrimination is responsible for the concentration of sojourners in middleman positions. She emphasizes that the gravitation to trading and independent positions is a matter of choice predicated on the sojourners' objectives. Bonacich believes that substantial discrimination begins only after sojourners have monopolized middleman positions. As Waldinger (1986) notes, "This orientation elicits a hostile reaction from the host society; that antagonism, in turn, strengthens solidaristic behaviors and in-group economic ties" (p. 253). Indeed, Bonacich (1973) suggests that it is the unwillingness of sojourners to relinquish their monopolies that causes discrimination to grow and "pushes host countries to even more extreme reactions" (p. 592).

When assessing intergroup relationships, Bonacich's sojourner theory parallels her split labor market theory. In her split labor market theory, even though white workers experience some discrimination from the elite, they benefit from the exploitation of blacks. In her sojourner theory, certain immigrant groups benefit from the exploitation of a native population. In both theories, even when privileged workers are threatened, they reject unity with black workers. In her split labor market theory, Bonacich claims that white workers gain a monopoly of unionized high-wage jobs, while in her sojourner theory, certain immigrant groups gain a monopoly in many primary positions. In her split labor market theory, white workers are able to circumvent attempts to break their monopoly, while in her sojourner theory, she contends that through "bribery" and "their economic and organizational power," these ethnic sojourners are able to circumvent attempts to dislodge them (Bonacich 1973, 592).

Bonacich's thesis is consistent with negative Jewish images.[4] For centuries, Jewish loyalty and business practices have been questioned. The resiliency of these attitudes is reflected in survey polls. Martire and Clark (1982) found that in 1981 48 percent of the non-Jewish public believed that Jews are more loyal to Israel than to the United States, an increase from the 1964 poll results of Selznick and Steinberg (1969).

In 1964, Gertrude Selznick and Stephen Steinberg (1969) found that 34 percent of non-Jews polled believed that Jews are "not as honest as other businessmen," 40 percent thought that Jews "are so shrewd and tricky that other people don't have a fair chance in competition," and 48 percent thought that "Jews are more willing than others to use shady practices" (p. 6). Casting their 1981 survey results in the most favorable way, Martire and Clark (1982) found that each of these percentages decreased by at most one-third.[5] Thus, even in 1981, the image of amoral Jewish merchants was held by close to 30 percent of the non-Jewish public and by 50 percent of those black Americans polled.

Critique of Bonacich's Sojourner Theory

Critics contend that there is little evidence that Zionist ideals have significantly influenced the economic behavior of American Jews. Before World War II, successful middleman positions were typical only among German Jews. While German Jews maintained ties to the Jewish community, Waldinger (1986) points out that assimilationism was a striking feature of German Jewry in both the United States and Germany. He notes that German Jews organized their own branch of Judaism, which rejected the clannish sojourner characteristics that Bonacich (1973) claims are so important. Indeed, Piore (1979) suggests that the rapid entrance of Jewish immigrants into nonindustrial occupations resulted because they did not have a sojourner outlook and thus invested more rapidly in businesses and education than other immigrant groups.

Bonacich (1973) emphasizes how strong ethnic ties within sojourner groups generate preferential economic treatment, especially with respect to employment. In contrast, Peled and Shafir (1987) describe how Jewish firms shifted away from Jewish workers in favor of Polish workers at the beginning of the twentieth century. Waldinger (1986) points out that competition was fierce among American Jewish firms and these firms had little preference for employment of Jews. Thus, there is extensive evidence that Jewish firms, both in the United States and in Europe, willingly hired Gentile workers rather than Jews.

Bonacich (1973) minimizes the extent to which the Jewish community contained a poor working class. Marxists (Gold 1984) and others (Beard 1942) struggled against theories that identified Jews with economic success. Nathan Goldberg (1947) notes that the 1900 census indicates that among U.S. Jews of Russian ancestry, less than 20 percent of those gainfully employed were owners, managers, or peddlers, while close to 60 percent were blue-collar workers.

Goldberg compares this occupational distribution to that of Jews in the 1897 Russian census. He finds that while 59.7 percent and 20.6 percent of U.S. Jews of Russian ancestry were engaged in manufacturing and trade respectively, the figures for Jews in the Russian census were 39.5 percent and 30.5 percent respectively. Whereas Bonacich (1973) contends that sojourners move to middleman positions in the host country, it appears that for Russian Jews the movement was in the opposite direction, away from trade and into blue-collar employment.

Even one and two generations later, the vast majority of American Jews were workers. Jacob Lestchinsky (1946) found that in 1940 only 27 percent of those Jews in the labor force were either self-employed, owners, or managers, while 65 percent were clerical or industrial workers. Lestchinsky (1942) points out that the occupational distribution was quite different in smaller cities. He estimates that the Jewish working class declined from 75 percent of the Jewish labor force in larger cities to about 20 percent in smaller cities, with the national average being about 63 percent. Thus, when Bonacich (1973) presents the Koenig (1942) study of Stamford, Connecticut, where the majority of Jews were owners or managers, she is generalizing from a highly unrepresentative sample.[6]

Not only does Bonacich (1973) misstate the proportion of Jews who were workers, but she also characterizes their behavior incorrectly. Bonacich chooses only those examples that support her contention that workers within the sojourner group would be antiunion and indifferent to social movements. This is completely at odds with the attitudes and actions of Jewish immigrant workers, who were extremely active in trade unions and movements for social change and were closely identified with demands for black civil rights.

During the 1930s, Jewish involvement in communist-led movements grew. While Jews were not the leaders at the highest level, Liebman (1986) estimates that "Jews alone in the 1930s and 1940s accounted for 40 to 50 percent of the membership of the Communist Party" (p. 339). Jews also were quite active in organizations, including Yiddish education clubs and the International Workers Organization (IWO), in which communists were influential. Albert Prago (1979) estimates that when the Communist party organized the Abraham Lincoln Brigade to fight in the Spanish civil war, at least 30 percent of the volunteers were Jewish.

As a result of this involvement, *Jew-communist* became a common phrase among anti-Semites. So strong was this linkage that it became a political force in the 1938 Minnesota gubernatorial race. Left-wing activists dominated the Farm-Labor party (FLP), within which Jews had visible positions. Literature claiming that the FLP was run by Jew-communists was widely distributed. As a result, Harold Stassen, a relative unknown, was able to defeat the FLP candidate (Berman 1976).

Much of the political activity of the AJC during the Depression era was to combat the attraction of Jews to communism and the identification of Jews with communism. During the 1940s, the AJC helped form the New York Liberal party to combat the support Jews were giving the communist-aligned American Labor party. The AJC took an active part in the communist witch-hunts following World War II, climaxing with its participation in the government case against the Rosenbergs. Naomi Cohen (1972), writing the official history of B'nai Brith, claims that the involvement of B'nai Brith and the AJC reflected a desire to demonstrate that Jews were loyal to the United States.

Thus, Bonacich (1973) overstates homogeneity within the Jewish community as well as its attainment of financially rewarding middleman positions. We find that most Jews did not attain these positions before World War II. Moreover, in contrast to Bonacich's model, Jewish immigrants to the United States were more likely to seek blue-collar employment and less likely to engage in entrepreneurial trade activities than in their country of origin. Bonacich claims that sojourner groups are unwilling to seek multiethnic unity. She uses this to justify the hostility many unions have had toward ethnic minorities. We found that a Jewish working class actively built unions and other working-class organizations.

According to Bonacich, we would expect the enmity toward Jewish immigrants to come from a native population being exploited by Jewish middlemen. Instead, a major source of anti-Semitism was from the elite, who associated Jews with progressive social legislation. Jews were so closely associated with militant social reform that the term *Jew-communist* was widely used by those opposed to change. So strong was this identification that major Jewish organizations adjusted their policies to demonstrate Jewish loyalty to the United States and opposition to communism.

Jews in the
Post–World War II Period

After World War II, the class composition of American Jewry changed. No longer was there a large Jewish proletariat. Instead, Jews became white-collar professionals employed as government administrators, teachers, and social workers. Table 11–1 summarizes the changing occupational distribution of Jews during the post–World War II period.[7] The percentage of Jews who were either professionals, self-employed, owners, or managers rose from less than 35 percent in 1935 to more than 60 percent by the mid-1970s.

Table 11–2 presents a comparison of the most recent Los Angeles survey and the 1980 U.S. Census figures for the non-Hispanic white population. While Jewish women and men are located more heavily in professional and managerial categories, more detailed data (Phillips 1986) indicate that differences are concentrated in a few areas. For males, almost the entire difference reflects the large number of Jews in medicine and law. The large percentage of Jews in teaching, writing/art, social work, and library science explains almost the entire female difference. The higher level of Jewish male managerial employment reflects the proportionately larger number of Jews who are retail managers, public administrators, and/or self-employed.

The fact that these most recent surveys find Jews concentrated in middleman positions is not a vindication of Bonacich's (1973) thesis. The attainment of middleman positions occurred two generations after the immigration process. This section explores alternative explanations for the gravitation of Jews to middleman positions and the evolution of black–Jewish relations.

In contrast to Bonacich's sojourner theory, liberal theorists do not believe that distinctive objectives are the principal explanation for the Jewish occupational distribution. Instead, liberals emphasize the restrictions anti-Semitism places on occupational choices available. Simon Kuznets (1960) notes that these restrictions "propel Jews toward pursuits different from those that would normally follow from an economic calculation of potential returns to given ability and resources" (p. 1624). Carey McWilliams (1948) claims that these restrictions force Jews to enter trades that have a high risk, are peripheral to the dominant centers of production, or have a social stigma.

Slavin and Pradt (1982) contend that the Jewish occupational distribution reflects the impact of statistical discrimination. They claim that Jews are perceived to have a distinctive type of intelligence that prepares them for certain jobs. As a result, corporations seek Jews for certain technical fields— accounting, computers, factoring, and so on—while shunning them in others.

One of the more widely held explanations of this occupational distribution is gap theory (Rinder 1958). Gap theory emphasizes that many mid-

Table 11–1
Jewish Male Occupational Distribution, 1935–1979
(percent)

Occupation	1935 (Detroit/ Pittsburgh)*	1951 (Los Angeles)	1957 (National)	1959 (Los Angeles)	1965 (Boston)	1967 (Los Angeles)	1970 (National)	1975 (Boston)	1979 (Los Angeles)
Managerial/executive/owner	24.6	35.5	35.1	30.5	37	23.5	26.5	27	28.8
Professional	9.2	15.3	20.3	24.9	32	35.4	27.3	40	33.7
Clerical/sales	40.8	28.3	22.1	24.2	15	20.8	28.0	21	21.5
Blue-collar/service	25.4	20.9	22.1	20.4	14	20.4	18.0	11	17.8

Sources: For Detroit and Pittsburgh, see Lestchinsky 1946; for Los Angeles, see Phillips 1986; for Boston, see Fowler 1975; for National, see Chiswick 1983.

*Unweighted average of surveys in Detroit and Pittsburgh.

Table 11–2

Los Angeles Occupational Distribution: Non-Hispanic and Jewish Populations, by Sex, 1979–1980

(percent)

Occupation	Male		Female	
	Jewish	Non-Hispanic	Jewish	Non-Hispanic
Executive/managerial/owner	28.8	17.8	14.3	11.9
Professional	33.7	20.1	36.0	18.2
Nonsupervisory sales	18.2	10.9	13.7	12.1
Administrative support	3.3	7.8	26.5	36.2
Service	4.2	6.8	4.6	12.0
Blue-collar	13.6	36.4	4.9	9.2

Source: Phillips 1986.

dleman positions have a social stigma because they are found in societies with a marked division between the elite and the masses. Examples include feudal societies with a gap between the peasantry and landed aristocracy or colonial societies with a gap between the imperial power and native community.

According to gap theory, ethnic outsiders attain middleman positions for a number of reasons. First, they are able to interact with the lower strata in ways the elite cannot (Stryker 1959). Second, they have fewer ethical constraints on business decision making than native entrepreneurs. Third, to the extent middlemen are required to exploit and manipulate the masses for the benefit of the elite, ethnic outsiders are most efficient.

Historically, it has been thought that middlemen played this role by serving feudal lords against the interests of peasants (Blalock 1967). More recently, Wilson and Portes (1980) have suggested that middleman capitalists in ethnic enclaves benefit larger firms in the center of the economy. Lower wages paid by middleman capitalists to their co-ethnic workers are passed along to customers in the form of lower prices. Since many of these ethnic firms sell intermediate goods to larger corporations, these larger corporations are the beneficiaries of the low wages paid by middleman capitalists. Middleman groups often act as a buffer for the elite, bearing a large portion of the hostility their actions generate.

Quoting Salo Baron, Aviva Cantor Zuckoff, and Stephen Isaacs, Slavin and Pradt (1982, 146) note that these middleman positions have had a long tradition within Jewish society. Baron contends that "Jews assumed the role of the gentry's agent in the exploitation of the peasantry and in effect became the scapegoat of the righteous wrath of the peasants." Zuckoff contends that Jews still play the role of "oppressor surrogate and the scapegoat." Isaacs suggests that "Jews served as moneylenders, brokers, and tax collectors" in their aid to feudal rulers and in the United States "Jews act as though those same roles were compulsory, although the job descriptions have, of course, changed with the times." Indeed, Abram Leon (1950) thought that the very survival of Judaism was a direct result of these middleman roles.

These theories suggest that the positions Jews take in black ghettos—whether as merchants, landlords, teachers, or social workers—may require unethical behavior. Ghetto businessmen and professionals may exploit black residents either directly or indirectly.[8] For example, the organization Jews for Urban Justice contends, "Jewish grocers . . . have been pressed by the ruling class—as grocers . . . not as Jews—to exploit . . . Black communities. Banks, wholesalers, and real estate owners have through high interest rates, high wholesale prices, and high rents pushed small grocers into charging high prices for marginal goods" (Slavin and Pradt 1982, 147). Similarly, others emphasize that ghetto businesses are often too small to take advantage of economies of scale. Unable to keep operating costs as low as more efficient large-scale stores, ghetto merchants must charge higher prices and/or pay lower wages. Although they might not be the ones who profit from the high prices and low wages, their black consumers and workers are exploited.

Some Marxists (see, for example, Tabb 1970) have applied gap theory to the black ghetto. In this model, the ghetto is considered a colony, with government professionals filling the gap between the white power structure and the black community. If schools and welfare agencies function to reproduce a low-wage work force, professionals in these government institutions facilitate the exploitation of ghetto residents.

The preceding analysis reinforces beliefs that Jews benefit from the oppression of blacks. In contrast, a traditional Marxist analysis, which emphasizes the primacy of class, suggests that Jews and blacks would benefit from unity. If the two groups are divided, the elite will benefit at the expense of both groups.

According to traditional Marxists, claims that Jews are "frontline controllers of Black children" are too simplistic (Slavin and Pradt 1982, 147). Many individuals enter teaching and social work because they genuinely wish to provide services. Some become demoralized and ineffective because of obstacles they face or because of their own racist attitudes. It is impossible to generalize about behavior, however. Some ghetto professionals become frontline controllers while many do not.

For traditional Marxists, the only acceptable generalization is that ghetto professionals are primary workers who may be harmed by racism. For example, Jewish professionals working in ghetto areas may be harmed when racism enables the government to lower its expenditures for social services. Not only might this reduce their incomes, if not their employment, but it also makes their jobs more difficult. Think how much harder it is to teach in ghetto schools if government support services, such as remediation funding, are reduced or class size is increased. Think how much harder it is to be a social worker if there are fewer funds for housing or child care. Thus, many observers, including Arthur Liebman (1979), expect Jewish professionals to move to the left in response to government spending cutbacks. Bill Tabb (1981) suggests, "Jewish professionals, many in socially involving jobs in the publicly financed sector . . . may well be radical[ized]" (p. 25).

In addition to Jews interacting with blacks through their role as providers of social services, both Jewish and black professionals also rely on government employment. Jews, especially women, continue to be located disproportionately in the government sector as teachers, social workers, and health professionals. Between 1970 and 1984, the government employed approximately 45 percent and 65 percent of black men and black women respectively as professionals, managers, or administrators (Bohmer 1985). Competition for government employment has intensified as a result of the slowdown in the growth of government employment. Whereas between 1950 and 1976 government employment grew at an annual rate of 3.8 percent, between 1976 and 1984 it grew at a rate of only 0.5 percent. Thus, Jewish professionals have a complex relationship with the black community; they support demands for more social services but not necessarily demands that the government hire more black professionals.

Traditional Marxists contend that the elite, instead of providing more private sector employment for black and Jewish professionals, encourages them to fight each other. Blacks are encouraged to believe that Jewish professionals monopolize government jobs and that they should be replaced by black professionals. The elite encourages racism among Jewish professionals so that they will not build a strong coalition against government social spending cutbacks. To the extent the elite is successful, each group fights the other while discrimination in private-sector hiring and deficient social spending continue.

These Marxists believe that organizations such as the AJC and ADL have made it more difficult to maintain the historic alliance between Jewish professionals and blacks. Marxists believe that for the past two decades, these organizations have struggled to convince Jewish professionals to side with those who wish to roll back social legislation. They also believe that these organizations have fought affirmative action programs, claiming that they are harmful to Jewish professionals. In a position paper prepared for the AJC, Samuel Rubinove (1979) questions this contention, saying, "[W]hile quotas and preferences in some instances may well have been injurious to individual Jews, there is no solid evidence that Jews as a group have been disproportionately hurt; in fact, many Jewish women may have benefited by them" (p. 5).

Whether Jewish professionals follow conservative leadership or unite with blacks is uncertain. However, one should not overstate the conservative drift among Jews.[9] In the electoral arena, Jews continue to be major funders and supporters of the Democratic party. In every presidential election since 1964, the majority of votes cast by every other white group went to the Republican candidate. In contrast, in each of these elections, the majority of Jewish votes went to the Democratic candidate. In the 1984 election, an estimated 65 percent of the Jewish vote went to Walter Mondale, the unsuccessful Democratic candidate (Hertzberg 1985). Thus, there is no reason to accept the view that Jews now have a class position that makes them unsympathetic to progressive reforms. To label them surrogate exploiters only increases the likelihood that Jewish professionals will accept the leadership of the AJC rather than joining progressive multiethnic movements.

Conclusions

Both Bonacich's sojourner theory and gap theory focus on the development of antagonistic relationships between certain immigrant groups and the native working class. These theories provide theoretical underpinnings to claims that anti-Jewish black attitudes are justified. This chapter suggests, however, that both theories rely on anecdotal evidence and stereotypic imagery rather than detailed assessments of the experience and behavior of American Jews.

While Bonacich's theory distorts the economic position of American Jewry, gap theory, whatever its historic significance, has been applied too easily to current situations. These theories hinder the formation of principled alliances between Jews and blacks. This chapter indicates that many have been too quick to accept these theories, which have such serious ramifications, without carefully assessing their applicability. Perhaps this chapter will result in a more thorough assessment of the economic position and behavior of American Jews rather than continued reliance on weakly documented theses.

Notes

1. For additional examples of black anti-Semitism, see Frazier (1962, 137–40), Marx (1967, 137–39), and Silberman (1985, 337–43).

2. Klausner (1987) believes that gentlemen's clubs are "not a source of economic power" and to the extent the business style of firms is "more universalistic, hiring practices more meritocratic, and more 'rationalized' around shareholder interests . . . [t]he particularistic social ties, such as represented by gentlemen's clubs, become less relevant for economic dealing in such an ambience" (p. 3).

3. Liebman Hersh (1946) found that for the entire period 1908 to 1943, 34 percent of all immigrants reemigrated back to their country of origin, while the rate for Jews was less than 5 percent.

4. Eugene Wong (1985) makes a similar point when discussing the implications of Bonacich's theory for black–Chinese relationships.

5. In both surveys, the percentage of respondents who rejected Jewish stereotypes remained constant; the only change was that in the 1981 survey a certain percentage of respondents shifted from affirming stereotypes to answering "don't know." Martire and Clark (1982) chose to eliminate "don't know" responses when calculating percentages. The reduction in anti-Semitic attitudes would have been much smaller if the "don't know" responses had been divided equally between the other two choices; if they had been included with the anti-Semitic responses, there would have been no change.

6. Bonacich's use of data on Chinese in Mississippi reflects a similar distortion (Wong 1985, 67–68).

7. Since the U.S. Census Bureau does not ask respondents their religion, national census data can only be used to estimate indirectly the Jewish occupational distribution. The 1957 and 1970 census data contained information on country of origin and/or language of parents, which enabled researchers to estimate the Jewish occupational distribution. The city estimates were all done by private Jewish organizations. For a discussion of the sampling techniques and sample sizes used in some of these surveys, see Brenner and Kiefer (1981).

8. Gary Marx (1967) found that blacks tended to believe that Jewish ghetto merchants and landlords were less exploitive than their non-Jewish counterparts.

9. There has been a consistent affiliation of even prominent corporate Jews, beginning with Julius Rosenwald (Backman 1976), with liberal policies. Noting the leadership Irving Shapiro (DuPont president) has given to the Business Round Table and Felix Rohatyn's masterminding of the New York City recovery from its 1976 fiscal crisis, Bill Tabb (1981) suggests, "I think there is a good case to be made that liberal Jewish capital has helped humanize the system even if most WASP elitists haven't always appreciated their services" (p. 25).

References

American Jewish Committee. 1973. *Summary of Reports on First Fifteen Banks*. New York: American Jewish Committee.

———. 1980. "Social Club Discrimination Survey 1968–1979." Memo, American Jewish Committee, New York.

Anderson, Scott, and John Anderson. *Inside the League*. New York: Dodd, Mead.

Anti-Defamation League. 1963. "Detroit Old Habits." *The ADL Bulletin*, November, 1–7.

———. 1968. "Insurance Industry Hiring Practices." *Rights*, June, 122–25.

Backman, Laurence P. 1976. "Julius Rosenwald." *American Jewish Quarterly Review* 66:89–105.

Beard, Miriam. 1942. "Anti-Semitism: Product of Economic Myths." In *Jews in a Gentile World*, ed. Isacque Graeber and Stewart Britt. New York: Macmillan, 362–401.

Berman, Hyman. 1976. "Political Anti-Semitism in Minnesota." *Jewish Social Studies* 38:247–64.

Blalock, Hubert. 1967. *Toward a Theory of Minority Group Relations.* New York: John Wiley and Sons.

Bohmer, Peter. 1985. "The Impact of Public Sector Employment on Racial Inequality: 1950 to 1984." Dissertation, University of Massachusetts.

Bonacich, Edna. 1972. "A Theory of Ethnic Antagonism: The Split Labor Market." *American Sociological Review* 37:547–59.

———. 1973. "A Theory of Middleman Minorities." *American Sociological Review* 38:583–94.

———. 1975. "Abolition, the Extension of Slavery, and the Position of Free Blacks," *American Journal of Sociology* 81:601–27.

———. 1976. "Advanced Capitalism and Black/White Relations in the United States: A Split Labor Market Interpretation." *American Sociological Review* 41:34–51.

Brenner, Reuven, and Nicholas Kiefer. 1981. "The Economics of the Diaspora: Discrimination and Occupational Structure." *Economic Development and Cultural Change* 29:517–33.

Carlson, Elliot. 1969. "Civil Rights and Clubs." *Wall Street Journal,* 10 September.

Chiswick, Barry. 1983. "The Earnings and Human Capital of American Jews." *Journal of Human Resources* 18:313–35.

Cohen, Naomi W. 1972. *Not Free to Desist: AJC History 1906–66.* Philadelphia: Jewish Publication Society of America.

Ellerin, Milton. 1982. "The AWAC Debate: Is There an Anti-Semitic Fallout?" memo, American Jewish Committee, New York, 17 February.

Finney, John W. 1974. "Chairman of Joint Chiefs Regrets Remarks on Jews." *New York Times,* 14 November, 1.

Forster, Arnold, and Benjamin R. Epstein. 1974. *The New Anti-Semitism.* New York: McGraw-Hill.

Fowler, Floyd. 1975. *Community Survey: A Study of the Jewish Population of Greater Boston.* Boston: The Combined Jewish Philanthropies of Greater Boston.

Frazier, E. Franklin. 1962. *The Black Bourgeoisie.* New York: Collier.

Gissen, Ira. 1978. "A Study of Jewish Employment Problems in the Big Six Oil Company Headquarters." *Rights* 9:3–10.

Gold, Michael. 1984. *Jews without Money.* New York: Carroll and Graf.

Goldberg, Nathan. 1947. *Occupational Patterns of American Jewry.* New York: J.T.S.P. University Press.

Heller, Celia, and Alphonso Pinkney. 1965. "The Attitudes of the Negro Toward Jews." *Social Forces* 43:364–69.

Hersh, Liebman. 1946. "Jewish Migration During the Last Hundred Years." *The Jewish People: Past and Present* 1:407–30.

Hertzberg, Arthur. 1985. "Reagan and Jews." *New York Review of Books,* 31 January, 11–14.

Kennedy, Eugene. 1988. "Anti-Semitism in Chicago: A Stunning Silence." *New York Times,* 26 July, A21.

Klausner, Samuel. 1987. "Jews in the Executive Suite: The Ambience of Jewish and Gentile Firms." Unpublished manuscript, July.

Koenig, Samuel. 1942. "Socioeconomic Status of an American Jewish Community." In *Jews in a Gentile World*, ed. Isacque Graeber and Stewart Brill. New York: Macmillan, 201–25.

Kuznets, Simon. 1960. "Economic Life and the Structure of Jews." In *The Jews: Their History, Culture, and Religion*, ed. Louis Finkelstein. New York: Harper and Row, 1597–1666.

Leon, Abram. 1950. *The Jewish Question: A Marxist Interpretation*. New York: Pathfinder.

Lestchinsky, Jacob. 1942. "The Position of the Jews in the Economic Life of America." In *Jews in a Gentile World*, ed. Isacque Graeber and Stewart Britt. New York: Macmillan, 402–16.

———. 1946. "The Economic Development of Jews in the United States." *The Jewish People: Past and Present* 1:391–406.

Liebman, Arthur. 1979. *Jews and the Left*. New York: John Wiley and Sons.

———. "Anti-Semitism in the Left?" In *Anti-Semitism in America*, ed. David Gerber. Urbana, IL: University of Illinois Press, 321–47.

Martire, Gregory, and Ruth Clark. 1982. *Anti-Semitism in the United States*. New York: Praeger.

Marx, Gary. 1967. *Protest and Prejudice*. New York: Harper and Row.

McWilliams, Carey. 1948. *Mask of Privilege*. Boston: Little, Brown.

Nelson, Lars-Erik. 1985/86. "Anti-Semitism and the Airwaves." *Foreign Policy* 61:180–96.

Nelson, Walter, and Terence Prittie. 1977. *Economic War against the Jews*. New York: Random House.

Peled, Yoav, and Gershon Shafir. 1987. "Split Labor-Market and the State—The Effect of Modernization on Jewish Industrial-Workers in Tsarist Russia." *American Journal of Sociology* 92:1435–60.

Perlmutter, Nathan. 1982. *The Real Anti-Semitism in America*. New York: Arbour House.

Phillips, Bruce A. 1986. "Los Angeles Jewry: A Demographic Portrait." *American Jewish Yearbook* 86:126–95.

Piore, Michael. 1979. *Birds of Passage*. New York: Cambridge University Press.

Prago, Al. 1979. "Jews in the International Brigades." *Jewish Currents* 33:15–21.

Rinder, Irwin D. 1958. "Strangers in the Land: Social Relations in the Status Gap." *Social Problems* 6:253–60.

Rubinove, Samuel. 1979. "Affirmative Action for the 1980s: Options for the AJC." Position paper prepared for the American Jewish Committee, December.

Selznick, Gertrude J., and Stephen Steinberg. 1969. *The Tenacity of Prejudice*. New York: Harper and Row.

Silberman, Charles E. 1985. *A Certain People: American Jews and Their Lives Today*. New York: Summit Books.

Slavin, Stephen, and Mary A. Pradt. 1982. *The Einstein Syndrome: Corporate Anti-Semitism in America Today*. Washington, DC: University Press of America.

Stryker, Sheldon. 1959. "Social Structure and Prejudice." *Social Problems* 6:340–54.

Tabb, William K. 1970. *The Political Economy of the Black Ghetto*. New York: W.W. Norton.

———. 1981. "Comment." *Jewish Currents* 35:24–25.

Waldinger, Roger. 1986. "Immigrant Enterprise: A Critique and Reformulation." *Theory and Practice* 15:249–85.

Wilson, Kenneth, and Alejandro Portes. 1980. "Immigrant Enclaves—An Analysis of the Labor-Market Experiences of Cubans in Miami." *American Journal of Sociology* 86:295–319.

Wong, Eugene. 1985. "Asian American Middleman Minority Theory: The Framework of an American Myth." *Journal of Ethnic Studies* 13:51–88.

Zweigenhaft, Richard L. 1982. "Recent Patterns of Jewish Representation in the Corporate and Social Elites." *Contemporary Jewry* 6:36–46.

———. 1984. *Who Gets to the Top? Executive Suite Discrimination in the Eighties*. New York: American Jewish Committee.

Zweigenhaft, Richard L., and G. William Domhoff. 1982. *Jews in the Protestant Establishment*. New York: Praeger.

12
Summing Up

T he purpose of this concluding chapter is twofold: to delineate the interrelationship of ideas found in various chapters and to offer my personal reflections on competing views.

Common Threads

This book has shown that there are common threads to various explanations of the impact of discrimination on the labor market behavior of blacks, women, and Jews. We found that conservatives consistently emphasize how cultural differences explain economic outcomes. For Glenn Loury and Walter Williams, the dysfunctional behavior of black youths explains their low employment rates. For Gary Becker and Solomon Polachek, the preference of women for household and child-rearing activities explains their part-time and low-wage employment. For Thomas Sowell and Barry Chiswick, the preference of Jews for learning has enabled them to have earnings well above the national average.

While some conservative economists believe that government policies are ineffective, others claim that they have worsened the situation. According to Sowell, sweatshops were indispensable for Jewish upward mobility and government occupation and safety standards would have been harmful. Sowell and Charles Murray also believe that compulsory education requirements have hindered the ability of black youths to develop the proper behavioral traits necessary for steady employment. For Martin Feldstein, unemployment insurance has encouraged discontinuous employment among adult women, while Charles Murray believes that welfare has discouraged the work effort and encouraged out-of-wedlock births among younger (black) women.

For all conservatives, government programs, however well intentioned, cannot help individuals overcome their personal inadequacies; only the market is capable of disciplining individuals. While some will fail, the market will encourage many to adopt the proper behavior and will reward them appropriately.

Liberals believe that the market is not strong enough to influence firms to end discriminatory hiring practices. For John Ballen and Richard Freeman, firms discriminate against black youths with spotty work records but not against comparable white youths. For Jonathan Leonard, firms continue to discriminate against black applicants because there is so little enforcement of affirmative action guidelines. For Barbara Bergmann, discrimination crowds women into low-paying, dead-end fields. For Simon Kuznets, discrimination within the corporate community forces Jews into peripheral, more uncertain lines of trade. Thus, the occupational choices of blacks, women, and Jews have been influenced by discrimination, not simply personal choice.

Liberals detail how statistical discrimination generates occupational patterns. For William Bielby and James Baron, even when women are in integrated occupations, they are concentrated in jobs that reflect gender stereotypes. For Stephen Slavin and Mary Pradt, the "Einstein syndrome" channels Jewish employment into specific trades.

While all liberals believe that discrimination persists, many liberals emphasize the adaptation of groups. For Gunnar Myrdal, blacks adapt by developing an inferiority complex and behavior that only reinforces negative stereotypes. For Michael Piore, women adapt by shifting from market employment to welfare and illegal activities. For Carey McWilliams, Jews adapt by shifting to trades that have a social stigma. While past discrimination may have initiated the process, dysfunctional behavior persists even after discrimination no longer exists.

Liberals emphasize the role of structural factors. For William Wilson, the suburbanization of manufacturing jobs is the major reason black male employment rates have declined. For the Kerner commission, skill mismatches help explain the black–white income gap. For feminists, child-rearing and household responsibilities impose restrictions on female labor market behavior. Thus, government urban planning and educational funding would decrease black employment problems, while day-care funding would reduce female labor market difficulties.

All radicals believe that liberals underestimate the importance of discrimination. Even those such as Bergmann, who are well aware of the discriminatory nature of hiring practices, believe that discrimination is not beneficial financially. In contrast, radicals believe that discriminatory practices persist because they are profitable to the elite. Discrimination against blacks and women enables capitalists to pay workers low wages and to rationalize cutbacks in social spending. Anti-Semitism enables capitalists to use Jews as scapegoats to deflect the anger of oppressed workers.

Some radicals believe that discrimination harms all workers. For Michael Reich, racism has harmed white workers by causing their wages to be lowered, reducing the ability of all workers to unionize, and enabling the elite to reduce social spending. For William Tabb and Arthur Hertzberg, anti-Semitism has resulted in the struggle between blacks and Jews over a declining number of new government jobs rather than a united fight against corporate anti-Semitism and cutbacks in government social spending. For

Julie Matthaei and Jane Humphries, men are harmed when they allow antiwoman and patriarchal attitudes to weaken a united struggle for change.

Many radicals, however, believe that majority workers benefit from discrimination against disadvantaged groups. For Harold Baron, white workers benefit when racism enables them to obtain good jobs with stable employment by shifting instability and low wages to a black secondary work force. For Heidi Hartmann, patriarchy enables men to obtain both material and psychological benefits. For Edna Bonacich, Jews gain monopolies in middleman positions by discriminating against non-Jews.

This summary indicates that each of the viewpoints can be divided into two distinct positions. Among conservatives, there are those who emphasize the damage of internal inadequacies and others who emphasize the damage done by government programs. Among liberals, there are those who emphasize the vicious cycle caused by discrimination and others who downplay discrimination and emphasize the culture of poverty. Indeed, sometimes liberals who emphasize the culture of poverty have more in common with conservatives who emphasize internal inadequacies than with other liberals. Among radicals, there are those who emphasize that majority workers are harmed by discrimination and others who emphasize how majority workers (along with the elite) benefit.

On a political level, each perspective infers a different strategy to overcome discrimination. For conservatives, discrimination is modest, so individual initiative is sufficient. Individuals should rely on themselves rather than on government. For liberals, individuals should rely on government programs, which are critical. For neo-Marxists, individuals should unite with others from their ethnic and/or gender group in a militant movement. For traditional Marxists, class solidarity is necessary.

Personal Perspective

Throughout this book, I have attempted to present material in as evenhanded a manner as possible and have avoided injecting my personal assessments. First, I believe this to be pedagogically sound; readers all too often are easily dominated by their own preconceived notions or the author's viewpoint. My approach forces readers to evaluate the basis of their own beliefs as well as contrasting viewpoints.

Second, this book has used research findings in a more measured manner than usual. Partisan presentations often overstate the value of empirical evidence that supports a particular position. Empirical evidence can be insightful but rarely decisive when judging competing viewpoints. Indeed, there were a number of cases in which different viewpoints had competing explanations of the same statistical relationships. Do blacks have higher rates of absenteeism because they have more dysfunctional behavior than whites or because they are forced to take secondary jobs to which they adapt? Do women have higher voluntary quit rates than men because they are crowded into high-turnover fields or because they are less career-oriented? Do Jews end up in middleman positions because of distinctive objectives or because of anti-Semitic restrictions?

Of course, it would be foolish to say that personal beliefs have had no impact on the presentations in individual chapters. These beliefs are always reflected in the organization, topic selection, and sources referenced. Although I have taken care in the foundation chapters to present the most persuasive case possible for each of the viewpoints, I have not always maintained perfect neutrality in later chapters. Sometimes this is reflected in situations where the claims made were so distant from the evidence presented that it would have been dishonest not to make clear that certain views should be firmly rejected. Sometimes, however, I have allowed my personal perspective to highlight those views that I believe are more credible than others. I hope that these instances have not detracted from the ability of readers to gain an understanding of the topics discussed.

Let me now identify directly my personal beliefs. I firmly believe that the traditional Marxist perspective provides the best foundation for an analysis of discrimination. Just as Michael Reich, I believe that the unadjusted ratio of black to white family income is the most appropriate measure of the discrimination black Americans face. While I do not discount the adaptation undertaken, the development of dysfunctional behavior, or the possible influence of personal initiative, I firmly believe that any differences in group income must fundamentally derive from the inequality experienced. Thus, when my son, after observing that all the sanitation workers in Paris were black, asked, "Is there just as much racism in France as there is in the United States?" I was gratified that he grasped the essence of racism. Let me briefly indicate some reasons why I reject other viewpoints.

The conservative view has some appeal, particularly for individuals who do not expect to experience discrimination. First, without experiencing discrimination, market mechanisms can easily appear more responsive to individual initiatives than regulated markets in noncapitalist societies. Not surprisingly, individuals who experienced arbitrary judgments in feudal societies perceive capitalist societies to be liberating. Indeed, Karl Marx generally agreed with Adam Smith on this count.

Second, communism continues to generate unequal status between highly educated and less educated members of society. While the income of manual workers is probably relatively higher in communist societies than in capitalist societies, formal education is the only access to status. Formal education may be less costly in socialist societies, but entrance examinations maintain inequality between social classes to the same extent that similar tests (SATs,

GMATs, and so on) do in the United States. Just as elite public schools in the United States have few students from working-class backgrounds, elite schools in socialist (communist) countries are devoid of proletariat children. While there have been attempts to change this—in the Soviet Union during the 1930s and in China during the Cultural Revolution—these attempts were short-lived. Thus, communist societies offer virtually no access to status for individuals who are unable to compete successfully in the formal educational system.

Capitalism, however, does offer the less educated an avenue to status—small-business ownership. Although individuals from poorer backgrounds face many disadvantages when opening their own business (for instance, undercapitalization and small-scale operation), for many, the chances of success are greater than those offered by the educational system. As a result, individuals who are willing to work hard but have negative attitudes concerning formal education will likely find capitalism to their liking despite its many shortcomings.

For many, the propensity of communist societies to monitor individual nonmarket behavior is threatening. While only the most committed ideologues believe that capitalism is capable of separating personal values from market behavior, many individuals believe that personal attitudes have little influence on the rights of others. In particular, many individuals are uncomfortable with having to defend their personal behavior and attitudes. This is especially true for white males, who often feel defensive about their attitudes concerning women and blacks.

Thus, I would argue that the broad base of support for capitalism has little to do with political freedom and freedom of the press. The right to seek status and financial gain through independent business and the lack of state intervention in personal behavior are central to this support. My own feeling is that until communist societies offer less educated persons an alternative avenue to status, many individuals will choose capitalism even if they believe it is a biased society. I also believe that the defeat of egalitarian policies in socialist societies has had a crucial impact on its acceptance. Not surprisingly, when communist societies have been unwilling to further equality between white-collar and blue-collar workers, they have been forced to allow small-business entrepreneurship in order to maintain broad-based support.

As for the issue of personal values, while I sympathize with many of the concerns voiced by defenders of nonintervention, I favor an aggressive government. It is clear to me that ethnic-based organizations have hindered the development of equality because they have insulated communities and allowed negative stereotypes to flourish. Male chauvinist attitudes are not benign, as they have rationalized the brutalization of women.

As for the narrow economic aspects of the conservative view, I find little evidence that competitive markets have undermined discriminatory behavior. Conservative ideologues who claim that smaller government programs are beneficial are mean spirited. While generating the view that compulsory education, safety regulations, welfare subsidies, and unemployment compensation only make things worse for the poor is an interesting intellectual exercise, this view serves only to oppress further the least powerful and most needy individuals. Even the more measured conservatives reject these views.

I reject liberal policies for many reasons. Liberal policies often reflect attempts at social control. Head start programs, training programs, and supplemental education can be useful, but just as Progressives attempted to "Americanize" immigrants, many of these liberal programs reflect attempts to impose values and attitudes on those who are oppressed by the capitalist system. These programs are often paternalistic, assuming that poor blacks are too ignorant and too dysfunctional to judge for themselves what is best. When black recipients demand more than the programs have to offer, liberals often withdraw from the struggle, claiming that these demands are unreasonable and that blacks are ungrateful. Liberals are willing to support antidiscrimination struggles only if they can control the process and the demands are modest. As a result, only a limited number of individuals in disadvantaged groups can expect to benefit from liberal initiatives, as few benefits will trickle down.

Liberals also are unwilling to confront capitalism in a fundamental manner. While they are well aware of the discriminatory nature of many private decisions, they are unwilling to undermine the profit motive. While they are well aware of the harmful role of insulated personal attitudes, they are unwilling to infringe upon social organizations that foster those attitudes. Thus, despite the benefits they are able to obtain in the short run, the source of discrimination remains: that is, the profit motive within a society that accepts inequality among groups. Just as the economic gains made by blacks during the early 1970s could not be sustained, so too the gains made by women in the early 1980s will not continue. As long as the profit motive dominates and chauvinist attitudes persist, it is likely that women will be channeled back into traditional roles.

I also find the neo-Marxist views wanting. Since blacks are a small minority in the United States, black nationalism never can be successful. I do believe, however, that black nationalism has enabled certain sections of the black population to benefit at the expense of the black working class. Black Muslims use nationalism as a means of lining their own pockets, coercing other blacks to buy from them rather than from white-owned businesses. Sections of the black middle class use nationalism to garner government patronage jobs. Mayor Harold Washington in Chicago did little for the black working class, as under his leadership schools deteriorated and police brutality continued. His election did, however, provide more government employment for black professionals.

The fact that black nationalism is limited because of the size of the black population and because certain sections of the black population use it for their own benefit is not the most important reasons why I reject the neo-Marxist view. After all, all reforms under capitalism are limited, and there are always those who gain personal advantages in any struggle. I reject black nationalism because it reinforces racism and undermines effective struggles for progressive change. Because nationalists encourage separatist attitudes in the black population, separatist attitudes in the white population are reinforced. If white support of antiracist struggles are discouraged and defamed, it becomes difficult to build antiracist support within the white population. Those whites who reject racism are politically paralyzed because they have no way of demonstrating their views; the only visible initiatives become those of white racists.

Second, nationalism has little to offer blacks who are victimized by police brutality and educational neglect once cities have black police commissioners and black school chancellors. Of course, leftist nationalists can then claim that these are not independent blacks—they are controlled by the white power structure—but for black nationalists who have gained the patronage, the struggle is over.

In addition, since many of these nationalists are unwilling to confront the capitalist system, they identify not the capitalist community but American Jewry as the controller. It was not surprising that when black nationalists in Chicago sought to rekindle a mass movement after the death of Mayor Washington, they identified the middle-class Jewish community as the enemy rather than the Chicago business elite.

My feelings toward left feminist views are mixed. Unlike black nationalism, left feminism has not been manipulated by some to divert struggles, nor has it fostered other types of discriminatory attitudes. Also, the resiliency of chauvinistic attitudes within society and their impact on the lives of women within the workplace and within the family cannot be dismissed. Moreover, whereas black nationalism has hindered the formation of multiracial organizations, the feminist movement has not undermined the ability of gender-integrated organizations to function. It is my feeling, however, that all nationalistic tendencies limit the success of the anticapitalist struggles I think are primary, and for this reason, I do not believe that left feminism can provide a foundation for political struggle.

I am well aware of the limitations class-based movements have had. In the past, there have been numerous examples of the inability or unwillingness of working-class movements to confront the chauvinistic attitudes of their members. While communist leaders have often been better in this regard, they have not always seen the necessity of maintaining the struggle against these harmful attitudes. Still, my reading of history—especially the organizing drives of the 1930s and the southern voter registration drives of the 1960s—indicates that only a unified multiracial, nonsexist working-class organization has the potential to generate meaningful reforms in a capitalist society.

Index

About the Author

Robert Cherry is an associate professor of Economics at Brooklyn College of the City University of New York. He has published articles on topics related to discrimination, including minimum wage legislation, welfare reform, black-Jewish relations, history of racial thought in the economics profession, class structure within the black community, and theories of racism. They have appeared in *Review of Social Economy, Review of Black Political Economy, Review of Radical Political Economics, Challenge Magazine, Jewish Currents,* and *Journal of Economic Issues.* He is also the author of *Macroeconomics* and coeditor of *The Imperiled Economy.*